RE-USA

20 american stories of adaptive reuse

A toolkit for post-industrial cities

Matteo Robiglio

Foreword

I first met Matteo Robiglio in 2014 in Bilbao, Spain, at an international conference on urban innovation and leadership. At that time I was writing my book, *Remaking Post-Industrial Cities: Lessons from North America and Europe* (Routledge, 2016). Matteo, a Professor of Architecture at Politecnico di Torino, was engaged in research in his home city of Torino on the reuse of abandoned industrial buildings. We were immediately on the same wavelength, and vowed to stay in touch.

Subsequently, in 2015, Matteo received a Fellowship from the German Marshall Fund of the United States to spend one month in the US to research adaptive reuse of industrial building and precincts. Fortunately, Matteo included Pittsburgh in his six-city itinerary. We reconnected and spent productive time together, not only visiting industrial sites in my home city of Pittsburgh, but also discussing the opportunities and difficulties of reusing industrial buildings. In 2016, I traveled to Torino where Matteo returned the favor, a tour of his city, and where we gave a joint presentation of our research.

Torino and Pittsburgh suffered greatly in the 1980s from the loss of tens of thousands of high-paying industrial jobs to low labor cost countries and from the abandonment of large portions of their industrial infrastructure. Our two cities were not alone in the Western democracies in that decline, with similar scenarios playing out in Detroit, the Midlands in England, and the Ruhr Valley in Germany, to name just three other regions. Yet some of these post-industrial cities have begun to come back in the last thirty years. That remarkable regeneration story is the focus of my book and was the impetus for Matteo's sojourn to the US.

RE–USA: 20 American Stories of Adaptive Reuse, is the outcome of that 2015 trip. It is an invaluable resource for architects, developers, government officials, and citizens. It will also be useful in academic programs in universities, not only in architecture, but also in urban design, economic development, and social science. In Part one, Matteo documents twenty reuse case studies in Philadelphia, Washington, D.C., Pittsburgh, Chicago, Detroit, and New York City. In words, photographs, and beautifully drawn plans, elevations, and sections he distills the essence of a wide range of reuse projects—from moving the headquarters of the clothing company Urban Outfitters into renovated historic buildings in the decommissioned Navy Yard in Philadelphia to locating new offices for Google Research in a repurposed bakery building in Pittsburgh. In Part two, "The adaptive reuse toolkit," Matteo presents eight strategies for adaptive reuse. Each strategy is illustrated with examples from the twenty projects he visited in 2015. I was particularly taken with the inspirational message of "Envision the future" and the incremental and bottom-up tactics of "Colonize the place." In Part three, "The adaptive reuse architecture," Matteo speaks directly to architects, laying out a theoretical and historic framework for adaptive reuse, including typologies of industrial space and a dissertation on the social practice of adaptive reuse. He concludes by making the case that Adaptive reuse architecture, "making old into the new new," requires a different design approach and a different set of skills for architects than those required for "making new."

Matteo and I continue to work together, not only in our research endeavors, remaking post-industrial cities and the adaptive reuse of industrial buildings, but also in facilitating student, faculty, and research exchanges between Carnegie Mellon University and Politecnico di Torino. Our most recent collaboration was a joint webinar in 2017 between our two universities on Re-Industry—exploring the potential of locating smaller scale manufacturers in old industrial buildings, not just the residential, retail, and entertainment uses that are typically associated with adaptive reuse. Clearly the emerging "maker economy" of additive manufacturing and automated production lends itself to locating in flexible spaces in abandoned and underused industrial buildings. That portends well for Matteo's reuse strategies for industrial buildings as the "future of work" evolves.

Industrial reuse projects are difficult to fund and to implement, especially in struggling post-industrial cities. Often there is no champion. The project seems too daunting to tackle. In RE–USA, Matteo Robiglio has been able to uncover the success factors of reuse projects and to synthesize those lessons into an easy-to-comprehend toolkit and a valuable resource guide for the adaptive use of industrial buildings.

Donald K. Carter, FAIA FAICP
Director, Remaking Cities Institute
Carnegie Mellon University
Pittsburgh, Pennsylvania, USA

To my friend and mentor Franco Corsico (1939–2015),
a maker of post-industrial Torino,
who introduced me to the ken of cities.

Preface

Several tracks brought me to write this book.
The first one is biographical. A regular, well-educated student, fascinated by the irregular creativity of squatted places and the beauty of industrial icons, I grew up as architect in the years while my city—Torino, the powerhouse of Italian manufacturing—saw 100 million square feet of factories emptied of workers and production within a few years. The instinctive attraction for the opposite became a professional commitment to urban regeneration and architectural reuse projects and, eventually, daily living experience—these lines are written from my desk, in a former coffee factory in the core of industrial Torino that is now home to my family.
The second is political. I believe in bottom-up action, and a long part of my professional life has focused on the issue of basing architectural design choices on a participatory process. I started practicing architecture in 1992 in a country that had just been shaken by a major political and economical scandal[1]—a shock Italy has still to recover from—which undermined citizens' trust in technicians and politicians. Public works and real estate were at the core of the unveiled system of corruption. Participation seemed a possible way to restore the legitimacy of architecture, experience brought inevitable disappointments. I grew skeptical about the effectiveness of formalized methodologies and the efficacy of steered processes. It seemed to me that a turn had occurred: from hands-up to hands-on participation. People took back city-making more when they acted directly to reshape places—with the support of professionals, when needed—rather than when they expressed their opinion in deliberative processes. And those places happened to be mostly reused spaces: where the legacy of the past—often industrial—provided the infrastructure for social, political, and economical innovation. As many stories in this book tell, it might prove difficult to build walls and a roof by yourself, but it is quite easy to occupy, adapt, and reuse an existing structure.
The third is theoretical. Teaching and researching in architecture, I always felt uncomfortable with the hype about "starchitects" and legendary heroes. The idea of architecture as the result of an individual act of genius is not only fake, as there is no art that requires more coordinated and interpersonal action than architecture, but also inherently authoritarian, not to mention frustrating for the vast majority of students and practitioners. The financial crisis in 2008 put a (temporary?) stop to the inflationary growth of unreasonable and budget-cracking projects.

The sudden, unprecedented availability of distressed assets and abandoned buildings all over the world led to an explosion of reuse projects, often directly led by communities abandoned by authorities and developers. Good architecture could be produced even with small budgets, with and not against communities, in inclusive and incremental processes. A happy heteronomy of architectural practices provided not only a way out of the crisis, but also an alternative to the ideal autonomy of architecture. Adaptive reuse testifies that architecture is the product of social practice, rather than an isolated, individual act of creation. It also redefines the role of the architect in society, as the creative enabler of social innovation in the city, whose invention is part of a broader conversation involving the many different actors of change.

The fourth is aesthetic. To appreciate (and to make) adaptive reuse architecture, you have to love hybrids, superpositions, overlayering, mix, contrast, contradiction. I suppose this is first of all a matter of taste—as were the late Renaissance paradoxical use of architectural orders, the Enlightenment passion for Chinese gardens and their irregular patterns, the Romantic love for ruins and contrasts, the Eclectic revival of styles that accompanied the first wave of industrialization, the Surrealists' use of ready-made trivial objects, the inclusion of commercial icons in Pop Art. What they have in common is the consciousness that we always work on a legacy and the capability to incorporate heterogeneous sources and materials into creative production. This attitude seems to me fit for an age when experts—artists or technicians—can no longer claim a monopoly on content and standards and the barrier between producer and consumer is weaker than ever.

The fifth is epistemological. Construction—from Latin "construere"—federates knowledge and techniques for the purpose of building. Specialization in practice and in research has increasingly traded the capability of integrating for the certainties of vertical excellency, supported by the multiplication of sectoral rules and assessments procedures. The inherently hybrid nature of reuse processes goes in the opposite direction and obliges disciplines—heritage preservation, building physics and technology, soil chemistry, real estate economy, urban planning, to mention the most involved—to rethink established frames and open to more holistic approaches in order to cope with emerging issues and demands.

The sixth is practical. At least in Europe and North America, the future urban construction market will be predominantly reconstruction, upgrade, or reuse. Most of the stuff we will be working on in the coming decades will be the legacy of the past, the recent past when the city became industrial and mass production introduced a new scale in city-making. And as economic growth and welfare grow in other areas, the attention to memory and demand for reuse will too. China is already shifting from the roughness of "clear & rebuild" to a more nuanced approach integrating preservation and reuse, and in the very days that these lines were written, the mayor of Moscow's plan to tear down and rebuild thousands of prefab Khrushchyovka estates—about ten percent of the city's housing stock—faces unexpected resistance both from intellectuals and inhabitants: in the name of reuse. It is a subject worth dealing with, if not out of curiosity, then at least out of opportunism.

The seventh, and last, is occasional. My undisciplined exploration of reused places found a more structured occasion of expansion in 2015 thanks to a German Marshall Fund Fellowship that enabled me to spend a month in US post-industrial cities to explore established and upcoming cases of adaptive reuse in a comparative transatlantic perspective.

This is a travel book, a manual, a theoretical essay.

As the first, it's meant to inspire the reader with top-down planned processes and grassroots situationist activism, ephemeral events and long term challenges, local volunteers and real estate developers, community and business, high architecture and architectural DIY, big money and low cost, large scale extensive comprehensive strategies and micro plot-by-plot incremental tactics. They all embody alternative approaches to and possible ingredients for adaptive reuse, locally brewed with the commitment, pragmatism, and openness I will always admire in American city makers.

As the second, it aims to be a tool for anyone interested in knowing more about adaptive reuse or becoming an actor of an adaptive reuse process in his or her community.

As the third, it attempts to explore the historical and theoretical implications of adaptive reuse practice, opening to future research. Written to be readable by all, it is mainly addressed to architects and professionals from related fields. Architects and professionals are the ones who most need to reframe their approach to city-making, which has been mainly shaped in a century when "new" was the watchword and authorship was the rule, to seize the opportunities and contribute to the growth of a promising activity field. It is completed by a selected bibliography that provides the reader with a chronology and references for further readings on the theme.

Part one

20 american stories of adaptive reuse

Part two

The adaptive reuse toolkit

Adaptive reuse is the process of reusing an existing site, building, or infrastructure that has lost the function it was designed for, by adapting it to new requirements and uses with minimal yet transformative means.
It has been the prevalent mode of building for generations, it will be the prevalent mode of building for the years to come in Europe and US. Its processes show how innovation can result from social practices that are generated independently from architecture, but can be enhanced and structured by architecture to achieve their full potential. Adaptive reuse architecture is inherently non-hierarchical and additive, heterogeneous and contradictory, pragmatic and specific. Incremental construction, redundancy of space, and freedom of distribution are its key features. Its beauty and efficacy depends on the capability of design to interpret existing infrastructures and organize the layout of new uses in shared and individual spaces through minimal yet transformative insertions, superpositions, and grafts. Its energy is drawn from the plurality of forces that design is able to summon and intercept around it. Its enduring vitality comes from its openness to time—to the past, to the future—and to life.

Old is the new new. Architecture and the adaptive reuse of industrial legacy

New ideas must use old buildings.
Jane Jacobs, 1961[1]

Processes of adaptive reuse of the industrial legacy of cities and their architectural outputs are a reminder of the proper relationship between architecture and society. In contrast to the concept of innovation supposedly being produced by formal and technical prowess and individual creativity, adaptive reuse experiences show that innovation is the result of enduring social practices[2] that are generated independently of architecture but reach their full potential if interpreted and enhanced by architecture.

It might seem contradictory to load a fluid social practice like adaptive reuse with the burdens of categories and abstractions. Nevertheless, some traits deserve to be outlined in order to understand the full potential implications of an approach to architecture and city-making based on the adaptive reuse of their industrial legacy.

What is adaptive reuse?

The current definition of adaptive reuse is: "the process of reusing an old site or building for a purpose other than which it was built or designed for."[3]

1 *The Death and Life of Great American Cities*, 1961, p. 188.

2 *In Sociology and Complexity Science* (2009), Brian Castellani and Frederic W. Hafferty define social practice as "any pattern of organization that emerges out of, and allows for, the intersection of symbolic interaction and social agency." The concept of social practice is introduced in French post-structuralist sociology to describe social behaviors in consumerist societies avoiding both utilitarian individualism—society is made up of rational individuals acting to maximize their utility—and structuralist determinism—individual action is the result of social and economic factors. Michel de Certeau, in his 1980 *L'invention du quotidien. 1. Arts de faire* proposes a double genealogy of the concept in Michel Foucault's "procedures" and Pierre Bourdieu's "strategies" (chapter IV) and affirms the political relevance of "spatial practices" "in the present conjuncture of a contradiction between the collective mode of governance and the individual mode of reappropriation" proposing a turn "from the concept of city to [study of] urban practices" (chapter VII). In *The Constitution of Society* (1984), Anthony Giddens uses a similar dialectic in his holistic approach to the study of modern societies based on the analysis of "agency" and "structure." The concept is still in use for social critique and policy design, see for instance the 2012 critical review of environmental policies by Elizabeth Shove, Mika Pantzar, and Matt Watson, *The Dynamics of Social Practice. Everyday Life and How it Changes*.

3 Wikipedia, "Adaptive Reuse," on 01.06.2017.

This definition is at the same time too extensive and too restrictive. It is too extensive because it could well define any reuse practice, without distinction, therefore making the adjective "adaptive" redundant. Derived from "adaptation," this is on the contrary the most important word in the term. It has a powerful root in natural philosophy and natural sciences. It expands the idea of adaptation as the way life assumes change and reacts to crises to architecture. Charles Darwin's idea of evolution as the "survival of the fittest"[4] was not an acknowledgment of sheer reproductive strength. Stephen Jay Gould explains it rather as "improved design," the fact of being —to quote the exact definition by Darwin—"better designed for an immediate, local environment."[5] Adaptive reuse in architecture could be also described as the "improved design" reaction to a critical change in a "local environment"—like, for instance, the loss of the original function of factories in deindustrialization processes—profiting from "immediate" environmental advantageous conditions—like, for instance, the availability of cheap, large, and robust spaces in central or accessible locations.[6] The forms of adaptation depend on the specific context and conditions and change over time, and cannot be described without reference to the situation in which they happen. We could not otherwise understand what a reuse was adapting to, and could not evaluate how effectively "adaptive" a reuse was: the idea of adaptation implies also a succession of limited changes rather than a single major

4 This famous expression was first used to summarize Darwin's idea by sociologist Herbert Spencer in his 1864 *Principles of Biology*. Spencer was also responsible for the translation of Darwin's concept from nature to society, and its diversion from adaptation to competition. Darwin introduces Spencer's expression in the fifth edition of *On the Origins of Species*, issued in 1869. For a critique of the teleological interpretations of evolution see *What Darwin Got Wrong* by Jerry Fodor and Massimo Piattelli-Palmarini, 2010.
5 In his 1976 article "Darwin's untimely burial," *Natural History*, 85. Darwin's natural selection has recurrently been used to sustain conservative political agendas and competitive visions of society. Peter Singer, in his 1999 book *A Darwinian Left: Politics, Evolution and Cooperation*, proposes to incorporate Darwin in a progressist perspective by recognizing the relevance of natural factors in human societies, while in the Marxist tradition society is determined mainly by economy and power structures.
6 The notion of a correspondence between site and architecture, and between local culture and universal civilization, is at the basis of Kenneth Frampton's notion of "critical regionalism" as a third way between the rootless International Style and Postmodern playful "quotationism." See his 1983 essay *Towards a Critical Regionalism: Six points for an architecture of resistance*.

disruption, and a frugal economy of means rather than a show of force. It is too restrictive in three ways. It omits infrastructures that are a key ingredient of the industrial city. It assumes that the building or site or infrastructures has to be "old," which is not necessary: to be "re"-used, it has simply to have already existed. It requires a change in purpose; what is necessary is the interruption and not necessarily a change in the purpose. Societal change in cities today, unlike in the 20th century, is traceable in the intrinsic transformation of uses and activities rather than in their simple substitution: additive manufacturing is reshaping production; cooperative consumption and online purchase are reshaping retail; ICT is reshaping office and work organization; off-soil cultivation is reshaping agriculture; demography and lifestyles are reshaping housing. By excluding mutated forms of the same purpose for the sake of last century's labels, we would miss a great deal of the most interesting ongoing social and economic innovation.

I propose therefore a definition of adaptive reuse as the process of reusing an existing site, building, or infrastructure that has lost the function it was designed for, by adapting it to new requirements and uses with minimal yet transformative means.

The tale of adaptive reuse

The canonic tale of adaptive reuse begins in Manhattan in 1953 with young Robert Rauschenberg who, coming back to New York City after touring North Africa and Europe with Cy Twombly, "found a loft" in 61 Fulton Street on the Lower East Side.[7] By dwelling in 19th and early 20th century industrial buildings—at the time Manhattan was still a place of production—artists were ready to trade substandard living and working conditions for raw but large, free, bright, cheap space, associated with the strong

7 The first to reconstruct the story of artists and abandoned buildings and analyze the social, cultural, and economic roots and consequences of the "loft lifestyle" was Sharon Zukin in her influential 1982 book *Loft Living. Culture and Capital in Urban Change*. Martina Baum and Kees Christiaanse (eds.) in their 2012 book *City as Loft. Adaptive reuse as a resource for Sustainable Urban Development* extend the concept of "loft" to the urban scale to discuss a worldwide repertory of adaptive reuse urban practices, while Liliane Wong's 2017 *Adaptive Reuse. Extending the Lives of Buildings* focuses rather on the scale of the building, to provide a complete theoretical and historical account of adaptive reuse in architecture.

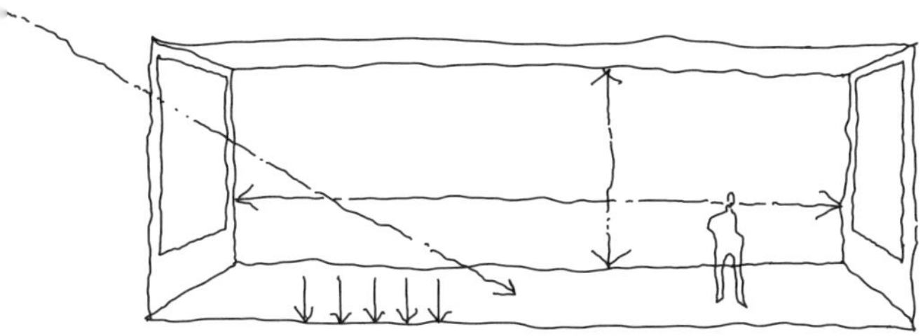

Fig. 1 Rauschenberg's finding

identity of places of production. For the studio itself—more than it already was for the Impressionists—was to become the center of gravity in the art scene, as making, action, and performance were increasingly incorporated in the meaning of artworks.
The loft as the scene of production was the perfect location for this new season that later peaked in Andy Warhol's Factory in Midtown between 1962 and 1968—his rent amounted to one hundred dollars per year. Unwittingly, they were not only revolutionizing art and habits, but also inaugurating what Sharon Zukin named the "Artistic Mode of Production" (AMP): the use of art by real estate developers as the key ingredient in a market strategy for repricing declined areas and answer new demands for authenticity and urbanity. An ancient Saxon word root referring to light, lift and air (Norsk lopt, German Luft, Dutch lucht), which had survived only as a term for a rural hayloft, was revived to brand this process as "loft lifestyle," rapidly turning an avant-garde posture into a lucrative new real estate business. Rauschenberg was an "early adopter" fond of having his studio among warehouses, docks, and workshops. His move was part of a regeneration process that would soon make space unaffordable for production—and eventually for the same creative community that "found" it.
In the same years, the New York City of "aged buildings" was endangered by "Bulldozer Bob" Moses' bold infrastructural and urban renewal projects. Jane Jacobs was to be its safeguard.[8]

8 Her book is the lasting legacy of her engagement in urban controversies, recently retraced by Matt Tyrnauer in his 2017 documentary *Citizen Jane: Battle for the City*. In 2009 Anthony Flint provided a journalistic yet documented account of Jacob's engagement against Moses' urban modernization projects in *Wrestling With Moses: How Jane Jacobs Took on New York's Master Builder and Transformed the American City*. It is interesting to note that neither Moses nor his biographers (i.e. Robert Caro in *The Power Broker*) ever mention Jacobs.

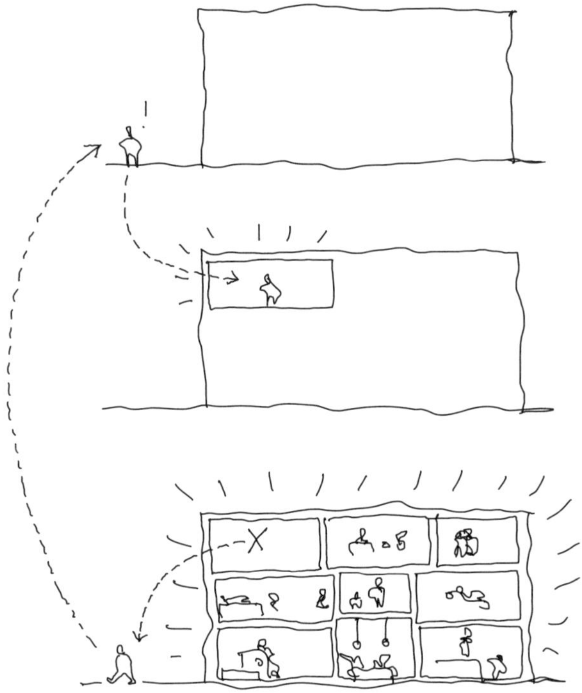

Fig. 2 The AMP cycle

Apparently against all odds, David knocked out Goliath—with a little help from the new taste for "authenticity"[9] of a growing number of loft lovers that made loft living a successful, mainstream trend.[10] The first loft users were sued for not complying with building codes and zoning rules. A decade later in the early 70s, Chester Rapkin had turned his sociological studies on the use of space in the area south of Houston Street

9 Sharon Zukin recently returned to the themes of Loft Living to explore the contradictions of the quest for "authenticity" by urban cultural elites and its consequences on urban economies and neighborhoods' livability in her 2010 *Naked City: The Death and Life of Authentic Urban Places*—a title which deliberately echoes Jane Jacobs.

10 Few markets are as conservative as residential real estate. The loft has been a way to introduce innovation into housing models by activating non-residential stock that had the right features to allow a more free and informal form of living in the house and organizing its layout. The use of the artist's atelier as an experimental field for testing solutions to be later applied to housing is already evident in Le Corbusier's atelier projects of the 1920s and 30s.

into a comprehensive preservation plan on behalf of Mayor Lindsay and invented a new destination, "SoHo." The first associations for industrial heritage were formed. Developers had both a new successful real estate commodity to market and a powerful tool to revive dangerous and marginal districts. Artists created their own tenants' association to fight evictions and rising prices—rents were capped and improvements imposed by the 1982 Loft Law. The term "gentrification" was coined to describe the paradox of "early adopters" being displaced by the increase in value they had generated.[11]

All of the ingredients of a powerful narrative are already there. The creative class inventing new lifestyles. People against power. David against Goliath. Makers reusing places where things were formerly made. Blight in central locations converted into new forms of urban liveliness. Bohemia and market. Spontaneity and planning. Bottom-up and top-down. Formal and informal. Preservation and modernization. Authenticity and falsification. Avant-garde and heritage. Artists, anarchists, activists, architects, speculators, and technocrats. Bricoleurs and engineers. The same narrative was staged in London and Paris in the mid 1970s, in Amsterdam and Berlin in the early 1980s, in Madrid, Lisbon and Barcelona after the 2008 real estate crash, and in Beijing and Shanghai in the late 2000s.

Each reenactment has its own story, but the key spatial ingredients and features were already in place in 1953 in New York City: generic, serial, robust, oversized, existing space repurposed for new uses with minimal effort and low cost tactics; non-professional communities appropriating assets out of need and turning their temporary market inefficiency into new economic value. Low threshold accessibility to space followed by a rise in value thanks to their cultural capital, social networks, and symbolic skills.[12]

11 The circle closes when art is purposely used as a placemaking strategy by developers—AMP engineered as a sophisticated development tool. Local activists opposing the upgrade of Boyle Heights in Los Angeles coined the term "artwashing" to define it, as art critic Jonathan Jones reported in *The Guardian*, 18 July 2016. The term soon gained worldwide diffusion.

12 Pierre Bourdieu, in *Forms of capital* (1985), distinguishes three forms of resources individuals can hold: economic capital (money, property), social capital (networks and relations) and cultural capital (education, language, symbols, credentials). The distinction is particularly useful in understanding contemporary urban societies, as the three capital forms, traditionally aligned, can now be present in uneven combinations. Robert Putnam's interpretation

The separation of old from new

What is interesting in squats and lofts is that they bring innovation where we would expect conservation. They make new inside the old. They hybridize the new with the old. They challenge the origin myth of the primitive hut[13]—the version of the first dwelling architecture treatises prefer, probably because it legitimates architecture as the creation of the new. The more probable history of humans dwelling in caves is for sure less heroic—the cave is already there and humans adapt it for the purpose of dwelling.[14] Robinson Crusoe—Daniel Defoe's 1719 archetypical bricoleur—merges both mythologies: he chooses a cave and completes it with a hut by reusing the wrecks of his ship, indeed a very up-to-date reuse.[15]

Squats and lofts challenge the separation of old and new, of present and past, which is a constitutive ingredient of the very idea of modernity. The Renaissance ushered in modernity by recognizing a discontinuity with the immediate past—the Middle Ages—and aspiring to restore a continuity with the distant past—the Classical Age. A lost and fragmented heritage has to be scientifically reconstructed—our contemporary idea of restoration in architecture has its root here—while the much

Fig. 3 New vs. adapted

in his *Bowling Alone: The Collapse and Revival of American Community* (2000) articulates social capital in "bonding ties" linking people who are similar and "bridging ties" linking people who are different, and underlines the importance of the latter for democracy and civic culture.

13 An erudite account of architectural myths of origins is in Joseph Rykwert's book *On Adam's House in Paradise: The Idea of the Primitive Hut in Architectural History* (1972).

14 It might be interesting to note that, while the largely dominant reading of the first chapter of Genesis interprets creation as addition—setting our idea of creativity as the capability of producing something new, a lesser version in the Lurianic Kabbalah of the mid-16th century sustains that God the infinite (Ein-Sof) has to contract (ṣimṣūm) to create a vacant space (khalal) for the world to be possible, as resumed by Gershom Scholem in Kabbalah, 1972, pp. 133–39.

15 In *La pensée sauvage* (1962), Claude Lévi-Strauss introduces the dichotomy engineer/bricoleur which will be repeatedly referred to in this essay. His goal as an anthropologist was to acknowledge the dignity of mythical thinking as "concrete science" in respect to modern scientific thinking (pp. 25–47). By comparing two opposed modes of transforming reality—the project of the engineer and the closed instrumental universe of the bricoleur, who has to make do with "les moyens du bord"—Lévi-Strauss escapes colonialist hierarchies and provides us with an interpretative tool to understand the logic of practices as adaptive reuse, that operate in closed instrumental universes like bricolage does.

easier ways that "barbarians" and "Goths" had dealt with ruins for centuries, dwelling in them and reusing their fragments as building materials, was rejected as incorrect. By dismembering classical buildings and reusing classical artifacts regardless of their correct position and meaning, they were applying Erwin Panofsky's "principle of disjunction" between content and form—exactly as we do today when repurposing old buildings for new uses. The new historical awareness pretended to restore the unity of the two.[16] It became imperative to document and to protect the traces of the past, for their knowledge was necessary to produce new and correct architecture legitimized by its classical lineage. It was not the matter that was to be reused, but the correct forms and their true meaning. Raffaello Sanzio, in his 1519 letter to Pope Leone X—considered as the birth certificate of the modern idea of conservation—claims to have surveyed Roman relics "without error" and "with true reason," and complains about their use by the Pope's predecessors as reserves of reusable pieces and materials—something we might praise and award with sustainability labels today. Classical ruins were measured to infer rules and models for making new architecture, but the results were not always consistent. Discrepancies required interpretations and conjectures, making any grammar disputable and providing more versions of orders and proportions than any classic purist ideal could assimilate into a single, coherent order. For the good fortune of architecture, Vitruvius left no drawings. Classical orders lost their normativity on the fields of archeological surveys, to be temporarily saved by being considered as a convention—something different from truth. And if we can convene on the beauty of classic architecture, why should we not enjoy the beauties of other traditions? The past was soon to become a repository of forms and symbols available for reuse in coherent style packages or more eclectic and free combinations. The "principle of disjunction" was at work again.[17]

While measuring ruins, one risks falling under their spell. They were not only relics to be enjoyed as traces of lost glory,

16 In his 1960 *Renaissance and Renascences in Western Art*, Panofsky recognizes the specific trait of Renaissance in the reconnection of "forms" and "content," putting an end to the "principle of disjunction" that granted the survival, appreciation, and reuse of classical pagan forms and symbols repurposed in a Christian context for centuries.

17 The crucial passage from the authority of ancient architecture to modern conventionalism is reconstructed by Joseph Rykwert in his 1980 lineage *The First Moderns: The Architects of the Eighteenth Century*.

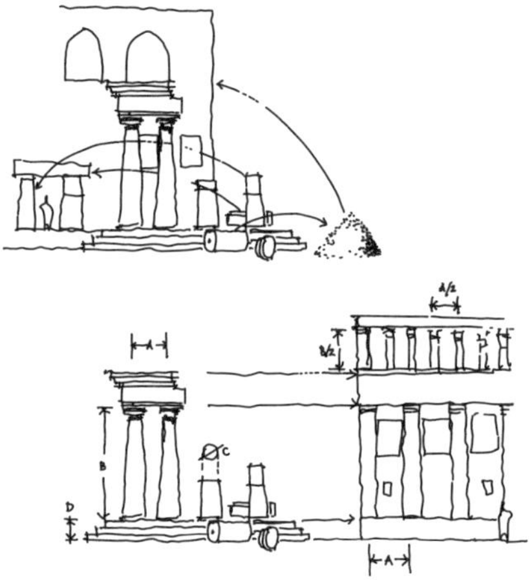

Fig. 4 Incorrect vs. correct

they had a beauty in and of themselves. Their incompletion reminded man of the frailty of existence, the passing of time, the revenge of nature over artifice. A new kind of aesthetic—sublime, irregular, and picturesque—arose when classical rationality slowly ceded to romantic experience, an aesthetic that praised stratification, hybrids, incompleteness, loved the palimpsest not only for what it testified, but also in and of itself, for its superpositions, voids, over writings, and fragments. It was less rigorous and elitist, more open and inclusive—the effects of the sublime are more various and accessible than the rules of proportion. It was also more adapted to the early steps of mass circulation and consumption of artifacts, images, and ideas that the printed illustrated accounts of the Grand Tour and the catalogs of historical styles—and their coming industrial production in the form of serialized artifacts for use of the general public—made possible. The upcoming "age of mechanization" celebrated by Sigfried Giedion[18] generously reused historical imagery to smuggle technologies we would today describe as "disruptive" to educated Victorian English and Second Empire French gentlemen, disguised under the familiar traits of eclectic serial reproductions of historicist artifacts.[19] The cornucopia of styles that the first post-war architectural avant-garde wanted to part from and even liquidated as a

18 In *Mechanization takes Command. A Contribution to Anonymous History*, 1948.
19 Early functionalism in industrial production was analyzed by Herwin Schaefer in his 1970 book *Nineteenth Century Modern: The Functional Tradition in Victorian Design*.

"crime" in the name of a new moral discipline[20] based on an abstract interpretation of the classical ideal and an idealization of the rationality of industry.[21] They drew an unwavering trust in the virtues of novelty as a means of constant improvement from the figurative arts movements and positivist technophilia: the old being always outmoded by the new. A misunderstood Darwinism seemed to confirm this idea: apparently in nature, selection was also at work to make the new—and not the fittest or the most adapted—prevail over the old. This commitment to purity, technology, and novelty was hegemonic for three decades. From the 50s on, angry young European and North American architects started to openly challenge the modernist International Style in the name of complexity, history, social responsibility, bottom-up design, vernacular architecture, and anti-authoritarian planning. Jane Jacobs was not alone in her plea for old buildings against forced modernization. In 1966, two of the most influential books of the 20th century were published: Robert Venturi's *Complexity and Contradiction in Architecture*, bridging from Mannerism to Pop Art and vernacular America to claim, in an ironic reversal of Mies van der Rohe's

20 This passage makes a long history short, with inevitable simplifications. Adolf Loos' famous 1908 lecture *Ornament und Verbrechen* is the clearest expression of the moralist implications of the purism of the Modern Movement. David Watkin, in his 1972 book *Morality and Architecture: The Development of a Theme in Architectural History and Theory from the Gothic Revival to the Modern Movement*, reconstructs the roots of this attitude. Roberto Gabetti and Carlo Olmo offer a complete historical analysis of the origins of mechanism and functionalism in modern architecture in their 1989 book *Alle Radici dell'Architettura Contemporanea*—unfortunately not yet available in English—while a more theoretical discussion can be found in *Architecture and the Crisis of Modern Sciences*, issued by Alberto Perez-Gomez in 1984.

21 In a global perspective, we have to note that this faith in the new has a deep root in a teleological idea of time specific to Judaism and Christianity, and is alien to most world cultures that see time rather as an endless circular cycle. Novelty itself does not hold any value for Buddhism, Hinduism, Confucianism, or Taoism, nor for African cultures, and is rather regarded with suspicion for breaking the continuity of tradition. Signs of time and irregularities are appreciated and enhance beauty more than novelty and perfection do. According to Daisetz T. Suzuki (*Zen and Japanese Culture*, 1959), Eastern philosophy defines this concept with the two complementary terms of wabi and sabi, 侘寂, roughly translated as imperfection, impermanence, and incompleteness. Maybe this appreciation of time explains the recent rapid diffusion of adaptive approaches to the reuse of industrial legacy in many Chinese post-industrial cities better than a Western influence, while modern approaches to restoration of heritage based on a Western modern notion of authenticity seem, on the contrary, to have a weaker hold on practices.

minimalist dogma, that "less is a bore" and Aldo Rossi's *L'architettura della città*, parting from modernist urban planning and architectural principles to reconstruct a typological, morphological, and iconical continuity with the history of the city. They were not architecture or urban historians: they lacked the methodological tools of a discipline that, in the same years, was gaining independence both from architectural design and from art history. They wanted to reopen access to a legacy that modernism had confined in the closed perimeter of heritage and monuments. They were in search of legitimacy in order to subvert the establishment, not an impossible reversion to history. Their approach was political and poetical, not philological. They practiced disjunction again: and the postmodern playful use of history was at hand.

Mass production and consumerism had turned the avant-garde ideal of "new and simple" into the more pervasive marketing idea of a kind of natural "obsolescence" of artifacts and goods. In 1973, the first global energy crisis marked the end of any confidence in infinite economic growth and technological progress, also for the general public. Environmental science —and soon, social awareness—started to question an economy transforming finished natural resources into goods to rapidly discard them as waste.[22]

Obsolescence of products was soon to become obsolescence of production—and producers. The factories, steel mills, and warehouses that had made modernity were starting to close at an unprecedented pace, leaving their material legacy in cities as a new form of post-industrial sublime:[23] industrial rusting ruins, soon rebranded as "archeology," invited to join the ever extending perimeter of historical heritage—and ready to be reused.

In spite of the modern insistence on newness, a more extended chronology of architecture would see the eventual overwhelming prevalence of adaptive reuse over new construction. Before

22 After the scarce results of the first 1972 United Nations Conference on the Human Environment, in 1983, the UN charged a commission led by former Swedish prime minister Gro Harlem Brundtland to report on the state of the global environment and its perspectives. Published in 1987 under the title *Our Common Future*, the Brundtland Commission Report reached a global audience and had a huge impact on public opinion.

23 The post-industrial relics merge two traditions of the sublime: the romantic notion of contrast between the immense—especially of nature—dwarfing the limitedness of humans, and the appreciation of the factory as a new landscape, where the power of man-made production rivals the generative forces of nature. For this second aspect see David E. Nye, *American Technological Sublime*, 1984.

being sanitized by archaeologists in 1840 in the name of history, the Arles Arena had hosted houses and workshops for a longer time than it had hosted gladiatorial games. Spared from the historicist zeal of restorers and the imperial ambitions of Mussolini, the Teatro Marcello is still inhabited today, as it has been since the fall of Rome. Abbeys and monasteries were reused as army barracks, hospitals, and schools after the French revolution. For the most of their time on this Earth, humans have produced most of their space by adapting existing artifacts to emerging needs and reused old stuff for new purposes. Sitting on the peak of the greatest growth wave humanity has ever seen—and probably will ever see—and imbued with a fatal attraction for the new embedded in the very roots of our culture, we are just starting to acknowledge this fact.

The social practice of adaptive reuse

All through modernity, reuse has been resisted as a stubborn, marginal, but pervasive social practice.
In the "glorious thirty" years of post-war reconstruction and growth,[24] the production of space was handed to the state or the market and the provision of space—for instance, the housing supply—became either a welfare service or a market sector.[25] People were dispossessed of the competence to build which they had proved for centuries, and forced to hand it over to specialized technicians like architects and engineers. But wherever people could retain some form of control over the production of space—in backyards, in allotments, in basements—the bricoleur was at work.[26] The enduring preference of Europeans and Americans for autonomous forms

24 The expression was proposed by French economist Jean Fourastié in 1979 in his book *Les Trente Glorieuses, ou la révolution invisible de 1946 à 1975*, and—although historically debated—has become a shortcut to summarize the impressive growth of welfare, economy, consumption, and population in Western countries after WWII.
25 The first international comparative analysis merging architectural history and political sociology is in *Architecture and the Welfare State*, edited by Mark Swenarton, Tom Avermaete, and Dirk Van Den Heuvel in 2015. Previous research at a national level was published under the title *Housing & the Welfare State. The Development of Housing Policy in Britain*, by Peter Malpass, 2005.
26 Christopher Alexander, in the first chapter of *The Production of Houses* (1985), opposes the "complexity" and "the process of minute adaptation" of

of housing has a solid base in the inherent adaptability of the single family house to the timely evolving needs of its users, and in the possibility for self-adaptation.[27] "Making" things may no longer have been a material necessity in consumerist societies, but, instead of disappearing, it remained as a form of fulfillment and expression of self, became a mass market rebranded as DIY, and was soon to be rediscovered as "authentic" by radical social movements criticizing the alienation of mass production and consumption.[28]

The first key to understand this endurance is identity. For the individual, the group, or the community, no top-down production process can provide identification with place, which is a crucial ingredient of social identity and cohesion—especially when modernization disrupts the traditional frames of experience, belief, and behavior, as happened and happens in the transition from rural to urban and from agriculture to industry.[29] It might come with time, through a slow process of adaptation to the new and of the new, as the troubled biographies of modernist public housing estates prove. This process' pace depends on social factors like income and social mobility, and on spatial factors like distribution and typology. Identity is instead a natural byproduct of autonomous production, self-help, do-it-yourself, and individual and communal mobilization. Making something by yourself incorporates it into your identity; making it with others incorporates it into the collective identity of the group or

biological systems (and self-built houses) to the "alienated character" of mass housing production, "categorically" asserting that no improvement can come by better design without a radical reorganization of process and power. Colin Ward has been the most convincing advocate of transferring the production of houses in *When We Build Again: Let's Have Housing That Works* (1985). Together with Dennis Hardy, he was the first to reconstruct a history of alternative, self-made, working class leisure housing in *Arcadia for All: The Legacy of a Makeshift Landscape* (1984).

27 See Peter Hall, "Arcadia for some. The strange story of autonomous housing," *Housing Studies*, 4.3, 1989.

28 Karl Marx, in his 1845 *German Ideology*, sees alienation (Entfremdung) as the loss of workers' control over their lives, work, and products due to the capitalist organization of production and society. Herbert Marcuse generalizes the concept to the interpretation of modern market societies and culture in his 1964 *One-Dimensional Man: Studies in the Ideology of Advanced Industrial Society*.

29 In *La Production de l'Espace* (1974), Henri Lefebvre defines the dichotomy "vécu-conçu" as the opposition between the "concrete" subjective space of users and the "abstract" space of experts like architects and planners (pp. 418–19). This leads him to praise the bidonvilles over the bourgeois neighborhoods as an example of "appropriation" (pp. 430–31).

community, be it a local community of place tied by proximity —i.e. residents of a neighborhood—or a community of interest with shared goals and motivational, political, cultural, and social ties—i.e. urban movements.[30] This voluntary and constructed identity is inherently cooperative and transformative, and should not be confused with the regressive notion of identity, understood as the conservation of the originary purity of a group. The social connection in the first case is dynamic and allows inclusion—anyone who shares our goal is welcome; in the second case it is entrenched and produces exclusion—anyone who does not belong to "us" is a danger to our identity. The first is positive, the second negative. The first is defined by future, the second by past.[31]

Various groups have sought to enhance and expand this progressive notion of identity attached to individual freedom, autonomous production, and social cooperation: young Team X architects attacking modernist pundits of International Style at 1959 CIAM in Otterlo, French Situationists exploring deep Paris and contesting its forced modernization, East coast hippies building geodesic domes with scrapped steel auto parts, London punks squatting Victorian townhouses and Amsterdam and Berlin radicals occupying abandoned warehouses and churches and turning them into social centers. It was the very same value that working class heroes were obstinately practicing in their suburban allotments, vegetable gardens, and Victorian backyards, and with the very same tools and methods.

The underlying shared goal was to reconquer control over the production of space, which had been increasingly

30 A useful classification of community types based on the distinction between "geography" and "choice" is in "Gemeinschaft revised. A critique reconstruction of the community concept" by Steve Brint, in *Sociological Theory*, 19:1, 2001. In his 2009 (or 1998) essay *Communitas. The Origin and Destiny of Community*, philosopher Roberto Esposito reverses the established notion of community as a social tie inherited from the past into the notion of a mutual engagement of individuals for the future. In his concept, identity is rather a project than a legacy.

31 According to Zygmunt Bauman, identity becomes a problematic notion when structured social frames are questioned by modernization processes; see *Identity*, 2004. The political construction of social identities was already discussed in the essays collected by Eric Hobsbawm and Terence Ranger in 1983 under the title *The Invention of Tradition*. For a recent review of the issue, see Richard Jenkins, *Social Identity*, 2004; in the second chapter, Jenkins situates the resurgence of a sociological debate on identity in the 1990s, while other authors date it back to the 1960s, referring especially to anthropology and psychology.

expropriated or delegated to technical bodies, public authorities, private developers, and housing institutions.[32] The second key is autonomy, or the decline in the monopoly of technicians and intellectuals in the production of content.[33] The 20th century modernist hero architect shared the socially recognized mission of innovating and the ownership of its results with the 19th century engineers, and even with their predecessor, the 19th century genius.[34] "New"—be it poetry or patent—was the product of a selected and specialized individual pushing forward the limits of human creation, and a special social status and legally reserved rights rewarded his effort. The inventor, the disruptor, and the groundbreaker are the modern institutionalized version of the romantic hero, deprived of his instable character and solidly connected to production and economy. Once ability and craftsmanship of execution have been downgraded to practicalities and creativity, concentrated in conception, is attributed to the individual as a personal and given talent, the author and the authority—from Latin augēre, to increase: the one who increases—can build their primacy in the separation of intellectual and manual work and the rule of the first over the second. The quality of things that for centuries had been the joint result of experience, knowledge, and skilled execution—in spite of all efforts by the many wishful followers of William Morris, scared by mechanization, to celebrate the talented craftsman and marry him with industry—had been wiped out by Frederick W. Taylor's and Henry Ford's "scientific" organization of work: split into repetitive elementary tasks

32 A review of radical urban practices and theories can be found in the essays collected in 2000 by Simon Sadler and Jonathan Hughes: *Non Plan. Essays on Freedom, Participation and Change in Modern Architecture and Urbanism*. The history of the Team X has been reconstructed in 2005 in the exhibition at the Rotterdam NAi, Team 10, 1953–1981, *In Search of A Utopia of the Present*, catalogue edited by Max Risselada and Dirk van den Heuvel.
33 The process was first discussed by Zygmunt Bauman in his *Legislators and Interpreters. On Modernity, Post-modernity and Intellectuals* (1987). Bruno Latour, interviewed in 2005 by François Ewald in *Un monde pluriel mais commun*, sees the function of experts in society as shifting from "truth" to "perplexity."
34 Edward Young, in his *Conjectures on Original Composition* (1759), first introduced the idea of an individual superior natural talent, different from any ability that can be acquired or trained, somehow similar to the Classical idea of a "divine madness" of the artist—for this pre-romantic root see Rudolf Wittkower's 1963 *Born Under Saturn: The Character and Conduct of Artists*. His influence on German *Sturm und Drang* and on Coleridge diffused a definition of creativity that still permeates current narratives with an inherently authoritarian and epistemologically useless, yet very fortunate, interpretation of human production.

requiring no skills, deprived of any creative value, sequenced in the production lines of massive industrial plants.

But, in the same post-war years that seemed to generalize this industrial organizational model to the whole society, contradictory and subversive tendencies emerged. Thanks to the universal access to education, the availability of free time, and the individual fulfillment promised by consumerism and pursued by libertarian movements, since the 1950s, starting from streetwear and rock'n'roll music, innovative cultural content was increasingly produced outside of established centers and institutions. This was not happening in the familiar and safe havens of folk, vernacular, or kitsch—where the separation of high and popular remained comfortably solid—but on the very brink of innovative lifestyles and symbolic production. Art, cinema, and fashion were ready to incorporate this shift, and elaborate and market it. Andy Warhol's New York City Factory was not only an early case of adaptive reuse, it was also one of the laboratories of this new form of cultural production. The unlimited availability and exchange of content on the web three decades later made it accessible to all.

The avant-garde techniques of the collage and the ready-made are today generalized in musical sampling, artistic copy-and-paste, cross-dressing, vintage furniture, and architectural reuse. At the same time, new technologies are revolutionizing the very logic of mass production—as it happens in additive manufacturing—allowing new forms of work organization that recompose tasks, question scale factors, and blur the boundaries separating production, distribution, and consumption, expanding the possibilities for individuals and communities. The 21st century "prosumer's"[35] and "maker's"[36] autonomous production of music, space, food, goods, and art, promises to reunify work, bridge the gap between intellectual and manual activities, and end alienation.[37] It does not necessarily question the capitalist mode of production, but it definitely breaks down the monopoly of intellectuals and technicians over content and innovation.

35 Marshall McLuhan and Barrington Nevitt, in their 1972 *Take Today*, were the first to suggest that technological change would turn the consumer into a producer. The term was coined by Alvin Toffler in his 1980 book *The Third Wave*.

36 This old word gained a new meaning and worldwide fortune thanks to Chris Anderson's 2012 best seller *Makers: the new industrial revolution*.

37 A philosophical and political elegy of new and old forms of work reconciling thinking and making can be found in Richard Sennett's 2008 book *The Craftsman*.

In this process, industrial buildings deprived of their original function, surviving as simulacra of a past powerful age, seem to play a central role. They are available for new purposes. They are big and cheap. They are iconic. They can accommodate any use and spatial configuration. It would be difficult to imagine a more ironic end to the corner stone of functionalism epitomized in the fortunate formula "form follows function."[38] Utilitarian buildings, supposedly strictly shaped by their function, survive their obsolescence thanks to the power of their forms and the mechanical robustness of their matter, in a posthumous victory of "firmitas" and "concinnitas" over "utilitas." The loss of the original rationale turns industrial architecture into an unexpected "open work." The original signification is still visible but no longer effective, leaving space to an active contribution by the users.[39]

The third key is memory. It is commonplace to stigmatize Le Corbusier's 1927 Plan Voisin for the center of Paris, but it has the undoubted merit of representing the short century's approach to the relationship between old and new with the clarity of provocation. The core of the Parisian Rive Droite can be cleared, as it is technically unfit for modern needs and is replaceable with improved substitutes: new high-rise, high-density housing, offices, and services connected by infrastructures floating in green space. It was the vision of a new, modern directional center for the capital of France, superposed to the existing city —with some subtleties. It generated a descendancy of less daring and more destructive urban reconstruction and renewal projects on both sides of the Atlantic. In many European cities, massive WWII bombings made the modernist planners' task easier,[40] and

38 The formula—originally "form ever follows function"—is by Louis Sullivan, from his article "The Tall Office Building Artistically Considered," in *Lippincott's Magazine*, March 1896.

39 The concept was proposed by Umberto Eco in his seminal 1962 essay *The Open Work*. Richard Sennett, in his 2006 Urban Age newspaper essay on "The Open City," relates form and process openness to democracy: "When the city operates as an open system—incorporating principles of porosity of territory, narrative indeterminacy and incomplete form—it becomes democratic not in a legal sense, but as physical experience" (p. 4).

40 The passion for aircrafts was shared between the two wars by military and planning theorists, a link that following events proved sinister. Airpower was theorized first by Italian general Giulio Douhet in his 1921 treatise *Il dominio dell'aria*, which was hugely influential on modern warfare theory; the book was translated into English in 1942 under the title *Command of the Air*. Le Corbusier published his *Aircraft. The New Vision* in 1935. His intuition of the design potential of aerial vision dates back to his South American journey of 1929.

were achieved by post-war reconstruction plans. In US cities, the rhetorics of slum clearance, traffic fluidification, and economic development (and, according to essayist and novelist James Baldwin, a hidden agenda of "Negro Removal") had a similar impact on inner cities, using wrecking balls instead of bombs. Le Corbusier was not interested in the ordinary history of the Marais more than Robert Moses was in Chelsea warehouses or Paul Rudolph was in the bricks and stones of Boston West End.[41] Everything should be cleared. Heritage was concentrated in some outstanding, isolated monuments. Their destiny was to be preserved and restored, deprived of any other function than embodying the past, freed from the city tissue that grew on and around them.[42]

Unfortunately for the modernizers, individual and collective memories are too complex and stratified to be easily channeled into the binary categories of past and future, old and new, heritage and modern. Memory is a continuous work of reconstruction incorporating identities and meanings into objects, sites, and buildings.[43] Unrespectful of hierarchies of value,

41 One of the first critics to contrast a comprehensive regard of the complex interplay between space, society, and memory with the simplifying approach of urban renewal was sociologist Herbert Gans in 1963. His seminal work, *The Urban Villagers*, portrays the vibrancy of the Boston West End working-class neighborhood before its destruction.

42 An opposite concept for the modernization of inner cities was elaborated by Gustavo Giovannoni simultaneous to the Plan Voisin in his *Vecchie Città ed Edilizia Nuova*, first published as an article in 1913 and later issued as a book in 1931. He applied this theory to the restoration and modernization of Italian historical cities. Giovannoni sees the city as a holistic "environment" in which "urban heritage" has to be integrated in the modern city and adapted to modern needs with careful cuts and punctual insertions respecting its peculiar features. His role in the cultural system of the Fascist regime led to his disfavor after the war—he died in 1947—although his writings remained influential in post-war debate. In 1951, the eighth CIAM in Hoddesdon discussed the theme of historical centers, and in 1961 the Associazione Nazionale Centri Storico-artistici (ANCSA) was founded in Italy to promote their protection. His idea of low-intensity extensive systems of cultural artifacts was a necessary step for the extension of preservation to the industrial legacy. We owe his rediscovery to the studies of Françoise Choay.

43 In his 1950 *La Mémoire Collective*, Maurice Halbwachs noted that "were the relationship between streets, homes, and groups inhabiting them wholly accidental and of short duration, then men might tear down their homes, district, and city, only to rebuild another on the same site according to a different set of plans. But even if stones are movable, relationships established between stones and men are not so easily altered. When a group has lived a long time in a place adapted to its habits, its thoughts as well as its movements

memory haunts monuments, but pervades also utilitarian buildings and daily objects. Contemporary art, architecture and photography have been incorporating and reframing the ordinary artifacts, landscapes, and structures of industry since the 20s—in Marcel Duchamp's ready-mades, in the Rationalist and Constructivist aesthetic, up to Robert Smithson's 1967 collection of anonymous New Jersey infrastructures relabeled the Monuments of the Passaic. Photography played a central role in the construction of this enlarged memory, for example Bernd and Hilla Becher's portraits of industrial infrastructure in the Ruhr area as early as 1959 and then in Europe from 1964 and North America from 1967, American "New Topographics" photographers of the 1970s such as Robert Adams and Lewis Baltz, Gabriele Basilico's 1981 "portraits" of Milano's factories and the French DATAR mission photographers who, between 1983 and 1989, simultaneously caught the early signs of deindustrialization and canonized the new industrial beauty in black and white frontal "typological" icons.[44] Movies also made a large contribution to this passion for industrial rusted landscapes by systematically incorporating post-industrial sets into dystopian sci-fi from the 70s onward, when the end of the post-war optimism opened the collective imaginary to non-linear cyberpunk visions of the city mixing past and future, as in Ridley Scott's 1982 celebrated *Bladerunner*.

All these different layers of cultural memory incorporated in industrial icons play an active role in raising attention, summoning supporters, and mobilizing energies: defensive in the first phase of fighting demolitions and proactive when in the

are in turn ordered by the succession of images from these external objects." The concept of "collective memory" was first proposed by Halbwachs in 1925 in his *Les cadres sociaux de la mémoire*. For more about the relationship between collective memory and narratives in Halbwachs, see the introductory essays by Éric Brian, "Portée du lexique halbwachsien de la mémoire," et Jean-Pierre Clèro, "Halbwachs et l'espace fictionnel de la ville," in the 2008 edition of Halbwachs's *La Topographie légendaire des évangiles en Terre sainte. Étude de mémoire collective*.

44 The work of the Bechers is described by Susanna Lange in her 2006 monograph *Bernd and Hilla Becher. Life And Work*, 2006. The exhibition *New Topographics: Photographs of a Man-Altered Landscape*, curated by William Jenkins, was held at the George Eastman House in Rochester, New York, in 1975. Basilico's *Ritratti di Fabbriche* was published in 1981. The DATAR mission was the first extended use of photography as a scientific description tool for the use of planning and is described by Vincent Guigueno in his "La France vue du sol, Une Histoire de la Mission photographique de la Datar (1983–1989)," *Études photographiques*, 18, 2006.

second phase reuse has to be devised.[45] Icons interact locally with the specific memories of single factories and working class neighborhoods, union fights, class solidarity, family stories, and individual remembrances: as industrialization, we shall not forget, has been and probably still is the engine of the most profound anthropological transformation of human societies in modern times, dramatically reshaping the lives of millions of Europeans and Americans in the 19th and 20th centuries, abruptly drawn from local rurality to global urbanity in the short time of one generation—much like the Chinese and Indians today. The permanence of this multiple layer of memories incorporated in cities and territories[46] explains the enduring attachment of local communities to industrial structures and infrastructures after they have lost their primary role in the community. Their material legacy holds a powerful communal energy that is activated whenever reuse enlivens these places again, and merges with the immaterial legacy of the skills and capabilities of people raised and trained to make things: like reuse, what we fashionably brand now as makers was in fact the ordinary condition for most humans for the vast majority of history. The delocalization of production of the 1990s and the idea of urban economies' inevitable turn from industry to services denied them existence and identity, confining their legacy in the safe but sterile realm of industrial heritage. The possible comeback of production to cities might reverse this destiny.[47]

45 Horst Bredekamp, in his 2007 treatise *Theorie des Bildaktes*, extends the notion of "agency" to images, recognizing their power not only to evoke emotion or produce aesthetic pleasure, but moreover, to induce action in reality. In this sense, images "act," rejoining the vast realm of impersonal "actants" that Bruno Latour explores in his *Action Network Theory*.

46 André Corboz, in his *Le territoire comme palimpseste et autres essays* (2001), proposes an interpretation of territory as the complex interference of incomplete material and immaterial traces inscribed in landscape by human actions over time.

47 The Urban Manufacturing Alliance (UMA) website summarizes "urban manufacturing is the oldest, newest thing going on." Nisha Mistry and Joan Byron, in their 2011 Brookings Metropolitan Policy Program report *The Federal Role in Supporting Urban Manufacturing*, provide a first complete review on "SUMs" (small urban manufacturers) and measure the "contraction and reinvention of the US manufacturing sector." Saskia Sassen gave a first critical account of urban manufacturing in her article "Cities today: A New Frontier for Major Developments" in *The Annals of the American Academy of Political and Social Science*, 626 (1), 2009.

Adaptive reuse and other "re"s

The three listed ingredients—identity, autonomy, and memory—are specific of adaptive reuse. They make it a case apart in a contradictory cloud of "re"s—regeneration, revitalization, renewal, reuse[48]—all sharing with the prefix "re" the idea of returning to the existing city to fix its failures. In the immediate post-WWII years, this was promoted by substitution: to be fixed, the inner city had to be cleared and remade.

The old city was renewed by replacing old pieces of it with new ones. The diffusion of less confident and more conservative "re"s in planning, policy, and literature, marked the end of growth management as the main political and technical concerns in the 1980s and the emergence of a new urban issue: what is to be done with the abandoned industrial areas opening voids inside cities as a consequence of the global reorganization of manufacturing and mass production?

Those voids were not intentional, they did not anticipate a planned renewal. Unexpected and unplanned, they were also distressing. They foreshadowed the end of modernity, or, more properly, of the modernity of the industrial city and the welfare state with its "good" jobs, its clear and simple social and political forms, its powerful mode of production, its simplified spatial patterns, and its established governance tools.[49] Conventionally, the turning point was the oil crisis of 1973, the first global event to show the frailty of the unlimited growth development model and reshape urban agendas.[50] For architects and urban planners, this year also saw the demolition of the Pruitt Igoe estate in St. Louis, a project completed in 1956 which, in less than twenty years had turned into a complete failure. This event is widely hailed as the end of the age of post-war mass housing and modernist estates.

What all "re"s have in common—in spite of their diverse practices—is the horror of void and the idea that it has to be filled in order to reestablish some form of completeness—an idea they owe to their common ancestor and an ancient lineage in the Latin term restauratio. In spite of its heavy

48 An exhaustive glossary is provided by Liliane Wong, *Adaptive reuse*, ibid.

49 For a comprehensive account, see David Harvey, *The Condition of Postmodernity*, 1990.

50 As Mirko Zardini and Giovanna Borasi documented with the exhibition *1973: Désolé, plus d'essence*, presented at the Canadian Center for Architecture in 2007, the energy crisis, brought on a rich season of architectural and urban experiments that anticipated the green urban policies of the 2000s.

political—Giustiniano's restauratio imperii—and theological meanings—one of ninety attributes of Christ listed by Thomas Aquinas is restaurator—in architecture, the term "restaurare" remained for centuries the rather innocent and neutral definition of works that fix or rebuild whatever existing architecture. In the middle of the 19th century, Eugène Viollet-Le-Duc brought about a profound ideological turn in the use of this term. In his words, "to restore a building is not to preserve it, to repair it or to rebuild it; it is to reinstate it in a condition of completeness which could never have existed at any given time."[51] He is fully aware that this notion breaks with millennia of pragmatic experience of dealing with the inconvenience of age by remaking, integrating, and reshaping with the same techniques and materials as ordinary construction. He proudly claims this rupture as a mark of modernity. His turn still haunts the current theoretical debate about conservation and has some paradoxical consequences as the number of artifacts entitled to conservation—and thus restoration—is in constant exponential growth. With the passing of years, products of mass production enter the appropriate age for being regarded as heritage—as has been the case for industrial buildings and infrastructure since the mid 1970s. What we consider of cultural value extends to include material heritage, natural heritage, industrial heritage, modern heritage, immaterial heritage, etc. Each artifact implies an extended conservation perimeter, expanding the number of heritage "systems" like historical centers and rural scenery. And we are also adding to "covenant history"—or maybe replacing it with—a kind of "private vernacular past," as John Brinckerhoff Jackson already warned in 1980.[52] The result is the virtuous extension of the perimeter of heritage—in terms of administrative procedure, legal status, and, more importantly, intervention paradigms based on restoration principles originally defined for a very selected realm of "artworks"—to an unprecedented set of artifacts in cities and landscapes. It is evident that most of them will have to negotiate new uses, their economic sustainability, and their practical requirements more heavily than artworks unless we pretend that a growing stock of built matter can be successfully preserved for the sole purpose of

51 Eugène Viollet-le-Duc, "Restauration," in *Dictionnaire raisonné de l'architecture française du XIe au XVIe siècle, vol. VIII*, 1854–1868. The quote is from Charles Wethered's 1875 translation.
52 In his article "The Necessity for Ruins," now in the collection *The Necessity for Ruins and other topics*, issued in 1980.

embodying collective history and memory—as it was and still properly happens for "covenant" monuments.[53]
Adaptive reuse practices are much more laic. They open a third way between the zeal of novelty, preserving only cathedrals, and the zeal of ancientness reaching from cathedrals to teaspoons —to quote the ironic formulation by Nathalie Heinrich, herself playing on Ernesto Nathan Rogers' famous 1952 claim that design was "from the spoon to the city." They adhere to the "modern cult of monuments"[54] with a refreshing pragmatism the ancients would appreciate, and imply a direct active engagement of actors that saves the past from the sanitization and commodification of the "heritage industry."[55] They often start in the silent shadow of abandonment or under the urgency of opposing planned demolitions, and invest buildings with previously unnoticed quality. They rarely have the budgets for deep restoration—if they have any at all. These two conditions provide a relative freedom of action conjugated with an inherent obligation to preservation, since even removal or cleaning might be too expensive, especially in places as extensive and robust as industrial settings are. The adjective "adaptive," as demonstrated above, describes reuse in terms of appropriateness both with regard to the existing form, state, structure, and matter and respective to the specific conditions in which the reuse process happens. With respect with other reuses, the adaptive is inherently more conservative, but does

53 The editorial inflation of titles on heritage is, in itself, a marker of this extension. As Jacques Le Goff noted in his 1978 entry *Documento/Monumento* for the Enciclopedia Einaudi (vol. V, pp. 38–43), the "revolution" of the new history of the Annales school has enormously expanded the "documents" historians deal with. Quoting Lucien Febvre, he lists an heterogeneous series of non-written sources to end with (my translation) "whatever, belonging to man, depends on man, serves man, expresses man, shows the presence, activity, tastes, and ways of being of man." Admittedly a very large and inclusive perimeter. It is not surprising that, consequently, also the list of "monuments" was expanded to include a similar extension of artifacts, with the risk that, in the end, everything is heritage. Nathalie Heinich, in her *La fabrique du patrimoine. De la cathédrale à la petite cuillère* (2009), describes the modern administrative procedures producing heritage and recognizes three categories of value that are attributed to artifacts from the past: historical, symbolic, functional. Adaptive reuse falls in the third—as it recognizes a potential new function of inherited buildings—and in the second—as preservation often originates in the recognition of a symbolic value for the local community.
54 The reference is obviously to Alois Riegl, *Der moderne Denkmalkultus* (1903).
55 The commodification of heritage was described with this term in 1987 by Robert Hewison in his *The Heritage Industry: Britain in a Climate of Decline*.

not have the ideal of "completeness"—this radically separates it from restoration. Adaptive reuses neither substitute the old with the new nor restore the old to its integrity. Adaptive reuses accept the void, cohabit with its anguish, and domesticate its enormity. They do it with undisciplined means, mixing ordinary maintenance, deliberate neglect, DIY simplifications, and clashing additions. They prove that the "competence to build" that old artifacts testify to modernity was not killed by the double stroke of mechanization and museification.[56]
William Morris would have cherished an operative condition imposing preservation without restoration, mobilizing diffused craftsmanship, unifying conception and execution, engaging a community for a shared vision, and producing beauty incorporating the layers of traces put down over time.[57]

A typology of adaptable industrial space

The production of space through adaptive reuse is ruled by a minimum effort law implicit in the adjective "adaptive." This differentiates adaptive reuse from other forms of reuse, and is possible thanks to the opportunities offered by the existing structure that is reused and the adaptive devices that make its reuse possible. Building for industry was an industrial activity in itself, with standard forms defined by the available technologies—steel, iron, concrete, wood—offering maximum freedom from internal constraint (and possibly fire resistance). This simplified and repetitive approach produced two main new types of buildings in cities: multi-story frames and big sheds.[58]
The frames were used as warehouses and for small manufacturing; the goal was to multiply space for light production by multiplying the natural ground in artificial vertical platforms. The sheds were used for wrapping space around heavy production. Both were generic, potentially infinite spaces with no distri-bution. The internal layout was defined later by the variable disposition of machines, the chains transmitting power,

56 Françoise Choay, in the last chapter of her 1992 *L'Allégorie du Patrimoine*, warns against the "syndrome patrimonial" and assigns a crucial role to heritage in the invention of the future: "Il nous sert directement à inventer notre avenir."
57 William Morris, *Speech Seconding a Resolution Against Restoration*, 1879.
58 The first to propose this rough but effective classification was Kurt Ackermann in his 1991 *Building for Industry*.

the organization of the assembly line, and the given forms of bigger engines and machines. They were thus abstract "ideal types"—in the meaning of Max Weber—of wrapped or layered empty space, rather than concrete building typologies. For typologies are defined by their distribution, here undefined—the presence of staircases and elevators in multi-story frames does not diminish the freedom of layout of each floor, as those were often arranged out of or on the floor perimeter. Their specific form was defined by the negotiation of the internal autonomous logic of production with the constraints imposed by the surrounding environment—the plot size and form, the neigh-boring buildings, etc.—, the requirements of production—light, air, load, power generation and transmission, etc.—and the characteristics of construction materials—maximum span, height, load, etc. Considered as a means of production, industrial architecture up to the mid 20th century was not submitted to the codes ruling civil construction in cities. This, together with standardization, explains the recurrence of a few repetitive schemes in different cities and times.
Both have initiators: the multi-story factory can be traced back to the first industrial textile mills, the big shed is a by-product of railway construction. Both were highly standardized: the construction of sheds through unifying steel profiles, joints, and geometries or by developing light concrete vaulted or trussed systems; the construction of multi-story frame even more so, with successful national and international patents.[59] The American "Kahnbar System" or the French "Hennebique" succeeded in transforming design and construction into a perfectly engineered and integrated serial production process, reducing the specific building into a simple application of the system. Both have noble ancestors—the Roman multi-story market and the multi-level arenas and theaters, the vaulted basilica, the Romanic cathedral, the Medieval hall, the Reform Hallenkirche—whose historically documented modes of use and reuse often foreshadow the contemporary strategies of adaptive reuses. Arenas were filled in with light partitions and wooden structures. Halls were regularly occupied by smaller often temporary and removable volumes and sub-structures. In both cases, minor architectures built to delimitate sub-spaces and provide locally required specific conditions

59 For industrial mass production, the definition of standards was similar to, if not more important, than the scientific organization of work. An account of its history can be found in Lawrence Bush's book *Standards. Recipes for Reality* (2011).

were introduced within the larger frame.[60] We see the same articulation today in reused docks.
Sheds and frames were not isolated. The industrial city went well beyond the factory fence. Around major plants, whole industrial neighborhoods grew in mixed regular grids of housing and services with smaller workshops and warehouses—the latter often echoing the sheds and frames in smaller size, proving that the logic of the ideal type is scalable. Today, we can see that they follow the same path of the main sites they were economically and functionally linked to in many cases, with scattered voids opening in the existing urban fabric—a process that is particularly evident in American post-industrial cities, due to the mobility of workforce that rapidly turns economic crisis into demographic decline and blight. From and to factories, a dense and interconnected network of life lines was necessary to supply and distribute: railways, pipes, roads, cables, etc. These infrastructures also lost their original function, and remain available for reuse. Their presence defined fronts and backs, determined differences in values, and segregated urban spaces and communities. Industrial linear infrastructure contributed to define hierarchies that persist in city geography even after their use ceases; reuse can weaken or even reverse them by connecting what was separated, making permeable what was inaccessible, and turning former backs into new fronts.
Sheds, frames, grids, and lines were all parts of a tightly connected network fed by a continuous flow of raw materials, finished products, resources, power, and workforce. We have to imagine a single distribution system from the suburban rails entering the city to the loading docks, from the elevators and cranes to the assembly lines inside the buildings, from

60 A history of the light structures that zealous restorers wiped away from ancient and medieval buildings has yet to be written. Some clues are offered by a rich iconography, often from sites whose extension and marginality prevented any attempt to restore a presumed integrity. One such example is the Diocleziano Palace in Split, filled in by a whole city, whose external wall was drawn by Robert Adam in 1764 showing small fishermen's houses clinging to its basement. The double arcade of the Arles Arena in the 1686 etching by Jean Baptiste Guilbert is filled in with houses, towers, and workshops, yet perfectly readable. Wenceslau Hollar's draws the temporary architectures accommodating the courts and the king in Westminster Hall West End with the Courts of Chancery and Kings in Session, ca. 1650. Pieter Jansz Saenredam accurately portrays partitions at floor level articulating the great Hallenkirche in smaller rooms in his 1649 painting of the Interior of Sint Odulphuskerch in Assendelft.

the warehouses back to the rails, from the workers' houses to the factory gates and back, from the intake pipes guzzling clear water from rivers to the outlet pipes spitting back waste water. Once this flow was arrested, the whole infrastructure serving it was deprived of its reason to be. The disappearance of productive uses meant the disappearance of productive distribution. Buildings were returned to their original genericity. They had become voids. When production leaves, the loft is what is left.

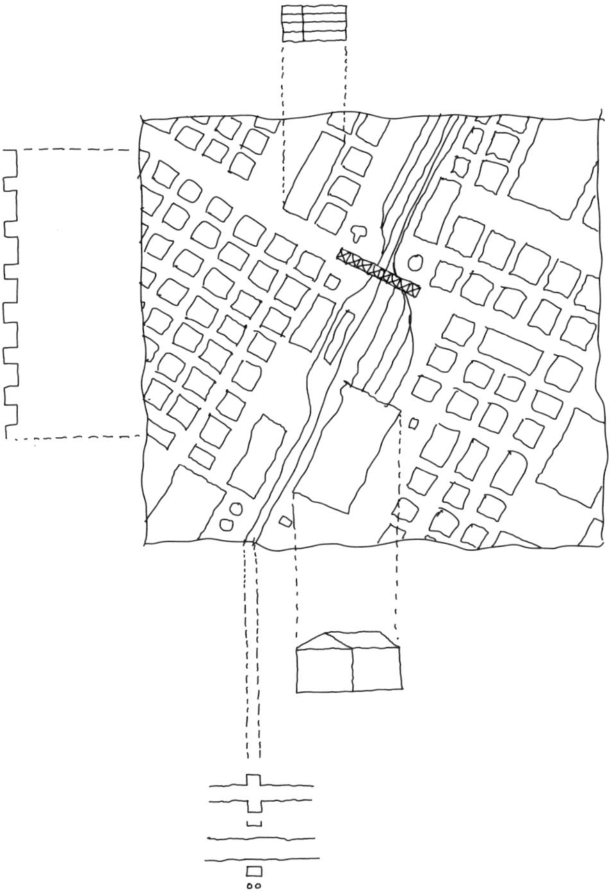

Fig. 5 Sheds, shelves, lines, and grids

The activation of potential and the reconstruction of place

The industrial city saw not only an unprecedented rise in the production of goods and commodities, but, also, an unprecedented incorporation of matter extracted from nature into a man-made world. And much of this material is still incorporated in the organized form of buildings: steel in the form of beams, sheets, and lattices, clay in the form of bricks, wood, concrete, and much more. The energy originally supplied to produce components and assemble buildings is still silently embodied in the built matter, and remains there even when uses are lost—a physiocrat vision of the production process that was revived by ecological economics in the 1970s to compare the energy saved by a product with the energy that was necessary to produce it, stressing the importance of understanding resources as limited and not entirely renewable.[61]

This energy is part of the more general potential all abandoned structures have: the capability of being reused and repurposed. In its Greek etymology as well as in physics and social sciences, potential is a power that has not yet been released, something tangible and measurable yet still generic, a tension that has yet to find its actual specific expression.[62] Georg Simmel, in his

61 Embodied energy is a powerful argument, which rapidly shifted policies from the construction of new buildings to a more general conservation of existing ones. The concept, proposed in 1966 by Wassily Leontief, in his *Input-Output Economics*, was generally diffused through the 1981 National Trust publication *New Energy from Old Buildings*. For a more recent overview, see Mike Jackson, "Embodied Energy and Historic Preservation: A Needed Reassessment" in *APT Bulletin*, 36.4, 2005. Most environmental assessment procedures for buildings now prize conservation over new construction, although without requiring a quantitative evaluation of alternatives.

62 Potential derives from the ancient Greek word "dunamis" (δύναμις), for possibility or capability. Its use by Aristotle as a concept contrasting with actuality made it a fundamental term in ancient philosophy and medieval theology. Galileo Galilei purified the term of its mystical implications and defined it in modern quantitative terms—what we call "potential energy"—in his 1638 writings on falling bodies. In spite of its fortune in the sciences, the term is surprisingly not used in architecture other than for its ordinary meaning. The recent research book *On the Potential of Abandoned Large Urban Structures*, edited by Jean-Pierre Chupin and Tiphaine Abenia in 2017, explores the concept but fails to specify its definition. The famous English landscaper Lancelot Brown (1716–1783) was nicknamed "Capability" for his peculiar way of appreciating the potential of a site to be transformed. The concept of "potential" has a main role in Chinese philosophy. Sun-Tzu's strategic thinking in

1919 essay *On Ruins*, saw the peculiarity of ruins in their state "between the not-yet and the no-longer," which opened their very existence to possibilities.[63] How can these possibilities be activated by reuse? The adjective "adaptive," as stated above, defines a line of minimal action particularly fit to current times —it is not by chance that many bottom-up and self-help adaptive reuse processes started as a response to the 2008 financial and real estate crisis. We might quote William Morris again and say that adaptive reuse is not much more than "keeping out wind and weather"[64]—not even that: some sheds brilliantly serve as urban roofs in parks and public spaces. In order to understand what is specific to it, we will instead outline its economic, legal, and environmental background and entailments.
Between the 1970s and the 2000s, the ordinary redevelopment strategy of an abandoned industrial area was quite established. The first step was to clear the whole site and clean it. Radical

The Art of War, VI century B. C. E., is based on the two complementary concepts of "situation" and "potential" (形勢, xing-shi). Unlike the western couple of site/context as inert and static, for Sun-Tzu's the context is a dynamic field of forces both active (the situation) and activating (the potential). The focus shifts from individual action to the transformative relationship of goals and means with outer conditions and forces. François Jullien, in his *A Treatise on Efficacy: Between Western and Chinese Thinking* (2004), offers a parallel reading of Western and Eastern notions of efficacy.

63 "It is as though a segment of existence must collapse before it can become unresistant to all currents and powers coming from all corners of reality. Perhaps this is the reason for our general fascination with decay and decadence, a fascination which goes beyond what is merely negative and degrading." Georg Simmel, *Die Ruine*, 1919 (translated by David Kettler, 1959). A similar remark is made by Marc Augè in *Le Temps en Ruines* (2003), by assimilating ruins to building sites as "poetic spaces, in the etymological sense of the world: something can be done in them; their incompleteness holds a promise." Less hopeful, in his essay "Anxious Landscapes: From Ruin to Rust" in *Grey Room. Architecture, Media, Politics*, n.1, 2000, Antoine Picon states that "we have gone from ruin to rust, from trace to waste" and asks "why does rust frighten us so while the ruin is adorned with a reassuring character? [...] The ruin, as we have said, restores man to nature. Rust, on the other hand, confines him in the middle of his productions as if within a prison, a prison all the more terrible since he is its builder. [...] The biggest fear suggested by the contemporary technological landscape is that of the death of humanity in the midst of the signs of its triumph over nature." Nevertheless, he concludes in a more optimistic tone: "After all, this is not the first time that the look that we cast over our surroundings has been modified. Each time, such a transformation proves inseparable from a mutation of the ideal image we project of ourselves." Adaptive reuse is such a transformation.

64 In Letter to the Editor of *The Athenaeum*, 5 March 1877.

off-site remediation techniques requiring preliminary massive soil asportation were preferred. Remediation was carried out before and separately from the redesign of the area, even without a planned redevelopment project. It solved problems of the past, and was not charged with imagining the future. The legal frame was (and still is) that the site has to be cleaned by the polluter—if any could be made liable. If none can be found, cleaning costs were (and still are) sustained by the public or incorporated into the value of land: but they were (and no longer are) a limited share of it. Unless specific buildings were under historical protection, nothing was kept on site. The economic assumption was that the value of the asset was in its location and its extension. No value was attributed to existing buildings and infrastructure. The real estate crisis of 2008 has permanently modified the fundamental steps and assumptions of this scheme. I suspect that, in places that do not belong to the restricted golden club of global cities and which have an extensive industrial legacy within their boundaries, the inflated pre-crash values will never come back: even if somebody were to find the magic recipe to bring back jobs and people, experience has forever wiped away any faith in unrealistic expectations.

Fig. 6 Substitution vs. adaptation

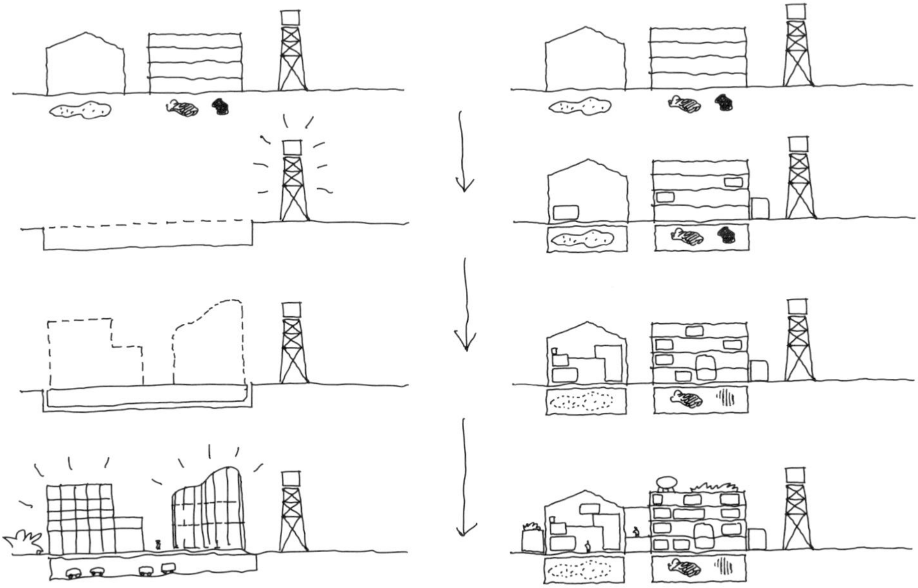

The opposite happened to remediation costs, due to stricter rules and enforcement. Today it is not uncommon that clean up costs in extensive sites are near or even outweigh land value. The result is the stalemate of so-called "mothball properties." No chance of capital gain, no deal, no clean up, no reuse. Stalemate can also occur when no heavy remediation is required simply if the mere supply of abandoned industrial sites far exceeds any possible local demand and no global player is in sight—as it is the case in many small and midsize post-industrial cities. Adaptive reuse promotes a completely different economy of place based on the activation of the fixed capital incorporated in the existing structures. The industrial legacy becomes the infrastructure for the new uses, enabling the reprise of some production of value—not comparable to the full power of industry but much better than the void of foreclosures, not competitive with the rapid value increases of speculative developments yet nevertheless slowly building up value. The focus shifts from stocks to flows, from one-shot capital gains to the incremental creation of value through progressive occupation, wise site management, and smart placemaking. Remediation and reuse are no longer incompatible thanks to new incremental, scalable, and partnership-based approaches.[65] Early adopters are lured by the affordability and availability of large unconventional spaces. Temporary events draw public and attention to the site.[66] Space redundancy (in surface and volume) provides a new form of flexibility at low cost, with the

65 Risk assessment was first introduced in the late 1980s to manage the environmental hazard in sites where activities were continuing. It is based on a probabilistic approach to site remediation based on future possible uses rather than on fixed thresholds or a supposed "clean" state of the site. Life Cycle Assessment (LCA) of remediation processes brought a more comprehensive understanding of the possible negative impacts of the massive off-site conditioning of polluted soil, including large excavations and demolitions. This approach is increasingly replaced by on-site risk prevention and remediation techniques, which is cheaper and more compatible with preservation and reuse. Further site-specificity is promised by soft bio- and nano-remediation techniques. Big impact funding is replaced by a more gradual and community-based approach that has reuse as a final goal for remediation actions. To this end, the Brownfields Action Agenda was launched in 1995 by the Environmental Protection Agency (EPA) to readdress the 1980 Superfund top-down and sectorial approach; see http://www.epa.gov/superfund/superfund-history (accessed 15.06.2017).

66 The role of temporary uses in urban regeneration and the inaugural function of informal activities in abandoned spaces is discussed by Philipp Oswalt, Klaus Overmeyer, Philipp Misselwitz in *Urban Catalyst. The Power of Temporary Use* (2013).

possibility of future expansion of uses in unused built space: something impossible in ordinary buildings, and very different from the modernist interpretation of flexibility as variable uses of the same space thanks to technological devices like sliding walls.[67] The redundancy in load bearing capacity also enhances flexibility, as it frees the layout of functions in space from structural constraints and allows to insert special functions requiring heavy machinery. Occupation can be gradual, works are carried out step by step, following the growth of demand. The actors in this process are mainly locals, who find the possibility to express desires and needs in adapted assets that standard real estate products do not meet. The sense of sharing a common challenge and having a common memory are powerful emotional ingredients and can prove attractive and contagious even beyond the natural watershed of the site. These performative narratives are strengthened by the production of iconographies building on the visual legacy of industry—lettering, trademarks, old advertisements—, the naming and branding of places, the enhancement of iconic landmarks, and the collection of industrial memorabilia. Adaptive reuse processes require the creative ability to reframe values and symbols—turning blight into vintage is the best possible example—that is a cultural capital only education can create, although global networking can inspire innovative practices in unexpected places. Therefore students, artists, start-uppers, and new craftsmen are the natural initiators of any reuse process, and its best catalysts. The incremental value-building strategy of adaptive reuses can, in some cases, eventually bring back values near pre-crisis levels, and even lead to the expulsion of the early adopters, replaced by more mainstream users attracted by the flair of a successful reuse. In any case, it is crucial that the physical infrastructure allowing progressive reuse is not eliminated and, on the contrary, this otherwise idle fixed capital is put to work as the enabling factor that sustains the reconstruction of value and the whole reuse process.[68]

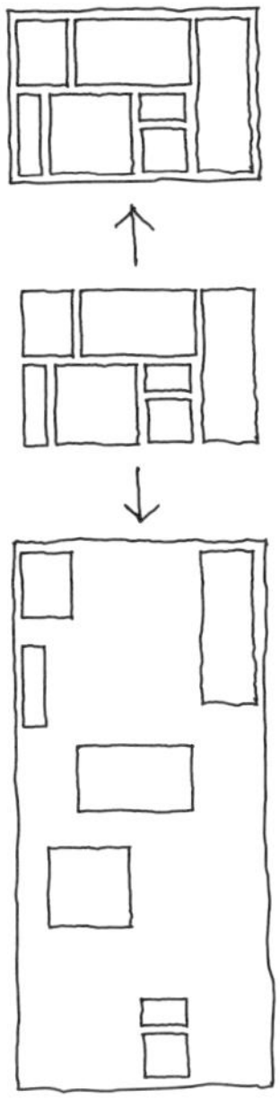

Fig. 7 Redundancy and flexibility

67 In *Flexible Housing* (2007), Tatjana Schneider and Jeremy Till describe the key factor as "one of attitude—of continually asking of the ability of that piece of design and construction to be adapted over time," and underline how industrial buildings offer the maximal flexibility due to their "generic principles" (pp. 181–82). Tom Bergevoet and Maarten van Tuijl in *The Flexible City, Sustainable Solutions For A Europe In Transition* (2016) extend the notion of flexibility beyond housing and to urban scale; many of their reuse examples prove the flexibility of industrial legacy.
68 This economic mechanism was already clear to Jane Jacobs when she advocated for old buildings' importance of offering cheap space for urban

In successful reuse stories, after a first phase of adaptive reuse inside the original envelope, new volumes might be built over or beside it. If the stock of original industrial space gets sold out, second phase developers might join the process by producing fake post-industrial lofts to satisfy demand for post-industrial flair plus full comfort.

It is not important how economic values go up in adaptive reuse. Its more relevant output is not the production of value, but the "production of locality" in the definition given by anthropologist Arjun Appadurai.[69] The end of industrial uses was also the end of the routines, codes, and habits of a daily life shaped by industrial spaces and times. The local space and social identity of the industrial city was the result of this original production of locality. Adaptive reuse initiates a second production of locality within the same spatial frame, through new patterns and new uses. As "physical spaces are part of the material that individuals work from, draw on, to some extent take for granted and in other instances highlight, sharpen, consciously use," in this renewed production of locality the existing industrial infrastructures "form part of the condition of its production, and they also form an important part of the object of that production."

In heritage preservation, locality is inherited, not produced, and has to be preserved. In adaptive reuse, the potential of legacy has to be activated in order to produce a new form of locality. Activation requires commitment and labor, and, more important, "collective ideas of what is possible." Producing collective ideas that extend the perimeter of what is possible might be a good description of the social role of the architect.[70]

economic activities in chapter ten in her *The Death and Life of Great American Cities* (ibid.). Far from any nostalgic romanticism, her plea for reuse is based on a solid understanding of urban economies. Her 1969 book *Cities and the Wealth of Nations* was listed by Robert Lucas among the sources of his research on the economies of innovation awarded with the 1995 Nobel Prize.

69 The first description of the "production of locality" is in chapter nine of *Modernity at Large. Cultural Dimensions of Globalization* (1996), previously issued as "The Production of Locality" in *Counterworks: Managing the Diversity of Knowledge*, edited by Richard Fardon in 1995.

70 Quotes are from "The Illusion of Permanence: Interview with Arjun Appadurai by Perspecta 34," *Perspecta*, Vol. 34 (2003), p. 46. In his 2010 article on *Transcultural Studies*, Appadurai writes that "we need to recognize that histories produce geographies and not vice versa. [...] Perceiving histories as producing geographies offers a better grasp of the knowledge produced in the humanities, the social sciences, and even the natural sciences about the way in which regions, areas, and even civilizations emerge from the work of human beings. This emergence includes what I previously called the "work of the imagination."

Some obstacles to adaptive reuse

Private property can be a severe limit to adaptive reuse initiatives. The absentee owner of a "mothball property" with no interest in development can be engaged by various means if local authorities and community act. Taxes, decency, or safety ordinances are possible legal means on the side of authority, and can lead to temporary seizures or permanent eviction and auction, further lowering the legal and economic access threshold to properties for reusers. On the side of the community, the recent economic and legal literature on the management of "commons" is providing the appropriate foundation—and growing experience and law—for collective actions for reclaiming unused assets and collectively managing property through "third forms" of ownership—neither public nor private—as for instance are Community Land Trusts (CLTs). These experiments renew a lasting conviction—rooted in Georgism, agrarian socialism, and Christian radical interpretations of the Gospels and Leviticus—that private land property is either illegitimate or legitimate only if contributing to the general welfare as a production mean, and that therefore, seizing unused property to reuse it is morally if not legally legitimate.[71] Public authorities using the right burdens and incentives can enormously affect the efficacy of the reuse processes. Punishing vacancy through tax evictions and prizing reuse with tax credits and tax increment financing stimulates reuse. On the contrary,

71 The 2009 Nobel Prize in Economics awarded to Elinor Ostrom, the author of *Governing the Commons: The Evolution of Institutions for Collective Action* (1990), marked a renewed mainstream interest in alternative and cooperative economies, the year after the subprime real estate loans bubble exploded in the most severe global financial crisis since 1929. In economic history, the end of the commons is a turning point into the construction of modern market economy based on private property, individual initiative, and state regulation. The expansion in the 2000s of the sharing economy, enabled by the web—see Rachel Botsman and Roo Rogers, *What's Mine is Yours. The Rise of Collaborative Consumption* (2010)—was seen as a possible combination of capitalism and mutuality, although forgetful of the conflictual nature of commons in a market society. Modern, more radical commoners are the legitimate heirs of the Diggers, who gathered in April 1649 at St. George's Hill in Surrey to pull down enclosures and plow the land in common. Woody Guthrie's famous 1940 refrain *This Land is Your Land*, often mistaken for a patriotic anthem, is instead a sharp critique of private poverty based on the harsh experience of the Depression years. It has to be noted that even Adam Smith, in his 1776 treatise *The Wealth of Nations*, describes land ownership as a specific form of monopoly and therefore the "proper subject of taxation."

reduced property taxes encourage inactivity, and impact or development fees, if applied in the early phases, prevent reuse from starting by raising the threshold the real estate crisis just lowered. Designed for capturing value in times of growth, some progressive city management tools can have reverse effects in periods of decline or stagnation. The same is true for zoning. The core tool of modern planning was forged in Bismarck's Germany at the end of the 19th century and imported to the United States at the very beginning of the 20th to rule the unprecedented growth of industrial cities and correct their failures by separating functions and controlling density; it was later refined during the 20th century to promote equal access to quality and services —a shift from the prevention of evil to the promotion of good.[72] But the tie between zoning and industrialization is deeper than historical contingency: the very rationale of disarticulating the complex—the city—into simple units—the zones—reflects Taylor's and Ford's scientific management mindset and its mechanist background; the prevision of future uses of greenfield developments reflects a solid trust in growth and in the efficacy of plans in organizing it. The first foreclosures of the 70s already undermined this trust, opening voids that cities were no longer able to fill with more prized services and uses, as it had been the rule for more than one century, pushing production away from central areas or delocalizing it to other countries.[73] In the

72 Peter Hall reconstructs the growing hegemony of zoning on 20th century planning—a contradictory outcome for a discipline whose roots he traces to the anarchist visionaries of the second half of the 19th century—in the chapter "New York discovers zoning" in his book *Cities of Tomorrow. An Intellectual History of Urban Planning and Design in the Twentieth Century*, 1988.
73 Up to the 1970s, cities maintained the competitive advantage of a concentrated skilled workforce, although, at metropolitan scale, production has massively left core areas since WWII. The delocalization to other countries breaks this tie. Diversifying the urban economy and shifting to services have become the main tasks for local governments across the Atlantic, integrating tools like strategic planning, urban marketing, incentives and tax policies, and planning and urban design. Donald K. Carter explores the ingredients of successful transformations in his 2016 *Remaking Post-Industrial Cities: Lessons from North America and Europe*. Tracy Neumann, in her 2016 *Remaking the Rust Belt. The Postindustrial Transformation of North America*, deconstructs the dominant narrative describing this policy turn as an inevitable necessity, to read it as a political option pursued by urban elites purposely ignoring possible alternatives. In spite of the decrease in scale, US metropolitan areas still hold the largest share of manufacturing, both traditional and innovative, as proved by Helper, Krueger, and Wial in their 2012 research for the Brookings Metropolitan Policy Program "Locating American Manufacturing: Trends in the Geography of Production."

2000s, the gap between rules and society in cities got wider. The task of classifying activities in space is increasingly frustrating: is a techshop production, education, or services? Is a loft production or residential? Is a workshop retail or production? From its very dawn in Lower Manhattan in the 1950s, loft living already implicitly questioned the separation of living and working at the basis of modernist spatial planning, bringing back a medieval mix previously condemned as backward and unhealthy. Contemporary lifestyle evolution, family demography, self-employment, light production, and the sharing economy are all processes challenging established classifications and weakening the legitimacy of enforcing the separation of uses by zoning.
On a more practical ground, bottom-up adaptive reuses often start with small actions that do not occupy the whole plot area, but rather grow incrementally by attracting other activities to build unique mixes whose force is heterogeneity and openness to change—often unforeseeable—over time. Top-down adaptive reuses break up large zoning areas into a finer grain of mixed uses to reach economic feasibility and provide urban liveliness. Both clash with the ties of zoning and require repeated variances to plans—planning has always had difficulties with time—when not the acceptance of "alegal" situations.[74] Innovation by definition is outside of established codes.
The answer of city planners in Europe and in the US has mainly been to complexify zoning by introducing "special" and "mixed" areas with predetermined composition or with flexible infill rules. This increasing complexity betrays the original promise of zoning, meant as a simplified yet effective tool to govern diversity in time and space through a general classification independent of site specificities. By introducing targeted and site-specific rules, comprehensive planning becomes more and more a tailored exercise, dangerously leaning on the idiosyncratic fields of architectural and urban design.
This practical shift should not go unnoticed in theory, as it undermines the efficacy of quantitative zoning and its very legitimacy as the keystone of modern urban planning. The future most probable scenario—at least in Europe and the US—for stable if not shrinking cities and intensive reuses requires

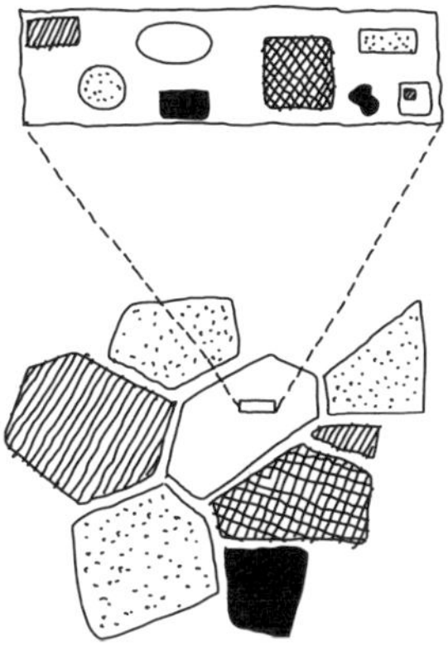

Fig. 8 Zoning and mixing

74 "Alegal" means neither legal nor illegal. Referred to the city, the concept was first used by philosopher and Barcelona deputy mayor to planning in the 1980s Jordi Borja in his book on public space, *L'espai públic: ciutat i ciutadania*, issued in 2001, to illustrate the need of a third space between legal and illegal to welcome emergent new social practices.

an urgent rethinking of planning tools, shifting the balance from regulating functions and quantities to regulating forms and consequences.[75] The conservation of progressive planning would otherwise have conservative effects, and hinder the social and economical innovation in cities it was originally meant to promote. Adaptive reuse processes are great test fields for the fresh thinking required.

Adaptive reuse architecture

After having questioned the role of the author in the production of narratives and symbols and his monopoly over content, recognized the emerging prosumer and celebrated his or her do-it-yourself skills, celebrated the virtues of bottom-up processes and adaptive variations in time, measured the risks of planning, and contrasted adaptive reuse, low-cost, incremental shared strategies to the high-end solitary achievements of starchitects, the reader might legitimately wonder what remains for architects in our adaptive reuse story. If adaptive reuse is a social practice that happens without architects, are architects needed at all? Are we reenacting Bernard Rudofsky's *Architecture without Architects*? If we remain tied into the opposition between spontaneous and educated, informal and formal, bottom-up and top-down, we might miss the most interesting point of adaptive reuse—and preserve each character of the story in his or her comfortable role. What is interesting in adaptive reuse for architecture is the mutual interplay, the contamination, the blurred boundaries, and the constant exchange between those terms of opposition. From the ones to the other, and the other way around.
Architecture draws inspiration and experience from the city—the same way fashion constantly incorporates signs and styles from streetwear and urban tribes and contemporary art incorporates pop icons, advertising, and graffiti. Containers, stacked boxes, pipes and valves, wagons, steel cranes, scratched plaster, burnt bricks, hooks, riveted metal plates, rails, text painted on walls, and signboards are materials adaptive reuse projects incorporate, combine, enhance, and reproduce. Architecture

75 A phenomenology of the codes and rules defining the form of the city is provided in historical perspective by Eran Ben-Joseph, *The Code of the City. Standards and the Hidden Language of Place Making* (2005) and with a comparative approach by Alex Lehnerer, *Grand Urban Rules* (2009).

offers inspiration and experience to the city. The popular industrial epic would not be so rooted if Impressionism had not portrayed the steel trusses of stations, Russian Constructivism had not made industrial buildings into revolutionary icons dramatized by Rodchenko's unconventional photographic angles, Gropius and Le Corbusier had not seen the signs of a new age in the American concrete grain elevators. Even the aesthetic appreciation of raw industrial materials like steel and concrete by the general public would not be possible without the modern ideal that materials have a specific natural expressivity and their many applications in modern architecture.

Architecture learns creative solutions for dry, light, and cheap construction using scrapped components assembled in unexpected ways from the urban bricoleurs of adaptive reuse. But bricoleurs also benefit from architectural research. The goal of simplifying construction and turning it into an assembly process of prefabricated elements has been a constant goal of architecture since industrialization proved the power of scientific production and the limits of craftsmanship, long before off-site prefabrication came to be seen as the appropriate answer to rising peacetime demands and a way to convert wartime plants' productive capacity.[76] Buckminster Fuller's 1920s research on prefabricated lightweight housing units leading to his 1951–1954 geodesic dome patent had its main large-scale application in WWII military shelters produced in the 40s but ended up inspiring peaceful California hippies' self-built domes in the 60s—and is still today embedded in contemporary fashionable "glamping."

The huge halls of steel mills and railway sheds needed no heating, but were often completed by closed sub-volumes where appropriate comfort was provided to personnel—the engineers' production line office, the control room, the watchman's shelter, the restrooms—or single production phases were isolated for hazard control and required conditions—as was the case for spray painting, fine mechanics, and electronics assembly. These boxes under the roof, laid on the floor, hanging from beams, accessible with flying staircases and suspended walkways, anticipated—before Space Age capsules and modules—the idea of confining comfort and providing specific

76 The conversion of war production into the engine of post-war welfare is described in *World War II and the American Dream. How Wartime Building Changed a Nation*, edited in 1995 by Donald Albrecht. The history of the industrialization of housing was reconstructed by Barry Bergdoll and Peter Christensen in *Home Delivery. Fabricating the Modern Dwelling* (2008).

technical conditions in limited environments, by constructing light, movable, and removable envelopes suited to specific needs. Whenever we have to negotiate standard local comfort with the diseconomies of non-standard, oversized volumes, we can profitably uncouple the external envelope and internal permanent use areas to create an intermediate space with intermediate comfort conditions, functioning as distribution, connection, a buffer, or as a temporary extension of internal space—and as a vital reserve of space for future additions.

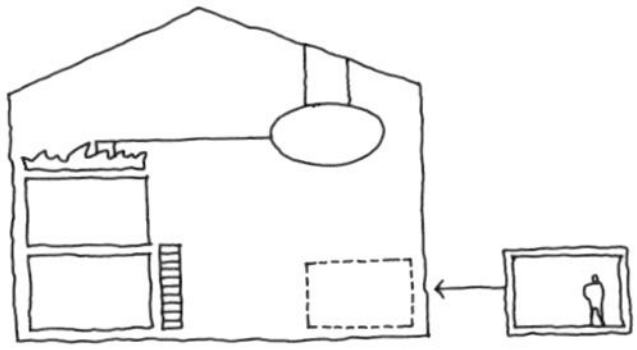

Fig. 9 Adaptive insertions in shed

The possibility of joining the free arrangement of space and exact technical provision, inspired especially from shipyard structures, was the promise of one of the most influential projects sprouting from Swinging London: Cedric Price's 1961 Fun Palace, commissioned by theater director John Littlewood to free his company's performances from any spatial constraint.[77] The Fun Palace was never built, but its differentiation of purposed yet variably arrangeable objects under a single canopy roof permanently influenced the design of convention and exhibition halls, entertainment venues, and airport halls—possibly anticipated by Mies van der Rohe's

77 In June 1966, Cedric Price publishes his "Potteries Thinkbelt" project in *New Society*: a groundbreaking proposal for a 20,000-student university to be located in North Staffordshire. The "thinkbelt" reuses the industrial infrastructure of the area—the signs of crisis in the local pottery industry, active since the early 18th century with worldwide impact, were already evident—to connect a geographically distributed system of temporary laboratories and movable housing units. Contrary to the segregated university campus, Price wanted to integrate technology students and working class communities, education and city. Issued in a more complete version in October of the same year on Architectural Design, the project has been recently reviewed in the 2007 *Cedric Price: Potteries Thinkbelt*, by Kester Rattenbury and Samantha Hardingham. In 1968, Price was invited to Detroit to promote a similar concept for the Oakland Community College, as Kathy Velikov reconstructs in her 2015 "Tuning Up the City: Cedric Price's Detroit Think Grid," *Journal of Architectural Education*, 69:1. Also in the Detroit "think grid" urban infrastructure and reused industrial legacy play a major iconic and logistic role.

famous 1942 collage concept for a concert hall.[78] It found a recent bottom-up declination in the extraordinary spaces of the NDSM "self-made city" Kunststad, grown from 2002 on under the roofs of the abandoned Amsterdam Ij drydocks based on a program autonomously defined and implemented by a collective of artists and activists.[79]

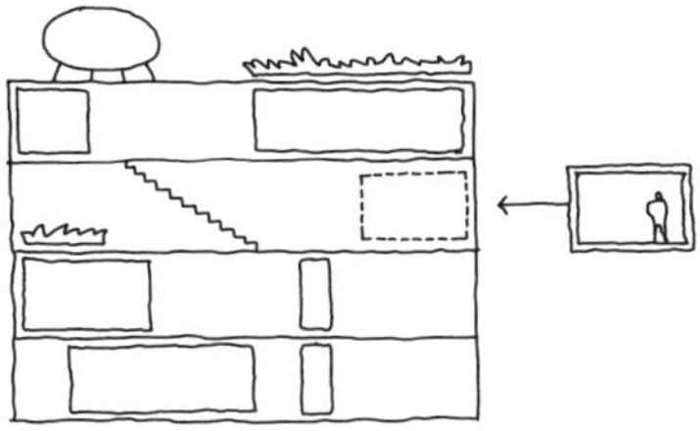

Fig. 10 Adaptive insertions in shelf

What we today call "parasite architecture"—autonomous small-scale architectures grafted in or on larger buildings—addresses the same need for comfort control and stems from the same ironic technophilia of the 60s, again with demonstrative projects such as David Green's 1966 Archigram Living Pod or installations between art and architecture by collectives like Austrian Haus-Rucker Co. with Oase nr. 7 at 1972 Kassel Documenta. In spite of their Space Age imagery and their supposed indifference to site,[80] such experiments and the many following variations continue the long history of minor architectures inserted in major spaces in order to adapt them to specific localized comfort or performance needs. Their lesson remains precious —flexible adaptation to evolving need—and technically wise—targeted and localized satisfaction of needs—especially when

78 First published in 1942 by *Architectural Forum* in a special issue on the "American city of the future," Mies uses a photo of the Baltimore aircraft assembly plant built in 1937 by Albert Kahn as background.
79 A summary of the making of the NDSM can be found at http://www.ndsm.nl/en/over-ndsm/ (accessed 15.06.2017). In 2007, the headquarters of MTV Media Benelux moved to the area, rebranded as Media Wharf, reusing another industrial dock, and in 2008, the Kraanspoor office building—repurposing an impressive horizontal concrete crane—was awarded the Urban Land Institute's prize for the most successful development at MIPIM; both marked the successful turn from DIY to mainstream development.
80 Oase nr. 7 hung from the severe neoclassical façade of Kassel's Museum Fridericianum. A 1966 drawing of the Living Pod by Ron Herron inserts the capsule in a 1756 Piranesi plate. Both hint at a more complex interplay of modules with context and a less innocent relationship of the future with the past and with history.

programs and purposes are heterogeneous and vary over time as it happens in adaptive reuse processes.

Those light temporary architectures were often erected in the occasion of special events—a contemporary art exhibition today, the king's wedding yesterday. Light and perishable architectures have always been used in cities—especially in moments of political change like successions or revolutions[81]—to mark the ongoing change by introducing visible innovation breaking the inherent continuity of the urban landscape. Their link with celebrations and public events—together with the 1960s playful and 1970s engaged relish for happenings and performances in urban space involving artists with public[82]—reminds us that this temporary layer of movable architectures was a powerful yet easy tool in the process of placemaking, long before this was made into a specialization of its own[83] and urban festivals became an unavoidable ingredient of city life and urban regeneration.[84] Adaptive reuse further weakens the borders of temporarity and permanence. Its evolutive incrementalism sees the "production of locality" as a possibly unending sequence of temporary stages, a permanent placemaking activity progressively giving form to space.

The uncoupling of container from content, of envelope from infill, happens in a different way when multi-story structures are reused with the insertion or superposition of new internal volumes supported by existing floors, acting as stacked layers of artificial ground. Industrial use also required the local delimitation of minor spaces and dedicated structures: small offices, made of light and removable materials such as wood,

81 From Mona Ozouf's studies on the architectural machineries of revolutionary France, inaugurated by her 1976 book *La Fête révolutionnaire 1789–1799*, to the 2011 account of Russian constructivist urban devices by Jean-Louis Cohen and Christina Lodder in the exhibition and book *Building the Revolution: Soviet Art and Architecture 1915–1935*.

82 See chapter four of Miwon Kwon, *One Place after Another. Site-specific Art and Locational Identity*, 2003.

83 The reference site on placemaking is the *Project for Public Spaces* at www.pps.org. See also the MIT DUSP 2013 report *Places in the Making. How Placemaking Builds Places and Communities*.

84 The "festivalization" of cities is part of a more general turn in cultural production from the institution to the event and from the ordinary to the exceptional. In urban sociology, the term was coined by Hartmut Häußermann and Walter Siebel in the 1993 special issue of *Leviathan* named *Festivalisierung der Stadtpolitik. Stadtentwicklung durch große Projekte*. In a more restricted meaning, Waldemar Cudny, in his 2016 *Festivalisation of Urban Spaces: Factors, Processes and Effects*, describes how festivals use and redefine public space.

were constructed next to production lines, laboratories, storage rooms, vestiaries. In reuse, the existing main structure loses —as happens for sheds—any definite functional meaning, to become a generic spatial infrastructure that enables evolutionary variations and a detailed program in specific positions. It was already the case for light medieval additions to multi-level buildings such as arenas or theaters, colonized by stacked houses and workshops. Le Corbusier used a similar approach to negotiate urban scale and individual preferences in his perspective detailing one of his 1933 Algeri Plan geographic buildings: the drawing clearly shows a standardized serial structure (deliberately drawn to appear infinite) with various content—services, public promenades, private gardens, and houses—and with a surprisingly multicultural touch.[85] A less visionary and more feasible version of the same concept is in his drawings for the "cellule-tiroir" related to the Unité d'Habitation in the 1940s. Already his most influential concept, the 1914 Maison Domino scheme, implicitly separates structure from envelope to freely accommodate variable infill. Yona Friedman's influential "mobile architecture" concepts for urban infrastructures supporting temporary living units employ the same logic.[86] American SITE architects, in their 1981 concept project Highrise of Homes, use a prefab parking structure to combine urban density and suburban freedom. Similar proposals were common already in 19th century urban utopias proposing to apply railway engineering solutions to cope with density and congestion issues; in the first years of the 20th century, they also gained attention in the general media.[87]

85 Le Corbusier wrote in his 1941 review of the 1933 *Chartes d'Athènes*: "Le noyau initial de l'urbanisme est une cellule d'habitation (un logis) et son insertion dans un groupe formant une unité d'habitation de grandeur efficace. Si la cellule est l'élément biologique primordial, le foyer, c'est-à-dire l'abri d'une famille, constitue la cellule sociale."

86 Yona Friedman's production of inspiring theoretical provocations gained renewed attention in the 2000s thanks to an impressive sequence of exhibitions all over the world. The most recent summary of his work is in the book *The Dilution of Architecture*, edited in 2015 with Manuel Orazi.

87 *LIFE*'s real estate magazine published a full-page cartoon showing conventional houses stacked on an open skyscraper frame in March 1909, with the caption "Buy a cozy cottage in our steel constructed choice lots, less than a mile above Broadway. Only ten minutes by elevator. All the comforts of the country with none of its disadvantages.—Celestial Real Estate Company." The image was ironic, but Richard Rummel's contemporary etchings portraying *The Future New York* were not: the idea of superposing steel structures to intensify urban life, multiply density, and reduce congestion was seriously discussed and

Hennebique and Kahnbar System structures and all their derivates scattered in post-industrial cities hold the same potential and the same design approach can make it real. Architectural research from the 1920s and 1960s—two crucial conjunctures of recent modernity, the reformist and revolutionary years of the first post-war, and the social liberation years after the second post-war period of mass consumerism—show how the most radical and visionary interpreters of the processes transforming production and society see the key for a renewed role of the architect going beyond decoration and style, pop provocations, and ephemeral performances in distribution rather than in form. If, in modernity, society is controlled by power by organizing time through space—as Michel Foucault showed in his writings on the discipline of bodies in prisons, schools, hospitals, and factories[88]—then new societal forms require architects to imagine new spatial distributive configurations, open and free layouts that redistribute positions, grant accessibility, maintain flexibility, reverse hierarchies, and blur distinctions. To become an ingredient of change, the generic potential of the loft has to be structured in new spatial sequences and arrangements, enabling new lifestyles and new production modes.

Fig. 11 Distribution, potential, redistribution

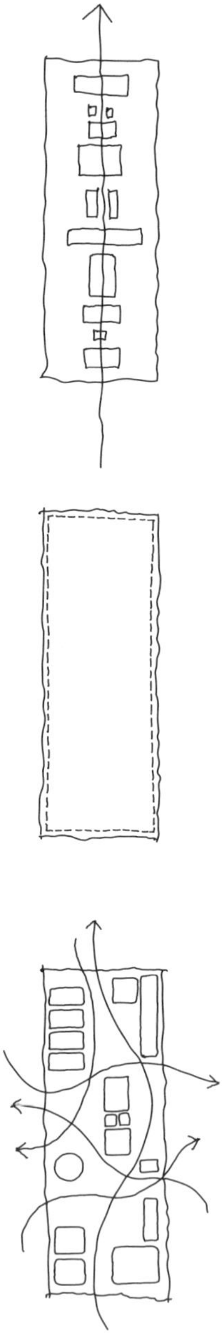

The adaptive reuse architect

Successful adaptive reuse architectures weld conflicting ideals together: preservation and innovation, individuality and collectivity, iconic and bottom-up, high-tech and DIY, low-cost and high-end.
Their lineage includes generations of anonymous reusers and centuries of minor and temporary architectures. Their aesthetic revives the powerful memory of industrial revolutions, while their technology builds on the embodied potential of structured matter. Their making reenacts the radical post-war ideals of individual expression and common action, combining the fulfillment of self with the fluidity offered by standardization—both modern ideals enhanced by globalization. Their separation of container and content joins the freedom of

somehow realized with the construction of overground and underground urban infrastructure. Rem Koolhaas features the 1903 *LIFE* cartoon as "the theorem" of the skyscraper in his 1987 *Delirious New York*.
88 In his 1975 book *Discipline and Punish: The Birth of the Prison*.

layout and evolution of uses with a permanent structure and recognizable identity. Their redundancy enables incremental action and allows flexibility over time.
Adaptive reuse architecture connects history and innovation in unexpected forms. Its dissonant balance of conservation and transformation drives the culture of heritage away from the quicksands of patrimonialization, injecting fresh content other than museum memories into old buildings, linking obsolete forms and emerging programs in fertile hybrids, and grafting new technical artifacts onto old relics. While heritage preservation confirms that the past is forever past and freezes it in one defined instant extracted from time, adaptive reuse reinserts the past in the time of the city and opens it to new uses and new significations, embodying simultaneously continuity and discontinuity, and permanence through social, technical, and economic change. Through the adaptive reuse, the legacy of the past becomes a lively ingredient of the future, sometimes literally the very incubator of the future: the place where innovation can emerge and grow thanks to the openness and the freedom gained by spaces that have lost their original function.
Adaptive reuse processes imply a relevant change in the architect's role. Making old into the "new new" is a wholly different design situation from making something new. When producing new architecture, the designer shapes space that did not exist before. The past is, at most, context: it surrounds the new space and might influence its design, but remains outside, around. The morphology of space is the result of relatively unconstrained design choices. Societal demand is summarized in the project's exposé, and users will come after the building is completed—hopefully they will be satisfied. Techniques are

Fig. 12 New vs. adaptive

selected and chosen to answer requirements and fit needs with the best performance available at the moment, as determined by the market and research. This has been the architect's main task and business in the unprecedented growth, which was sparked by the industrial revolution and peaked in the "glorious thirty."

In adaptive reuse, the situation is inverted. The context here is not just the site, but—in a more constraining way—the actual container of the new architecture. There is no autonomy of form, form here literally depends on the context, is context. The main spatial frame of architecture is inherited, not created. It already has its specific form, size, position, matter, and distribution. The designer defines how new elements are inserted within this existing frame to adapt it to new uses and demands. He might fix the existing frame, if needed, lightly clean it, or keep it as it is. Infills are of smaller scale than the container hosting them. They are not necessarily faithful or coherent with the container. They might introduce contradictions and enhance complexity or accept and promote incongruity and heterogeneity. Their insertion induces—to use Guy Debord's expression[89]—a "détournement" that completely changes the meaning of the original architecture as a whole, although conserving most, if not all, its space, form, and matter. This "diversion" is what makes adaptive reuse an alternative way to renovate what Halbwachs named "le lien vivant des générations" and not a lesser form of restoration. It belongs to the fluid realm of "collective memory" rather than to the established field of "historical memory."[90] People worked there, lived there, and are still there. Communities saw, and maybe see again, future in those familiar yet industrial built forms. Users already project expectations and sometimes start appropriation, eased by what they find on site.

89 The "détournement" is a critical, political, and artistic tactic at the core of the situationist approach to society and city. First described in 1956 in the article by Guy Debord and Gil J. Wolman "Mode d'emploi du détournement," which was published in the Belgian surrealist journal *Les Lèvres Nues* #8, the concept is defined in the 1958 inaugural issue of Internationale Situationniste as "the integration of present or past artistic productions into a superior construction of a milieu." The concept is presented as a synonym of appropriation (réappropriation) by Guy Debord in theses 206–9 of *La Société du Spectacle* (1967). For a complete account of the urban practices and influences of Situationism, see *The Situationist City* by Simon Sadler, 1998.

90 Both the distinction and the quote are from chapter two of *La Mémoire Collective*, ibid.

The way the architect works here is not different from the ordinary practices of grassroots reusers, though it may differ in quality, timing, scale, and budget. Both are repurposing the existing and rewriting the context with mild and discontinuous means. Both work on second-hand materials. For both, the pre-existing building is a found palimpsest that has to be interpreted and interpolated, not a white page yet to be written. Working as the "interpreter" in a conversation with a plurality of social actors—users, the community, city authorities, clients—and material and immaterial "actants"[91]—trusses, beams, pipes, slabs, walls, tanks, chimneys, pollutants, rust; memories, history, icons—the architect's legitimacy relies not on the capacity of creating something new, but rather on his capability to "federate" actors and actants through design for the process of reuse and draw the greatest possible benefit from the situation and the potentials that it holds. Far from grand gestures and expression of self, what matters is the "negative capability" the architect has to continue the past while subtly diverting it and negotiating with multiple actors and mutable conditions.[92] His creative skills are called to enable transformation, empower the actors, and accompany the process that, together, make adaptive reuse. His technical prowess is to negotiate new technologies with legacy techniques—aptness proves more important than excellency. Adaptive reuse has been the predominant mode of building for generations and will be the predominant mode of building for the years to come, at least in Europe and the US.[93]

91 As defined by Bruno Latour in the glossary (p. 237) of his *Politics of Nature. How to bring the Sciences into Democracy* (2004). The concept is central to his "Action Network Theory" (ANT) and allows the incorporation of non-human factors in process description, where the term "actor" refers only to individuals or social bodies. We use the term here to underline that the pre-existing form directly influences design choices, therefore "acting" on the architectural project.
92 In a 1817 letter to his brothers, Keats writes: "I mean Negative Capability, that is, when a man is capable of being in uncertainties, mysteries, doubts, without any irritable reaching after fact and reason." The line is used by John Dewey in *Art as Experience* (1934, pp. 33–35) to underline the role of imagination and intuition—and eventually beauty—in understanding "life and experience, in all its uncertainty, mystery, doubt and half-knowledge," as opposed both to the pretended "full" knowledges of rational reasoning and revelated truth.
93 In the US and the EU, the rate of new construction over existing stock is between one and one and a half percent per year; in the EU, ninety percent of the existing stock was built before 1990, sixty percent before 1960 (source: *Sustainable (Re)Construction. The Potential of the Renovation Market*, The Hague Center for Strategic Studies and TNO, 2013).

The architect's mission in adaptive reuse might seem narrower than in mainstream architectural tasks—you do not design the entire structure—but it is also broader—you have to reach out for additional possible ingredients and be ready for future inclusions. But ever crucial will be his or her ability to imagine and give a form to these ingredients through distribution at all scales: in urban space, at the building scale, and in interior design. The potential of the loft will otherwise remain unfulfilled, and, paradoxically, its apparent freedom will perpetuate the industrial hierarchy that generated it, due to the inevitable inertia of built matter. The designer has the power and responsibility to break this inertia, and to order new values and desires in a new organization of space materialized in a new distribution, thereby defining private and public, intimate and exposed, restricted and free, shared and individual. He will define public space and its accessibility. He will preserve openness for future changes. The resulting architecture will be inherently non-hierarchical and additive, yet fluid and comfortable, heterogeneous and contradictory, yet concrete and site-specific. Its richness will be achieved by minimizing resources, accepting differences, and drawing the most from the given conditions. Its energy will be drawn from the plurality of forces that it is able to summon and intercept. Its enduring vitality will come from its openness to time—to the past, to the future—and to life.

The past is another country that everyone can visit.
Charles Jeffrey, 2017[94]

94 Charles Jeffrey is an emerging British fashion designer. His quote is from the Lauren Cochrane article on his 2017 *Loverboy* show, in *The Guardian*, 11 June 2017.

Adaptive reuse architecture: selected readings and timeline

Elena Vigliocco

Adaptive reuse of old buildings

The complete set of strategies and procedures devised for the active conservation of architectural heritage, in particular industrial architectural heritage, is defined in the theory and practice of contemporary conservation. Synonyms of adaptive reuse are "remodeling," "retrofitting," "conversion," "adaptation," "reworking," and "rehabilitation." Change of use is the most obvious case of adaptive reuse since all other interventions must maintain integrity with the pre-existing building. The adaptive project must be evident and, possibly, reversible (Brooker, Stone, 2004).
Making alterations to existing buildings, by introducing new functions or tampering with their original structures, is an old practice: in the past, many solid and immutable buildings were transformed when a different need arose without any theoretical issue. A pragmatic approach and the lack of any intent to conserve or protect the cultural heritage of the buildings were common factors in all these cases.
A theoretical approach to reuse arose in the 19th century with Eugéne Emmanuel Viollet-le-Duc (1814–1879) who recognized the potential contribution of reuse to the conservation of historical monuments. However, his idea was strongly opposed by John Ruskin (1819–1900) and his student William Morris (1843–1896), who affirmed that such interventions should be considered "impossible, as impossible as to raise the dead" (Ruskin, 1849). The conflict between these two opposing theories reemerged in a more subdued manner in the work of Alois Riegl (1858–1900), who made a distinction between the commemorative value of monuments (including their historical and artistic value) and their contemporary value (including occupancy value, artistic value, and novelty value). Proffering the concept that a commercial use value could be attributed to monuments, he recognized that the practice of reuse of buildings was an intrinsic part of contemporary conservation projects.
In the first half of the 20th century, an architectural culture was sought from the two wars and new buildings and projects broke with traditional ones. At the same time a new interest in the conservation of antique buildings developed as a direct result of the devastation caused by WWII aerial bombardment campaigns. From the intervention at the Castelvecchio museum in Verona to the Tate Modern Gallery in London, the second half of the 20th century was characterized by a growing interest in adaptive reuse.

L. Wong, *Adaptive REUSE: Extending the Lives of Buildings*, Birkhäuser, Basel, 2016.

Reclaim: Remediate Reuse Recycle, vol. 39–40 of *A+T* magazine, 2012.

B. Plevoets, K. Van Cleempoel, "Adaptive Reuse as a Strategy Towards Conservation of Cultural Heritage: A Literature Review," in C. A. Brebbia, L. Binda (eds.), *Structural Studies, Repairs and Maintenance of Heritage Architecture*, Wit Press, Southampton, UK, 2011, pp. 155–64.

M. Berger, L. Wong (eds.), *Adaptive Reuse*, vol. 1 of *Interventions Adaptive Reuse*, Department of Interior Architecture, Rhode Island School of Design, Autumn 2009.

J. S. Rabun, R. M. Kelso, *Building Evaluation for Adaptive Reuse and Preservation*, Wiley, Hoboken, New Jersey, 2009.

F. Scott, *On Altering Architecture*, Routledge, London, 2008.

G. Brooker, S. Stone, *Re-Readings: Interior Architecture and the Design Principles*

of Remodelling Existing Buildings, RIBA Enterprises, London, 2004.

K. Powell, *Architecture Reborn: Converting Old Buildings for New Uses*, Rizzoli International Publications, New York, 1999.

P. Cunnington, *Change of Use: The Conversion of Old Buildings*, Alpha Books, London, 1988.

D. G. Woodcock, W.C. Steward, R.A. Forrester (eds.), *Adaptive Reuse: Issues and Case Studies in Building Preservation*, Van Nostrand Reinhold, New York, 1988.

National Trust for Historic Preservation, *Old and New Architecture: Design Relationships*, The Preservation Press, Washington D.C., 1980.

S. Cantacuzino, S. Brandt, *Saving Old Buildings*, Architectural Press, London, 1980.

T. Markus, *Building Conversion and Rehabilitation*, Butterworth, London, 1979.

L. E. Reiner, *How to Recycle Buildings*, McGraw-Hill, New York, 1979.

J. H. U. Boykin, *Industrial Potential of the Central City: An Investigation of Regulatory Barriers to the Reuse of Existing Buildings—A Team Investigation* sponsored by the National Bureau of Standards Centre of Building Technology, MIT Press, London, 1978.

R. Pérez De Arce, "Urban Transformations and the Architecture of Additions," in *Architectural Design*, n. 4, 1978, pp. 237–66.

R. Machado, "Old Buildings as Palimpsest: Towards a Theory of Remodeling," in *Progressive Architecture*, n. 11, 1976, pp. 46–49.

S. Cantacuzino, *New Uses for Old Buildings*, Architectural Press, London, 1975.

S. Cantacuzino, "New Uses for Old Buildings," in *Architectural Review*, 1972, pp. 262–324.

A. Riegl, *Der Moderne Denkmalkultus: Sein Wesen und seine Entstehung*, ed. Dr. Benno Filser Verlag, Augsburg-Wien, 1928, pp. 144–93 [1903].

E. Viollet-Le-Duc, *The Foundations of Architecture*, George Braziller, New York, 1990 [1854].

J. Ruskin, *The Seven Lamps of Architecture*, Smith Elder, London, 1849.

Contemporary theories on adaptive reuse

Regarding the interpretation of Bie Plevoets and Koenraad Van Cleempoel (2011), a classification with three different theoretical approaches is proposed. Typological, technical, and strategic approaches are discussed and presented independently but different works, belonging to separate categories, are linked to more than one approach. The following studies include only those that deal with architecture and the conservation of architectural heritage.

Typological approach

The first publication regarding adaptive reuse is the 1975 text *New Uses for Old Buildings* by Sherban Cantacuzino. Following the introduction to adaptive reuse, the author provides a selection of international examples organized on the basis of their building classification prior to conversion. However, in 1989, the author published a new study where the typological catalogue is organized according to the six main building types, featured as the main focus of the work. Consequently, many other authors chose to adopt the same approach to

the subject: James Douglas (2006) organized part of his important work on the reuse and conversion of buildings on the basis of the typology of the use of space, despite the limited nature of the variety of building types considered. In his work there are few new projects for each typology while the difficulties inherent with the specific reuse of each building category are highlighted. In fact, many authors preferred to focus on specific building types, such as religious or industrial buildings, with detailed analysis. Finally, certain authors, including Peter Eley and John Worthington (1984) and Kenneth Powell (1999), organized the categories according to the contemporary transformation program, thereby shifting the focus to a contemporary interpretation of the architecture and to the adaptive reuse intervention, moving away from the historical classification of the buildings.

I. Alavedra, *Converted Churches*, Tectum Publishers, Antwerp, 2007.

J. Douglas, *Building Adaptation*, Elsevier, Oxford, 2006.

L. Morisset, L. Noppen, T. Coomans, *Quel avenir pour quelles églises? What future for which churches?*, Presses de l'Université du Québec, Québec, 2005.

English Heritage, *The Future of Historic School Buildings*, English Heritage, London, 2005.

D. Henehan, D. Woodson, S. Culbert, *Building Change-of-Use: Renovation, Adapting, and Altering Commercial, Institutional, and Industrial Properties*, McGraw-Hill, New York, 2004.

English Heritage, *New Work in Historic Places of Worship*, English Heritage, London, 2003.

D. Latham, *Creative Re-use of Buildings: Vols. 1 & 2*, Donhead, Shaftesbury, UK, 2000.

Icomos, *The Nara Document on Authenticity in Relation to the World Heritage Convention*, ICOMOS, Nara, 1–6 November 1994.

A. Fisher, *Neue Architektur durch Umnutzung alter Gebäude und Anlagen. New Life in Old Buildings*, Karl Krämer Verlag, Stuttgart and Zurich, 1992.

S. Cantacuzino, *Re/Architecture: Old Buildings/New Uses*, Thames and Hudson, London, 1989.

M. Mackeith, *The History and Conservation of Shopping Arcades*, Mansell Publishing Limited, London and New York, 1986.

Typological approach—industrial buildings

D. K. Carter (ed.), *Remaking Post-Industrial Cities: Lessons from North America and Europe*, Routledge, New York, 2016.

M. Baum, K. Christiaanse (eds.), *City as Loft: Adaptive Reuse as a Resource for Sustainable Urban Development*, gta publishers, Zurich, 2012.

M. Berger and L. Wong (eds.), *Adapting Industrial Structures*, vol. 2 of *Interventions Adaptive Reuse,* Department of Interior Architecture, Rhode Island School of Design, February 2011.

C. Schittich (ed.), *Building in Existing Fabric: Refurbishment, Extensions, New Design*, Birkhäuser, Basel, 2003.

F. Bordage, F. Faure, *The Factories: Conversions for Urban Culture*, Birkhäuser, Basel, 2002.

M. Stratton, *Industrial Buildings Conservation and Regeneration*, Taylor and Francis, London, 2000.

P. Eley, J. Worthington, *Industrial Rehabilitation: The Use of Redundant Buildings for Small Enterprises*, Architectural Press, London, 1984.

Technical approach

Some authors have dealt with the theme of adaptive reuse by focusing on the technical sense of the term and, in some cases, have published "guides" or manuals that serve to illustrate how a building can be converted for reuse. In the book by David Highfield (1987), *The Rehabilitation and Re-use of Old Buildings*, the first macro differentiation is between residential buildings and non-residential buildings, followed by a comprehensive technical section with performance indicators for the improvement of the pre-existing buildings—fire resistance, sound and heat insulation, and so on. The last section offers a series of case studies discussed from a purely technical and infrastructural point of view. In the following years the author extended his research to cover additional case studies while maintaining the same approach to his work. In common with the works of D. Highfield, James Douglas (2006) included a technical analysis, paying little attention to the conservation of the heritage of pre-existing structures. In contrast, other authors focused on an interdisciplinary approach to the theme of adaptive reuse of historical buildings (Rabun, Kelso, 2009).

G. Giebeler, R. Fisch, H. Krause, F. Musso, K. Petzinka, A. Rudolphi, *Refurbishment Manual: Maintenance, Conversions, Extensions*, Birkhäuser, Basel, 2009.

C. Gorse, D. Highfield, *Refurbishment and Upgrading of Buildings, 2nd Edition*, Spon Press, Abingdon, Oxford, 2009.

J. Rabun, R. Kelso, *Building Evaluation for Adaptive Reuse and Preservation*, John Wiley & Sons, Hoboken, New Jersey, 2009.

D. Highfield, *Refurbishment and Upgrading of Existing Buildings*, 1st Edition, Spon Press, Abingdon, Oxfordshire, 2000.

D. Highfield, *The Rehabilitation and Re-use of Old Buildings*, Spon Press, Abingdon, Oxfordshire, 1990.

Strategic approach

The strategic approach to adaptive reuse focuses its attention on the processes and strategies behind the necessary change in significance of the buildings. Rodolfo Machado (1976) proposes a series of metaphors to suggest different ways of thinking about adaptive reuse of historical buildings. Similarly, Philippe Robert (1989), without making specific reference to Machado's study, discusses the concept of conversion using the metaphor of a schedule. He presents seven categories or concepts representing an equal number of specific physical interventions that he identifies by the analysis of many examples from ancient times to the postmodern period: 1. building within; 2. building over; 3. building around; 4. building alongside; 5. recycling material or vestiges; 6. adapting to a new function; 7. building in the style of. Another approach is proposed by Graeme Brooker and Sally Stone (2004). They outline three different intervention strategies for pre-existing buildings, analyzing a large number of cases of contemporary conversion: 1. intervention; 2. insertion; 3. installation. Furthermore, the approach of the two authors begins with a consideration of the physical dimension of the conversion before focusing on the sentimental and participatory aspects of each reuse. In their opinion, the most important aspect of the entire process is the original building and what it represents. Frank Peter Jäger (2010) uses a similar approach consisting in a discussion on selected case studies classified on the basis of the conversion strategy adopted: 1. addition;

2. transformation; 3. conversion. The case studies were selected on the basis of their architectural quality and originality. Conversely, Johannes Cramer and Stefan Breitling (2007) make a distinction between "project strategy" and "architectural expressiveness," including the expressive and aesthetic qualities of the intervention: this distinction appears less effective than later studies where the examples illustrated seem to fluctuate between the different categories of interpretation.

F. Jäger (ed.), *Old & New: Design Manual for Revitalizing Existing Buildings*, Birkhäuser, Basel, 2010.

G. Brooker, "Infected Interiors: Remodelling Contaminated Buildings," in *IDEA Journal*, 2006, pp. 1–13.

E. van Hooydonk, *Soft Values of Seaports: A Strategy for the Restoration of Public Support for Seaports*, Garant Publishers, Antwerp, 2007.

J. Cramer, S. Breitling, *Architecture in Existing Fabric*, Birkhäuser, Berlin, 2007.

P. Robert, *Adaptations: New Uses for Old Buildings*, Editions du Moniteur, Paris, 1989.

Industrial archeology and industrial heritage

As for many other disciplines, industrial archeology and the history of industrial heritage have had a complex evolution. From a historical point of view, Great Britain is considered by many the first country that recognized the role played by industrialization in its history and manifested the need of studying the process in greater depth. The expression "industrial archaeology," despite already in use in learned circles in Great Britain at that time (Cossons, 1975), was proposed by Michael Rix in 1955. The Council of British Archaeology made it official in 1959. Nevertheless, it was only with the demolition of the historic building of Euston Station in 1962 and the ensuing protests that the discipline of industrial archeology gained traction. In his paper from 1963, Rodney Richey Green highlights that Great Britain should have produced a catalogue of the derelict buildings from the first part of the industrialization era (18th and 19th centuries) based on a method of work derived from "classical" archeology. The results of this "cataloging" would then have been the subject of subsequent studies by economic and technological historians. The same attention to the buildings is evident in the work of Michael Rix (1967), who regards early Industrial Revolution buildings as true monuments. Subsequently, having superseded the effect of the "semantic disturbance" caused by the name (a reminder that the English write archaeology while in Ameri-can English and elsewhere it is written archeology), today, it is agreed that if archeology is the science that studies artifacts and the evidence of the activity of man in ancient times, then industrial archeology is the science that studies the artifacts and evidence from the age of the Industrial Revolution, in all its aspects and physical manifestations (machines, buildings, technology, infrastructure) and the economic and social consequences which followed (Hudson, 1979). However, thanks to a multi-disciplinary approach to the study, the term "industrial heritage" is preferred to industrial archeology. Once the meaning of the term "industrial archeology" is understood and it has been ascertained that the term industrial heritage is more functional and articulated, researchers begin to wonder what will happen after the work of identification, cataloging, and study. Although the expansion of the industrial base during the

first phase of industrialization and after WWII was seen in a negative light due to its intrusive impact on the landscape, today the factories are generally agreed to constitute the founding stone of our contemporary culture (Harrison, Schofield, 2010). The need for refurbishment and the closing down of many industrial sites, especially those which remained within the confines of the expanding cities in the 20th century, helped to shift the debate towards the need to safeguard this cultural heritage. Authors began to make a true appraisal of these sites, conferring symbolic and cultural values and not just economic ones on the components of the industrial age (Bergeron, 2014).

H. Orange, *Reanimating Industrial Spaces: Conducting Memory Work in Post-Industrial Societies*, Routledge, New York, 2016.

L. Bergeron, "Gasholders as a heritage," in *Patrimoine de l'industrie. Ressources, pratiques, cultures*, n. 32, 2014, pp. 63–70.

J.-F. Belhoste, P. Smith, P.-O. Deschamps, *Architectures et Paysages Industriels: L'invention d'un Patrimoine*, Editions de La Martinière, Paris, 2012.

R. Harrison, J. Schofield, *After Modernity: Archaeological Approaches to the Contemporary Past*, Oxford University Press, Oxford, 2010.

P. Dambron, *Patrimoine industriel et développement local: le patrimoine industriel et sa réappropriation territoriale*, Delaville, Paris, 2004.

J. Cowie, J. Heathcott, *Beyond the Ruins: The Meanings of Deindustrialization*, Cornell University Press, New York, 2003.

I. Tognarini, A. Nesti, *Archeologia Industriale. L'oggetto, i metodi, le figure professionali*, Carocci, Rome, 2003.

C. Cartier, *L'héritage industriel, un patrimoine*, CRDP, Besançon, 2002.

F. Bordage, F. Faure, *The Factories: Conversions for Urban Culture*, Birkhäuser, Basel, 2002.

F. Bordage, *TransEuropeHalles, Factories of the Imagination*, Birkhäuser, Basel, 2002.

B. H. Bradley, *The Works: The Industrial Architecture of the United States*, Oxford University Press, New York, 1999.

M. Palmer, P. Neaverson, *Industrial Archeology: Principles and Practice*, Routledge, London, 1998.

L. Bergeron, G. Dorel-Ferré, *Le patrimoine industriel: un nouveau territoire*, Liris, Paris, 1996.

P. A. Shackel, *Culture Change and New Technology. An Archaeology of the American Industrial Era*, Plenum Press, New York, 1996.

D. L. Uzzell, "Create Place Identity through Heritage Interpretation," in *International Journal of Heritage Studies*, n. 1, 1996, pp. 219–28.

J. Alfrey, T. Putnam, *The Industrial Heritage: Managing Resouces and Uses*, Routledge, London, 1992.

J.-Y. Andrieux, *Le Patrimoine Industriel*, PUF, Paris, 1992.

M. J. Choffel-Mailfert, J. Romano, *Vers une Transition Culturelle? Sciences et Techniques en Diffusion: Patrimoines Reconnus, Cultures Menacées*, PUN, Nancy, 1991.

L'étude et la mise en valeur du patrimoine industriel, Edition du CNRS, Paris, 1985.

J. Pinard, *L'archéologie Industrielle*, PUF, Paris, 1985.

B. Trinder, *The Making of the Industrial Landscape*, Phoenix, London, 1982.

R. Gould, M. Schiffer (eds.), *Modern Material Culture: The Archeology of Us*, Academic Press, New York, 1981.

M. Daumas, *L'archéologie industrielle en France*, Robert Laffont, Paris, 1980.

K. Hudson, *World Industrial Archaeology*, Cambridge University Press, Cambridge, 1979.

T. E. Leary, "Industrial Archeology and Industrial Ecology," in *Radical History Review*, no. 21, 1979, pp. 177–82.

T. A. Sande, *Industrial Archeology: A New Look at the American Heritage*, S. Greene Press, Brattleboro, Vermont, 1976.

Transactions of the First International Congress on the Conservation of Industrial Monuments, Ironbridge, 29 May–5 June 1973, Ironbridge Gorge Museum Trust, Ironbridge, 1975.

N. Cossons, *The BP Book of Industrial Archaeology*, David and Charles, Newton Abbot, 1975.

K. Hudson, *Exploring Our Industrial Past*, Hodder & Stoughton, London, 1975.

J. K. Major, *Fieldwork in Industrial Archaeology*, Batsford, London, 1975.

A. Buchanan, *The Theory and Practice of Industrial Archeology*, Bath University Press, Bath, 1974.

R. A. Buchanan, *Industrial Archaeology in Great Britain*, Penguin, London, 1972.

A. Raistrick, *Industrial Archaeology: An Historical Survey*, Eyre Methuen, London, 1972.

M. Rix, *Industrial Archaeology*, Historical Association, London, 1967.

R. R. Green, *The Industrial Archaeology of County Down*, HMSO, Belfast, 1963.

K. Hudson, *Industrial Archeology: An Introduction*, Baker, London, 1963.

L. Mumford, *Technics and Civilization*, Routledge & Kegan, London, 1934.

Ecological approach and urban sustainable development

Contemporary planning, which developed in the 1960s, acknowledges the earlier fundamental political errors in the management of environmental resources. It also announces a new awareness of the need for a radical change in thinking and approaching the environmental management (Bateson, 1977).
The first error observed by those authors who dedicated themselves to the subject was the supposed linearity response of the human ecosystems, capable of prediction and controllable. The second error is the assumption that human and natural ecosystems could be considered independently from each other. The city is regarded as the epicenter of the contemporary crisis—an economic, political, cultural, and environmental crisis—and the analysis of the texts reveals how the various authors concur on the dual nature of the challenge faced by the administrators of modern urban areas. On the one hand, they have to deal with economic, social, and environmental problems, which are increasingly interrelated and cannot be resolved separately.

On the other hand, they have to confront a political disposition and actions oriented to a vision of the future in order to earn the greatest consensus.
The concept of urban sustainability represents the response formulated from a theoretical point of view, while the planning strategy constitutes the most efficient instrument available from a practical point of view.
The first of the two terms is still a long way from having an univocal definition, not only because the same concept can be interpreted in different ways (James, 2015) but also because a brief transposition of the concept of urban sustainability is not possible. In any case it implies two premises: first, the maximization of positive synergies and the minimization of the negative external factors that develop among the underlying political, economic, social, and environmental systems of the city; second, the presence of a collective social learning process that can trigger cultural change, in terms of mentality, value systems, and lifestyle through the direct participation of the urban players. Studies such as that by Carl Folke (2002) assert the concept of resilience, or the capacity of complex systems to learn, evolve, and adapt themselves to a reality that is well articulated and involves rapid change.
Strategic planning represents the most appropriate instrument for launching and supporting this process of change (Scott Armstrong, 1986). It represents the most recent and sophisticated means available which, on the one hand, reverts to the systemic approach adopted in the structural plans of the 1970s and coordinates the interventions respecting each of these dimensions; on the other hand, it also encourages stakeholder involvement, not limited solely to the major players in urban development but expanding it to a wider range of interested parties (Wood, Landry, 2008).
Since natural and social systems have non-linear behavior and they are inherently dynamic and interact in a synergetic way, it is necessary to employ complex plans and approaches in order to transform urban systems in a controlled and integrated way.
A recent work (James, 2015) reiterates the need for a holistic approach to the study of urban phenomena.

P. James, *Urban Sustainability in Theory and Practice: Circles of Sustainability*, Routledge, London, 2015.

A. Scerri, *Greening Citizenship: Sustainable Development, the State and Ideology*, Palgrave McMillan, Basingstoke, 2013.

L. Fabian, E. Giannotti, P. Viganò, *Recycling City: Lifecycles, Embodied Energy, Inclusion*, Giavedoni editore, Pordenone, 2012.

W. Fawcett, "Flexible Strategies for Long-term Sustainability under Uncertainty," in *Building Research & Information*, vol. 40, 2012.

UN-Habitat, *State of the Cities Report 2012/2013: Prosperity of Cities*, Earthscan, London, 2012.

M. Alberti, *Advances in Urban Ecology: Integrating Humans and Ecological Processes in Urban Ecosystems*, Springer, New York, 2008.

N. B. Grimm et al, "Global Change and Ecological of Cities," *Science*, n. 319, 2008, pp. 756–60.

P. Wood, C. Landry, *The Intercultural City: Planning for Diversity Advantage*, Earthscan, London, 2008.

S. Bell, S. Morse, *Measuring Sustainability: Learning from Doing*, Earthscan Publications, London, 2003.

C. Folke, S. Carpenter, T. Elmqvist, L. Gunderson, C. S. Holling, B. Walker, "Resilience and Sustainable Development:

Building Adaptive Capacity in a World of Transformations," in *AMBIO: A Journal of the Human Environment*, n. 32, 2002, pp. 437–40.

S. Campbell, "Green Cities, Growing Cities, Just Cities? Urban Planning and the Contradictions of Sustainable Development," in *Journal of the American Planning Association*, Summer 1996, pp. 296–312.

W. Rees, M. Wackernagel, "Urban Ecological Footprints: Why Cities Cannot Be Sustainable and Why They Are a Key to Sustainability," in *Environmental Impact Assessment Review*, n. 16, 1996, pp. 223–48.

P. Söderbaum, *Economics and Ecological Sustainability. An Actor-Network Approach to Evaluation*, Third International Workshop on Evaluation in Theory and Practice, London, 1996.

H. Mintzberg, *The Rise and Fall of Strategic Planning*, Prentice Hall Europe, Glasgow, 1994.

D. Pearce (ed.), *Blueprint 2: Greening the World Economy*, Earthscan Publications, London, 1991.

Commission of the European Communities, *Green Paper on the Urban Environment*, EEC, Brussels, 1990.

F. Archibugi, P. Nijkamp, *Economy and Ecology: Towards Sustainable Development*, Kluwer Academic, Dordrecht, 1989.

A. Bramwell, *Ecology in the Twentieth Century: A History*, Yale University Press, New Haven, 1989.

P. Hall, *Cities of Tomorrow*, Basil Blackwell, Oxford, 1988.

A. Faludi, *A Decision-centred View of Environmental Planning*, Pergamon Press, Oxford, 1987.

World Commission on Environment and Development, *Our Common Future*, Oxford University Press, Oxford, 1987.

J. L. Kaufman, H. M. Jacobs, "A Public Planning Perspective on Strategic Planning," in *APA Journal*, n. 53, 1987, pp. 23–31.

D. L. Sorkind, N. B. Ferris, J. Hudak, *Strategies for Cities and Countries: A Strategic Planning Guide*, Public Technology, Washington, D.C., 1984.

G. Bateson, *Steps To An Ecology of Mind*, Balantine, New York, 1977.

D. H. Meadows, D. L. Meadows, J. Randers, W. W. Behrens, *The Limits to Growth: A Report for the Club of Rome's Project on the Predicament of Mankind*, Universe Books, New York, 1972.

From the culture of transformation to the culture of conservation

Pope Pius II, *Cum almam nostram urbaem* 1492

Pope Pius II empowers the papal bull that prevents the plundering of ruins

Letter from Raffaello Sanzio to Pope Leone X 1519

for the protection and preservation of the vestiges of ancient Rome

French Revolution 1789

Declaration of the Rights of Man and of the Citizen

DEMOCRACY AND INCLUSION

Ruskin, *The Seven Lamps of Architecture* 1849

"It is impossible, as impossible as to raise the dead, to restore anything that has ever been great or beautiful in architecture."

Great Exhibition of London 1851

Viollet-le-Duc, *Restauration* 1866

"Restaurer un édifice, ce n'est pas l'entretenir, le réparer ou le refaire, c'est le rétablir dans un état complet qui peut n'avoir jamais existé à un moment donné."

Great Exhibition of Washington 1876

Wagner, Puck Building in New York 1886

Great Exhibition of Paris 1889

UNDEMOCRACY AND EXLUSION

1830 Delacroix, *La Liberte guidant le peuple*

1844 Turner, *Rain, Steam and Speed*

1871 Levi Strauss & Co. begins the production of the 501

1875 Monet, *Train dans la neige*

Tour Eiffel

Romanticism

Post-Impressionism

Art Nouveau

#society

#buildings

Sullivan, Bayard Building in New York 1898

Riegl, *Die Stimmung als Inhalt der modernen Kunst* 1899

Behrens, AEG's Turbine Factory in Berlin 1909

Gropius, Fagus Factory in Alfeld 1913

WW1

First edition of the CIAM 1928

Congrès International d'Architecture Moderne, La Sarraz

The Athens Charter 1931

for the Restoration of Historic Monuments

Le Corbusier, *Athens Charter* 1933

Fourth edition of the CIAM

WW2

Concept of Public Property Protection 1954

UNESCO Convention for the Protection of Cultural Property in the Event of Armed Conflict

#art

1901 Pellizza da Volpedo, *Il quarto stato*

Artist's house in avenue de Reille 53, Paris

Russolo, *Dinamismo di un treno*

1912 Picasso, *Naturaleza muerta con silla*

1914 Sant'Elia, *La Citta Nuova*

1917 Duchamp, *Fountain*

Thayaht, *Tuta*

Höch, *Cut with the Dada Kitchen Knife through the Last Weimar Beer-*

1919 *Belly Cultural Epoch in Germany*

1922 Le Corbusier designs the artist's house

Evans starts documenting small-town life and the rural communities during the depression

1936 Chaplin, *Modern Times*

1937 501s are published in *Vogue* for the first time

Art Nouveau

Vienna Secession

Futurism

Dada

Bauhaus

American social realist photography

Castelvecchio Museum is completed in Verona 1957

11th and last edition of the CIAM 1958

Concept of Industrial Archeology 1959

London's Ironbridge is appointed monument 1962
after the demolition of Euston Arch

The Venice Charter 1964
for the Conservation and Restoration of Monuments and Sites

Concept of Cultural Heritage 1972
UNESCO, World Heritage Convention

UN Conference on Human Environment in Stockholm

1st International Congress of TICCIH 1973
The International Committee for the Conservation of the Industrial Heritage

International Conference "Old into New" and "Old and New Architecture" 1977

CULTURAL

Ironbridge: UNESCO's first industrial site 1986

1956 James Dean wears 501s in *Giant*

Warhol opens the Factory at 231 East 47th Street in Midtown Manhattan

1963 Dylan performs at the Newport Folk Festival wearing 501s

1967 Debord, *La Société du Spectacle*

1970 New Westbeth artists colony in New York

Situationist International

Pop Art

Land Art

ECOLOGY

1975 Matta-Clark, *Conical Instersect*, Paris (demolished)

Inauguration of the Gare d'Orsay Museum

Concept of Sustainable Development 1987

The Berlin Wall is opened 1989

Concept of Cultural Landscape 1992

Earth Summit in Rio de Janeiro

Start of the Euroméditerranée project in Marseille 1995

Kyoto Protocol 1997

Inauguration of Centrale Montemartini in Rome

Concept of Landscape 2000

Council of Europe, European Landscape Convention

Concept of Intangible Cultural Heritage 2003

UNESCO, Convention for the Safeguarding of the Intangible Cultural Heritage

United Nations Conference on Sustainable Development in Rio de Janeiro 2012

Officine Fagus in UNESCO's list 2013

Paris Climate Agreement 2015

XVI International Congress of TICCIH 2016

IBA Emscher Park is inaugurated

1990 Zucker, *Ghost*: the loft is stigmatized

Düsseldorf School of Photograpy

1998 TV show *Will & Grace* starts using Puck Building for outdoor shots

2002 Becher und Becher, *Industrielandschaften*

Inauguration of the Tate Modern building

Acknowledgments

All books are the result of a network of reflexive brains that the author catalyzes in his work—and a book on adaptive reuse drawing so much from inspiring experiences and insightful discussions even more.

My passion for American culture has been nurtured since childhood by the deep passion of my uncle Sisto Giriodi, architect and photographer, which he transmitted through movies, readings, records, and tales. My parents Daniele and Giovanna insisted that English was important in times when globalization was not even a word, and apparently this made me confident enough to dare to write this book directly in English—I count on the indulgence of my native readers for the inevitable mistakes.

The first idea of this research originated in the friendly and provocative conversations I had with Franco Corsico, urban planner and designer, while preparing the application for the 2015 German Marshall Fund (GMF) of the US Urban and Regional Policy (URP) Fellowship. I have to say that I miss those conversations—and Franco's excellent cooking that often went with them. Geraldine Gardner, director of the URP at GMF, supported with Bartek Starodaj my application process, the preliminary research, the preparation of the study trip and the editing of the first document from which this book stems—the policy paper "The Adaptive Reuse Toolkit—How Cities Can Turn their Industrial Legacy into Infrastructure for Innovation and Growth," published on the GMF's website in September 2016. The toolkit in this book is a revised version. I continue to share thoughts with Geraldine and I am proud of being part of the GMF community. GMF is an impressive and enduring effort for promoting transatlantic exchange of practices and ideas on cities. It is a precious work especially today, when the two sides of the Atlantic seem to be more distant than they were.

Donald K. Carter, founder and director of the Remaking Cities Institute at Carnegie Mellon University in Pittsburgh and author of *Remaking Post-Industrial Cities: Lessons from North America and Europe* (2016), before honoring me with the introduction to this book, has been an unfailing source of knowledge and understanding of Rust Belt cities' present and past. His rich experience as architect and urban designer made our conversations and walks in Pittsburgh a vivid lesson in city making. I am happy that the program of exchanges we promoted between Politecnico di Torino and CMU with the support of Steve Lee, head of the School of Architecture, gives us the chance of extending them to our colleagues and students.

Doug Cooper, Andrew Mellon Professor at CMU, guided us during our visit of CMU Campus. His 200-foot-long mural for Carnegie Mellon Center (1996) is an epic visual narrative of Pittsburgh's past and present and a lesson in urban history. The impressive quality of the drawing proves that nothing can rival the refinement and expression of talented craftsmanship.

Marisa Novara, program director at the Metropolitan Planning Council of Chicago helped us in organizing the Chicago field research and framing what we were seeing in a more general picture of planning policies.

During our field research we could count on support and information offered on site by local practitioners, scholars, experts, artists, managers, and activists who helped us in understanding the processes behind the places we were visiting. Nothing compares to the direct experience of places, but without interviewing the actors of its making no place can be fully understood. Each name in the following list is a person strongly committed to make his or her city a better place to live, and I am grateful to each of them—I can still recall our conversations as I write—for welcoming us and sharing with us their time and experience.

In Philadephia, Tim McDonald, founder of Onionflats, gave a passionate account of his work as architect-developer; Will Agate, senior vice president of real estate at PIDC, explained to us the strategies behind the Navy Yard project; Zoe Kaufmann and Disha Andapalling, PhD students, led our visit to the Penn State-CMU energy innovation hub; Shawn McCaney, program director of the Penn Foundation's Creative Communities, has been helpful with contacts.

In Washington, my meetings in the Federal Triangle have been fundamental to understand the financial and regulatory framework of adaptive reuse, thanks to: Brian Goeken, chief of the National Park Services' Technical Preservation Services office, Matthew Dalbey, director of the Office of Sustainable Communities, and David Lloyd, director of the Office of Brownfields and Land Revitalization, both at the Environmental Protection Agency. Andrea Limauro, Washington D.C.'s neighborhood sustainability and industrial policy coordinator, led us in the discovery of the unexpected industrial past of the capital and its most interesting reuse projects.

In Pittsburgh, Todd Reidbord, principal and president of Bakery Square developers Walnut Capital offered us a thorough visit of his achievements and a passionate account of their making and numbers; Robert Rubinstein, executive director of the Urban Redevelopment Authority of Pittsburgh, was a source

of information about seventy years of urban transformations in the city. Deborah Lange, executive director of the Western Pennsylvania Brownfields Center at CMU guided us on a journey in time and space around Steel City and along its rivers. Her database on brownfield reclamation in the area has been a precious and reliable source in writing the case studies of this book, and she photographed for us Carnegie Robotics as our status of foreign visitors did not allows us to take pictures in a plant that develops defense technologies.
In Chicago, Charlie Vinz and Caitlin Grey at Rebuilding Exchange introduced us to the art of deconstruction; James Lewis of the Heartland Alliance showed us the impressive impact of social investments at Harvest Commons and Town Hall apartments; John Mulrow, energy manager, and John Edel, founder and executive director, illustrated the visions and achievements of The Plant; Bob Dean, planner with Chicago Metropolitan Agency for Planning helped us in understanding how industrial infrastructure reuse is promoted in the Windy City.
In Detroit, we were offered insights on the city strategies in business attraction and urban regeneration by Matthew Clayson, former director of the Detroit Creative Corridor Center and Daniel Kinkead, formerly of Detroit Future City. We were guided in our tour of Shinola by its president Jacques Panis. Thanks to Charlie and Caitlin of Rebuilding Exchange we got in touch with Charlie O'Geen, architect and artist, who led us to discover the amazing reuse projects of Klinger Street. Eric Novack of Russell Industrial Center, whose business cards read "manager of nothing," explained the site and how it works to us—we hope that the RIC will be soon back and safe. Kari Smith, director of development at the Packard Plant, gave us a complete and accurate explanation of the past and future of the most amazing industrial plant we ever visited—I learned later that she is an architectural historian. In New York City, we concluded our tour with an interesting conversation with Toni L. Griffin, urban planner, founder of Urban Planning and Design for the American City, and former director of Detroit Work Project, that went well beyond the Detroit case study.
This book would not have seen the light without the energy and drive of its graphic designer Francesca Tambussi and would not be so beautiful without her skillful creativity. The drawings of Angelo Caccese with their clarity and accuracy describe the urban architecture of each case study better than many words—and with much more beauty. Anja Bippus at JOVIS was a patient and committed editor, supporting the making of the book through all its phases. The enthusiastic response of

Artbook D.A.P. to the book project has been a constant source of motivation when writing it was getting hard. Elena Vigliocco has enriched the book with her bibliographical research and timeline summary on adaptive reuse in history—and pushed me to take the responsibility of writing footnotes and properly quote sources.

Carlo Olmo, who I met in 1986 as a young architecture student attending his unforgettable lessons in history of contemporary architecture—a course I took twice—and now a dear friend and colleague at the Department of Architecture and Design of Politecnico di Torino, has had the patience to read the draft essay, in spite of the historical and theoretical shortcuts a designer takes when dealing with issues with complex backgrounds. Its final quality owes much to his precious critiques and comments, but he is accountable for none of its many possible errors.

Last, the careful reader will have noticed a recurrent use of "we" in the text. My spouse in life and associate in practice at TRA, Isabelle Toussaint, has been taking the ride through the States with me, sharing encounters, visits and thoughts, comments and reflections. I could not tell what is mine and what is hers in this book, but I am sure that without her I would never have developed neither the interest in adaptive reuse that is the reason of this book—nor other more important things in life.

Our two sons Pierre and Thomas sustained a struggling father for some weeks, and will hopefully appreciate the result of his efforts.

This is a toolkit for post-industrial cities and their citizens. Industrial activity has deeply shaped these places in physical and economic terms, but the prefix "post" means that this industry belongs more to their past than to their present. This could be the case in your city. Your city might be full of closed factories. Maybe you or your family members have spent some part of your life working in one of those factories. Or perhaps you were not even born when your city was bursting with industrial energy. Yet you can still feel this energy in the air. Part of this is the collective memory of what used to be. But an equally significant part is the identity and the physical legacy of this industry.

All over the world, industrial infrastructure is being creatively repurposed. Culture, leisure, sports, research, education, design, services, production, housing, and even agriculture are bringing life back into abandoned factories. This process is called adaptive reuse.

Adaptive reuse can be sparked by whoever feels the power of the industrial past and dares to imagine a future for its legacy. No matter if you are a professional, an activist, a decision-maker, an investor, or simply a committed citizen: if you feel that the

abandoned factory on your way could become part of your community's future, this toolkit is for you.

American cities faced unprecedented challenges in reviving large industrial spaces. They did it without the safety nets of European urban policies and public spending, but also with fewer constraints than the European planning system and a stronger tradition of civic commitment. Finally, while European cities can rely on a rich historical legacy and rooted social capital, higher mobility within the United States compels cities to innovate in order to retain and attract individuals, families, and investment.

This toolkit draws from this experience in creating an eight-step approach for how to make adaptive reuse work in your community. Written in a transatlantic comparative perspective, it outlines some specific features of adaptive reuse projects in North American post-industrial cities that could inspire European policy makers and US practitioners in making adaptive reuse an ingredient of successful city-making.

Reuse happens when individuals or groups introduce new content into an existing container (building, infrastructure, place, area), content that

differs from the one the container was originally designed for. Adaptive reuse is carried out by adapting the content to the container rather than the contrary; it involves maximum conservation and minimal transformation. It is the most radical approach to reuse: instead of keeping what still fits, you make fit so that you can keep everything. Examples from the US cities visited prove that existing form can host new functions through adaptive reuse. Reuse often proves better than demolition and reconstruction for a number of reasons. It's good for local culture, because the industrial legacy is part of the urban landscape, is rooted into the city's identity, and offers astonishing spaces and structures. It draws investment, as innovative activities seem to be attracted by the flexibility of space and freedom of use offered by existing industrial buildings. Reuse is better for the environment, as "the greenest building is the one that is already built." Finally, reuse strengthens a feeling of community by positively linking a city's past to its future, and offering cheap and robust infrastructure to emerging needs, thus sparking holistic renewal processes.

Explore possibilities

Deindustrialization leaves cities with a large stock of opportunities. To minimize required resources and budget, an adaptive reuse project starts with the selection of the appropriate infrastructure or building to reuse. This phase is important to build community awareness around potential opportunities, but there needs to be some structure to support this exploration.

Cities should keep track of private and public assets and their current status in order to prevent blight and promote reuse. In Pittsburgh, the Urban Redevelopment Authority constantly updates an online map of vacant properties based on tax foreclosures. Any individual, local group, entrepreneur or developer can freely browse it to select opportunities for reuse and redevelopment projects. In 2014, The Detroit Blight Removal Task Force produced a similar on-line dynamic tool, the Motor City Mapping. It is the result of a mix of public authority data as tax foreclosures and a web-based collaborative assessment named "blexting" in which anyone could contribute with photos and data to build a complete and an accurate knowledge of the city's 380,217 vacant properties.

These examples show that blending "cold" knowledge from public databases with "warm" local experience supported by open source or free web-based tools is enormously effective. The possibility of constant improvement and update, the availability on portable devices, and the possibility of adding other relevant geo-referred data layers offer unprecedented transparency and knowledge to city actors at all levels. This bridges the historical gap between city planners and on-the-ground citizens.

Mapping in itself can become a task that aggregates community energy around a reuse project. Urban explorers all over the world often break into abandoned industrial sites to explore them and share their knowledge through social media. Participatory tools such as urban transect walks can be used not only to map but also to raise awareness and promote commitment in local communities. For example, the celebrated High Line ● in New York City was saved by a bottom-up action

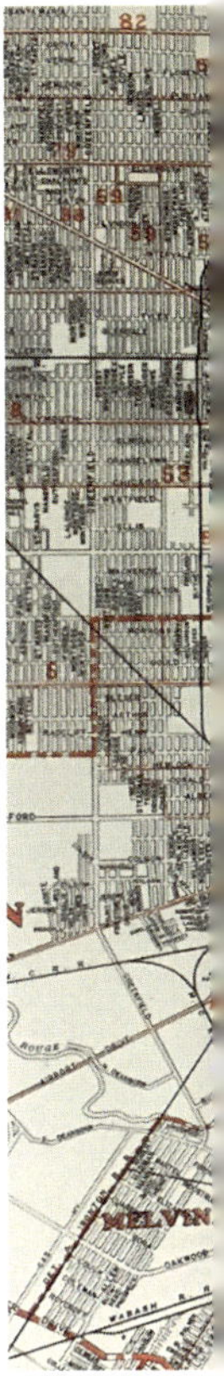

19

by local activists—the "Friends of The High Line"—that fought in court against scheduled demolition but also promoted community and heritage walks on the abandoned railway to win support.

Assess potential

Any abandoned industrial area or building has its peculiar
features. Before falling under the spell of your industrial icon
—and investing large amounts of time and energy in a reuse
project—it is important to understand what its specific positive
and negative features are and how they can influence the reuse
process. Successful projects visited during this research were
all based on a deep understanding of the existing market reality
and clear preliminary strategic choices.

First, one must chose the right place. Location plays a central
role in reuse, as in any city-making process. Location includes
accessibility, connections, services, neighboring areas, visibility,
and views. All these factors are incorporated in site and have to
be carefully weighed in advance. Some of these factors might be
potential negative influences, while others will provide positive
ones. Bakery Square is along a main city axis, near existing 6
public transport, between deprived and wealthy neighborhoods.
Russell Industrial Center is near an important highway 14
junction, and is therefore visible and accessible to the larger
public. The Plant might seem to be in the middle of nowhere, 10
in a place where land is cheap enough to experiment, but it is
just a quarter of an hour by car from Downtown Chicago and a
ten-minute walking distance from two main bus lines.

Second, comes the determination of the appropriate scale of
intervention. Context and goals define the right size and form
of projects. Where property is fragmented and multiple small
actors will be engaged in a long-term incremental strategy, reuse
will be a sort of "urban acupuncture" by tenths of square feet
as in Corktown or in Fishtown. Where assets have a single 16 2
owner and investor, you can foresee massive engagement in
steps measurable in acres, as at the Packard Plant. Where the 18
goal is the extensive and complete reuse of a whole part of the
city, reuse will assume the form of a comprehensive area master
plan, as at the Navy Yard in Philadelphia. Where reuse should 1
be the catalyst of a more general regeneration process, as
along the Monongahela, a line as thin as a walking and biking 4
lane is enough to reconnect and revive different sites over an
extended region.

B

Third, can the potential of existing structures be maximized? The specific qualities of any existing industrial infrastructure offer opportunities for their reuse. Load bearing capacity is what makes old multi-story industrial buildings attractive for artists and makers. Serial spaces can be easily portioned to fit users as different as Google and the local artist. Small plots are perfect for incremental reuse, either at urban scale—as
in Pittsburgh's Penn Avenue ● regeneration—but also large 7
spaces can be reused by inserting small scale sub-structures
for multiple users, such as the food stalls at Union Market ● in 3
Washington D.C., the former food delivery hub of the capital that has become a destination for foodies and will soon be at the core of an ambitious redevelopment plan. Large spans can accommodate new forms of working and/or living; high ceilings can host oversized art or industrial production, but also allow the insertion of minor volumes and intermediate spaces such as the
Urban Outfitters' headquarters at the Navy Yard; ● bridge cranes 1
that once lifted raw steel beams can now lift high-tech but still
heavy machinery at Carnegie Robotics. ● 9

Fourth, the art of linking a contemporary story to a powerful memory: in most industrial cities, civic identity has been shaped through and by industrialization, which involves a constant process of creative destruction, innovation, economic growth,

and social change that are the ingredients of a legacy that can sustain new narratives. Pittsburgh-born Andy Warhol in 1962 labeled his New York City creative platform experiment "The Factory"—and located it in a former firehouse in East Midtown Manhattan, with no heat or running water. Nearly all the places visited for this research openly link the future to the past by reusing an industrial legacy. Their communication uses industrial imagery, adopts vintage graphics, echoes factory culture in slogans and style, and offers a reconstruction of the past history and often a photographic archive enriched with interviews and original documents.

At the same time, potential can also be negative and even turn into hazard. A site could be polluted; clean-up might prove an unsustainable burden for any reuse project since inexpensive space is a key factor in the reuse process—Warhol rented the Factory for one hundred dollars per year. Nonetheless, regulatory burdens in both the United States and Europe often discourage reuse in sites that have been contaminated. Decontamination can and has to be incorporated in the reuse process—for instance, by defining a development timeline that allows the use of slower but cheaper techniques such as phytoremediation, or by laying out new uses according to the cleaning requirements

imposed on existing spaces, as was the case in the Navy Yard 1
master planning. If communicated well, organizers can even generate related public funding for decontamination.
To get a preliminary understanding of contamination from past production processes, local knowledge by retired workers or neighbors can prove useful, and can be easily collected through interviews, focus groups, and public walks. This collection of local knowledge is also an opportunity to reconnect to the history and culture of a place. To evaluate its possible impact at the preliminary stage, technical support to communities and local governments by external bodies such as the US EPA can be a great resource when no previous assessment or general mapping has been carried out.

B

Envision the future

What attracts users, residents, entrepreneurs, innovators, and eventually investors to reuse projects is a compelling positive vision of the future rooted in the past. This positive projection of legacy into future is not exclusive to post-industrial cities: it is inherent to physical permanence and the living continuity of all cities and urban communities. In industrial cities, the predominance of a recent, homogeneous, and pervasive past over any other identity layer just makes this process clearer than elsewhere.

Industrial cities and communities have often endured a long period of negative narratives: decline, blight, unemployment. The future was uncertain and dark—as it was for New York City from the 1970s to the 1990s, when the city's story was industrial decline, economic stagnation, white and middle class flight, and crime.

Industrial legacy often brought clean-up and demolition costs: visit the Pittsburgh Technology Center along the Monongahela, redeveloped by the Regional Industrial Development Corporation (RIDC) in the 1990s, and you'll see no trace of its previous use neither on the site nor in the architecture. Reuse was simply not on the agenda. No potential was seen in the industrial material legacy. Often sites were cleared and cleaned before any redevelopment project was in sight: it was simply a way to move ahead in the redevelopment schedule. But even if the Texas-based shareholders of Shinola ● decided to settle in Detroit 15
after visiting available vacant spaces in the very core of Midtown, what brought people like the current president Jacques Panis to Detroit was more than the possibility of having vast space for little money. It was the possibility of reviving a mythology of American industry and marketing it. Material and immaterial legacy were equally relevant and the Argonaut building (today: A. Alfred Taubman Center for Design Education) significantly embodied both. Shinola adaptive reuse was the right way to link this rich legacy to profound trends in society and consumption. Being at the Argonaut connects Shinola to the desire for well-designed, carefully crafted, robust, and durable goods—like the best American cars in the 1950s and 1960s. Being in Detroit

shows Shinola's commitment to socially responsible production modes that create jobs in deprived communities. No new building could deliver this message as effectively.
Not all visions fit all places: East Market in Detroit is the natural location for food innovation, as Union Market ● is in Washington 3
D.C., but both would poorly brand as "tech" places. The Plant ● 10
is about feeding the city—as industrialized meatpacking was in the same district around 1900; John Edel's previous project, the Chicago Sustainable Manufacturing Center a few blocks away in the same area, builds on a different narrative—one of production innovation—but still rooted in the place.
Building an appropriate vision thus requires linking the existing infrastructure and its potential to local and global large-scale trends and challenges. Renewed attraction for urban life, extended active life expectancy, attention to quality food, new family structures, etc., are general drivers you can explore in creating a vision for a site. What do people want? What do people love? What do they fear? What do they dream of?
You can look for evidence in research and references, and draw inspiration from examples and comparables. You have to root this to the specific place you are working on, and include its legacy in your vision: project future onto the past, build the future upon the past. It's better to be foolish than reasonable —visionaries always are.

Involve partners

Another aspect all projects visited have in common is a kind of "snowball effect," or the capability of attracting forces and gaining momentum while running. It might simply be something that happens, as in the incremental regeneration of the Strip District ● in Pittsburgh or the attraction of activities at Russell Industrial Center, ● or that is designed purposefully, as in the redevelopment of Packard. ● Successful projects have to be able to convince early adopters—start-ups, artists, innovators, creative businesses, young families and users—and welcome established joiners—big firms, universities, major investors, middle-class wealthier residents.

8
14
18

Todd Reidbord's key to successful reuse of the Bakery Square ● area was his ability to build a broad and inclusive "growth coalition." Bakery Square effectively partnered with public bodies—the Urban Redevelopment Authority of Pittsburgh (URA), the Housing Finance Agency, the Building Trades Union Pension Funds of Western Pennsylvania, the Pennsylvania Department of Community and Economic Development—and

6

involved local community in the planning process through regular public hearings and meetings. In a process that took about three years, it also attracted private equity from Walnut Capital and RCG Longview Fund and gained preliminary interest from big players such as Google Inc., UPMC Technology Development Center, the University of Pittsburgh Department of Rehabilitation Sciences, and the Veterans Administration Human Engineering Research Laboratory, and established brands such as Marriott and Anthropologie. Most importantly, when Google asked Todd to double its capacity, he could rely on the established private-public partnership to gain the city's, county's, and school district's approval to buy an abandoned school building built in the 1970s just across Penn Avenue. The building was torn down to build the Bakery extension, launching the second phase of the project. The two buildings will be linked by a pedestrian bridge over the street. Bakery Square 2.0 doubles the project's capacity, investment, and number of jobs created, and diversifies the functional mix by introducing housing and services.
In a positive exchange between top-down planning and bottom-up initiatives, grassroots projects such as the community gardens of Latham Street Commons in a side street off Penn Avenue contribute to the picture. Temporary uses occupy vacant lots and unused properties, providing residents tangible signs that regeneration processes will not leave them behind. Along Penn Avenue, plots cleared due to tax foreclosures and abandoned houses are being reused for open air public art projects, and vacant shops are given over to community services such as thrift shops and child care or start to be occupied by trendy cafes.
The involvement of partners at all scales is inherent to reuse projects in a way that is largely unknown in greenfield development. Reuse happens in existing urban space. Even when a place is abandoned, there is a community around it. The fate of existing places mobilizes opinion leaders, decision makers, possible donors, potential investors, and media. These places face the loss and lack of uses and activities, so there is no need to be exclusive: in an abandoned factory or industrial area, there is usually room for more than one story, and mixed uses grant liveliness, vitality, and resilience to projects. Sharing must be incorporated into the design process by using community design tools and by taking advantage of the fact that place and space are already there. On-site activities promote a deeper understanding of the site in participants, generate shared creativity from reaction to the site, and show that reuse is already going on.

Colonize the place

Bring people to your space as soon as it is feasible to do so. This is a practice rooted in the very early phases of adaptive reuse, when it was a bottom-up practice promoted by marginal communities seeking cheap or free space and squatting spaces nobody was interested in. Adaptive reuse is a tactic that occupies abandoned spaces, as squatters often did in the 1970s in cities such as London and New York. Colonization can start from scratch and at the very beginning of a reuse process: street art painting and temporary events are enough to open the way. Some uses might be feasible now, some later; some users could be "early adopters" that give way to more established tenants later—or become more established themselves. Informality can stimulate experiments, especially in the early phases. The challenge of winning back derelict iconic spaces can mobilize local and urban communities. Reuse of Russell Industrial Center ● started with the "People's Art Festival" 14

organized by The Russell Center for Creative Arts, a non-profit where early artist tenants volunteered, subsidized by the developer. The group's communication and program explicitly referred and appealed to urban "off" cultures—the highway front of Russell displays a bold, full-height manga-style robot chimera by street artist Kobie Solomon, roaring at drivers. Street art was a winning low-cost way for keeping the Eastern Market in Detroit alive and attractive even in Motown's worst years. The area is becoming a lively cultural district where street food and fancy restaurants mix with art galleries and residential lofts, and the 2015 Murals in the Market public art festival contributes to the process while continuing a 45-year-old strategy.

In Washington D.C., the booming food industry of the capital reuses old warehouses and docks as catering infrastructure. The Mess Hall culinary incubator and the temporary restaurants
in the 40 stalls of the Union Market, ● a location where food 3
has been the core business for more than 200 years, will soon become the anchor of a huge mixed development that promises the creation of 20,000 new jobs. In both cases, real estate developers adopted guerrilla tactics learned from underground practices to create a sense of place, make it a destination, test attractiveness, brand the site, and create value through placemaking. This is a process that creates cultural and social value and later fully develops it into market value.

Some critics might label this as artwashing. In cases where real estate pressure is high, art could be regarded as a subtle way to spark gentrification—although one should not forget that places like Chelsea in New York City or Shoreditch in London were derelict only twenty years ago. But in the places we visited, no economic value was in sight when placemaking started through art and culture: early adopters and seed investors were daring enough to bet on places and visions that many would have dismissed as unrealistic.

In addition, even if success was eventually to induce early adopters to move, there will always be room enough for new experiments in post-industrial cities. Through an art project supported by the Kresge Foundation, Detroit-based young architect Charlie O'Geen is turning abandoned detached
houses of the working class neighborhood of Klinger Street ● 17
into small community facilities like a theater or a squash hall. His ingredients are abandoned houses, passionate volunteers, scrap materials, community engagement, and personal commitment. His results prove that creativity can ignite urban regeneration even where you would least expect it to happen—an ordinary blighted street of Detroit.

Design to reuse

After the reuse process has been started—the abandoned industrial site has been explored and assessed, a new vision has been shared, a network of partners committed to its revitalization is active, and colonization has started by early adopters, temporary uses, and events—a more comprehensive design approach is necessary to create a concept that fits them. To undertake this step, you need a clear understanding of what is specific to reuse planning and design.

When you plan new, you start from a concept and draw up an urban scheme accordingly. When you reuse and adapt, you start from specific site conditions and infrastructure and create a concept that fits them. In the early steps, an open concept is conducive to reuse: framed by a clear and bold vision, keeping goals relatively loose can attract new and unexpected players, allow for incremental development, and keep the process open, flexible, and reversible. This is something major top-down
developments such as the Navy Yard ● or Bakery Square ● 1 6
have in common with minor bottom-up regenerations like in
Corktown ● or Penn Avenue. ● In most cases, planning can be 16 7
useful after reuse processes have started, in order to sustain them, scale them up, and include them in a new urban vision.

In the United States—as in Europe—up until the late 1990s, industrial infrastructure was assumed to be an obstacle that should be removed. Pittsburgh offers clear examples. The agenda of its urban redevelopment authority focused on clearing brownfield sites and then cleaning them up, often without any solid redevelopment plans. Projects like the Pittsburgh Technology Center show how the existing structures of the Jones and Laughlin Steel Company, constructed in 1886, were completely demolished in 1983 to give way to a suburban high-tech campus. It was only in 2007 that the redevelopment authority launched a densification scheme to inject new energy into the location, and the only surviving infrastructure, the hot metal bridge, which originally carried crucibles of molten iron from the blast furnaces to the open hearth furnaces on the opposite bank to be converted to steel, was restored as a pedestrian and bicycle bridge.

When you design for reuse, you are in a completely different mindset. Place is already there, encumbered by existing structures, sometimes polluted, always loaded with dense memories, old pride, and new hopes, and often without any actual economic value. In reuse, the potential of the site is a central part of the concept. The given situation—location, existing buildings, site specific assets and infrastructures—is the starting point, as we saw in the first steps of this toolkit. Instead of being an obstacle, it is the frame in which reuse will happen and which will make reuse possible.

To make the most of this potential, the reuse project has to find the best mutual adaptation between use, users, and spaces. This brings us to the core of successful adaptive reuses: an effective distribution of activities and spaces within and around the existing adapted container. Regardless of their date of construction, industrial sites were designed to make flows of workers, energy, materials, and products as lean and efficient as possible. The freedom of arrangement that industrial space offers is an exceptional resource that should be designed to:

1. Create common space. The size and scale of space offers the possibility to create amazing internal covered streets, squares, elevated walkways, staircases, and ramps that connect areas and levels, multiply access possibilities, and can accommodate shared services and facilities. Adaptive reuses of these spaces should be clear, generous, and spectacular, taking advantage of the unique possibilities of oversize structures.

2. Wrap functions according to their size and comfort needs. Requirements for new uses do not match the original roughness of industrial production; sub-volumes inserted within the primary container can easily accommodate new uses, satisfy their needs and avoid unnecessary energy consumption, while offering an exceptional chance for creative arrangements which enhance the individual character of each use.

3. Save space for further reuse. The redundancy of space is the most effective form of future flexibility, and some parts should be preserved for unexpected growth or new activities. Saturation deprives adaptive reuse of its most interesting feature: the ability to evolve in time.

Many of the sites visited by the author had a specific adaptive reuse aesthetic and similar design tactics. For example,
the Urban Outfitters headquarters at the Navy Yard ● in 1
Philadelphia, which was fully professionally designed, has smaller “boxes” which occupy the large dock buildings, thereby confining the usable environments and allowing the structure to meet comfort requirements without requiring general heating

of the huge, triple-height halls. Examples like the main Nabisco building at Bakery Square ● or the infill housing schemes of 6
Onionflats ● in Philadelphia, which are all LEED certified to high 2
environmental standards, provide further evidence that smart reuse design can revive existing industrial structures and reach top energetic performances and comfort standards. Elements that are usually hidden in civil buildings, like pipes, wires, cables, panes, or shades, can be openly integrated into a post-industrial aesthetic that simplifies construction and reduces costs. Layering styles gives a tasteful vintage look and also avoids unnecessary finishings. Huge graphics define a bold urban image—and are also the cheapest way to brand a blind wall. Thus, industrial appearance is part of the charm of reused places but also sets the stage for low-cost construction techniques. Oversize buildings and infrastructure can be "frozen" and landscaped for extensive leisure and open-air uses, as the inspiring example of the German Ruhr Emscher Park coal and steel district successfully proves.
Furthermore, condemned parts and structures can become raw materials and ready-made details for original design medleys that incorporate old pieces into new settings—in interiors, like at Russell Industrial Center ● or Carnegie Robotics, ● or in the 14 9

landscaping at the Navy Yard: ● a labor intensive procedure 1
that can become a business in itself. Rebuilding Exchange ● in 12
Chicago has diverted 10,000 tons of building materials from the landfill, made over two million dollars worth of quality materials available for reuse, and hired eighty-two people with barriers to employment since 2009.

F

Placemaking and funding

Funding of reuse projects can also benefit from the inherently incremental structure of the reuse process. The existing infrastructure can be progressively activated without requiring large amounts of funding in the early steps of placemaking. Community events, cultural festivals, art installations, and temporary markets are all activities that can be organized by or with bottom-up players to temporarily occupy existing assets. One needs only the carrying the costs of making the site accessible and safe on the best preserved parts of a site, while other parts can await the larger budgets needed for full reuse. Early and partial occupation already creates a positive micro-economy of rents, fees, tickets, crowdfunding, donations, sales, and initial maintenance work. This generates economic and organizational resources that will be precious for the following phases and draws attention to formerly forgotten places, thereby creating value through placemaking.
Public funding is often available to support the very early phases of reuse processes. This happens through small seed grants handed to local players. During my talks with NPS and EPA officers in Washington, it was clear that both bodies pay attention to community engagement. Federal agencies are not entitled to local action unless directly called in by cities or communities—they otherwise risk violating state power. For the EPA, the lackluster results of the so-called "Superfund" launched in the 1980—a top-down program that involved huge sums of money—has led to an alternative approach that mainly prizes bottom-up actions. Projects start with small grants and technical support and adopt a holistic approach that sees cleanup as part of more general sustainable redevelopment. At the EPA, they call this "work with the willing." No matter who takes the initiative—a local committee, a determined mayor, a neighborhood group, a school director—the EPA provides on-demand technical advice and seed grants to local actors.
After the early colonization phases, large reuse projects often require a private-public partnership and become eligible for more extensive public funding. In an age of shrinking public budgets on both sides of the Atlantic, it is important to

understand how this can be done. While in Europe there is still a solid belief that the state or the European Union should extensively fund urban regeneration through general grants, as was the case for decades, from post-war reconstruction until the 1990s, the projects visited in the United States prove that public funding can be more effective if targeted at earlier phases and provided as a loan or tax credit rather than as a grant.
Public funding works as seed investment in the most delicate phase of a redevelopment process, when the risk is higher and private funding cannot yet be guaranteed by mortgages, and is clearly related to private beneficiaries' achievement of agreed and measurable goals of general interest such as heritage preservation, site remediation and environmental improvement, public transport and sustainable mobility, and water management.
This becomes clear when examining the funding for a successful private-public partnership project such as Bakery Square ● 6
in Pittsburgh. Direct public funding (grants) was modest, comprising only six percent of total funding. It compensated local public agencies for public works, environmental protection, and site reclamation. Tax credits and public mortgage loans made up a further ten percent of total funding. But in the first step of the project, they contributed to twenty-seven percent of funding, declining in later phases. Public support is thus mainly used not to lower private investment but rather to reduce risk in early project phases. Public support is also mainly revolving: payback in time rebuilds finances for future projects, multiplying the impact of public money.
Restoring sustainable environmental conditions and preserving industrial heritage are public goals in the US and in Europe.
In most of the projects examined, tax credits for heritage preservation—managed at the federal level by the National Park Service—and brownfield cleanup funding from the EPA (in form of a tax incentive until 2011, afterwards as a revolving loan) make the difference by encouraging preservation over demolition and sustaining brownfield rather than greenfield development.

Run and evolve

Without exception, all of the adaptive reuse projects visited have somebody leading and running them: no matter whether a community or business leader, a professional manager, or an activist volunteering his/her time. Adaptive reuse is a long-term process of evolution rather than a pre-set project, and most processes see their goals change completely along the way. Even at larger sites with more established investors, institutional partnerships, and structured strategies, we see that these have been constantly adapted and modified to grasp opportunities and incorporate uncertainty. To see this process through and take advantage of opportunities, an inspirer, a caretaker, an enabler is needed—either one person or a team. Often, steering is more important for a successful

reuse than design. This role always includes more tasks than would be included in a standard development or facility management. The makers of reuse should create a story they are able to transmit to others in order to involve them. This narrative appears to be the most effective tool to steer a complex, uncertain, and pluralistic process. Each new settler, tenant, user, visitor, each event, each new achievement has to fit in and add to the story. Public events, press, and a strong digital presence should disseminate this story while building a virtual community around the reuse process and the real community involved in it. A successful reuse process often means that some of the preliminary assumptions have to be reviewed on the run, for instance by intensifying some spaces or redefining some uses.

A successful reuse brings in new players who add new layers to the story and change the needs and goals of the project itself.

The abundance of space is a key resource in this evolutionary process. Reuse can profit from redundancy to allow future expansion of activities and uses within existing frames. This inherently incremental and evolutive structure is what makes even the most daring reuse schemes feasible and reasonable.

None of the reuse processes observed during the author's visit could be considered concluded. Within the fences of reused factories, acres of built space were still available. Around reused industrial sites, more areas awaited reclamation. Around rebuilt properties in industrial neighborhoods, boarded buildings and foreclosed plots were available for the ones wishing to join in. A simple tour (even virtual) within and around the areas described would reveal the potential still awaiting to be activated and the possibilities lying ahead. Fortunately, industrial buildings are mostly well made and can wait many years for reuse.

The complex interplay of infrastructure, community, and place makes adaptive reuse projects long-term tasks offering both early short-term outputs and lasting benefits to cities. This toolkit shows the high degree of value that adaptive reuse can provide, and the process that individuals should go through when considering reuse of an industrial site. Because adaptive reuse is an evolution, the eight-step path described here can often be relevant several times for the same site, from exploration to evolution, to reclaim more space, welcome new users, and re-adapt what was already adapted.

Part three

Adaptive reuse architecture

Issued in 1979, Neil Young's Rust Never Sleeps album remains one of my favorites. Rumor has it that the title was drawn from an advertising campaign for the product Rust-oleum, a rust inhibitor. The refrain of the first and last track was "it's better to burn out / than it is to rust": juvenile rocker's despise for aging—heroes die young.
I travelled across the US to learn more about adaptive reuse strategies and tactics. My Urban & Regional Studies Fellowship brought me through the birthplaces of American industry and to the very places where this powerful past is being reshaped into future. This is nothing unfamiliar to a native from Torino, Italy's Motown, Fordist city and company town if there is one in Europe. Torino has even recently been re-linked to Detroit. Fiat Founder Senator Giovanni Agnelli visited Albert Kahn's plants in Detroit twice before WWI. He had his engineer Giacomo Mattè Trucco incorporate this model of modern production layout into the iconic Lingotto factory. On July 21, 2011, Fiat bought the Chrysler shares held by the United States Treasury after the 2008 financial crisis. Fiat Chrysler Automobiles (FCA) is today a transatlantic global industrial partnership that closes a circle initiated

one century ago. So do I not have enough rust at home? Of course I do—one hundred million square feet in Torino in 1985, less than forty million square feet left today. But there is always something refreshing for a European researcher and practitioner in US case studies. It is the hardness of falling and the strength to recover that binds people, communities, entrepreneurs, and cities in the comeback struggle of industrial cities. The EU planning and welfare systems are a safety net: they reduce dangers and losses—but also hinder initiative and invention. US cities have to walk the rope without it. Further, EU urban population mobility is negligible if compared to the pace at which US residents flee their hometowns when they start to fail. So US cities really have to retain and attract to survive and revive—or at least to creatively manage shrinking. And they often have to cope with the dubious oversized legacy of a past, which is much larger than the present. How do they turn blight and emptiness into a positive asset, abandoned space into a potential resource? How do they reuse industrial infrastructure for innovation? How do they make longtime silent factories into vibrant urban spaces, open to new lifestyles for new generations? How do

they join private and public, community and market, local and global? How do they adapt old structures to emerging needs, forging a new identity that incorporates memory and icons of the past? These are my reasons for being here. Because here, rust actually never sleeps: it struggles to come back, and often succeeds. There are lessons to be learned here.

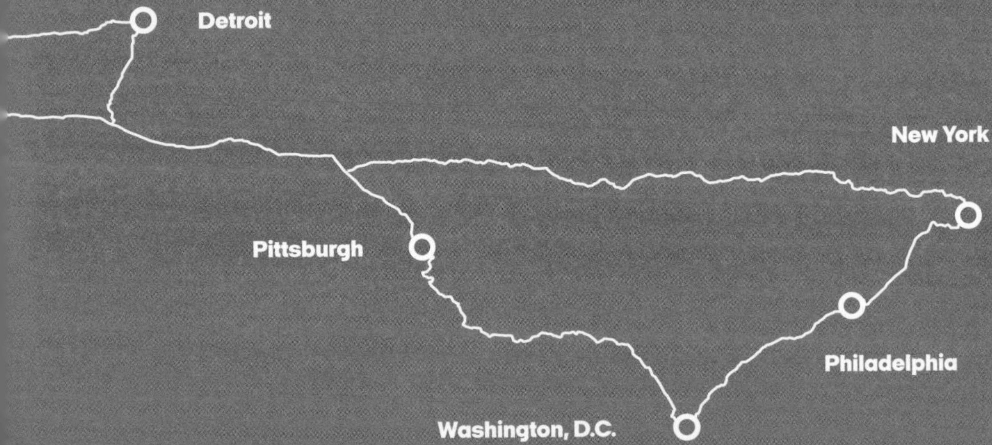

This adaptive reuse journey through US post-industrial cities began in New York on the 28th of June and ended there on the 20th of July, 2015. Unless otherwise stated, all photos were shot by me or Isabelle Toussaint with our iPhone 6 built-in cameras, as visual field notes. Drawings were made by Angelo Caccese in 2016 and 2017. Stories were written by the author in spring 2017 and are based on preparatory research, field notes, collected materials, and web sources.

Philadelphia
1

2

Rebranding the Navy Yard

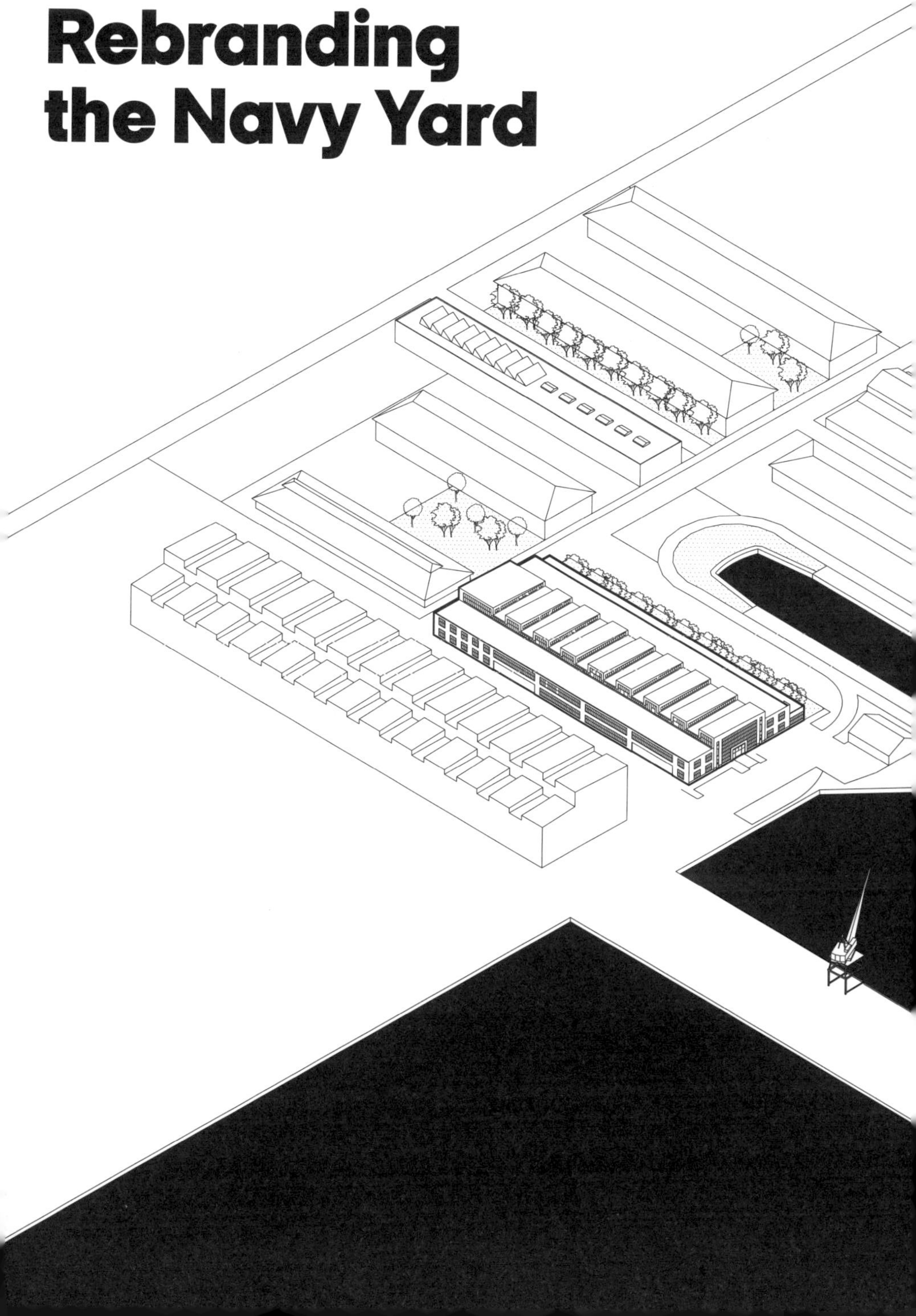

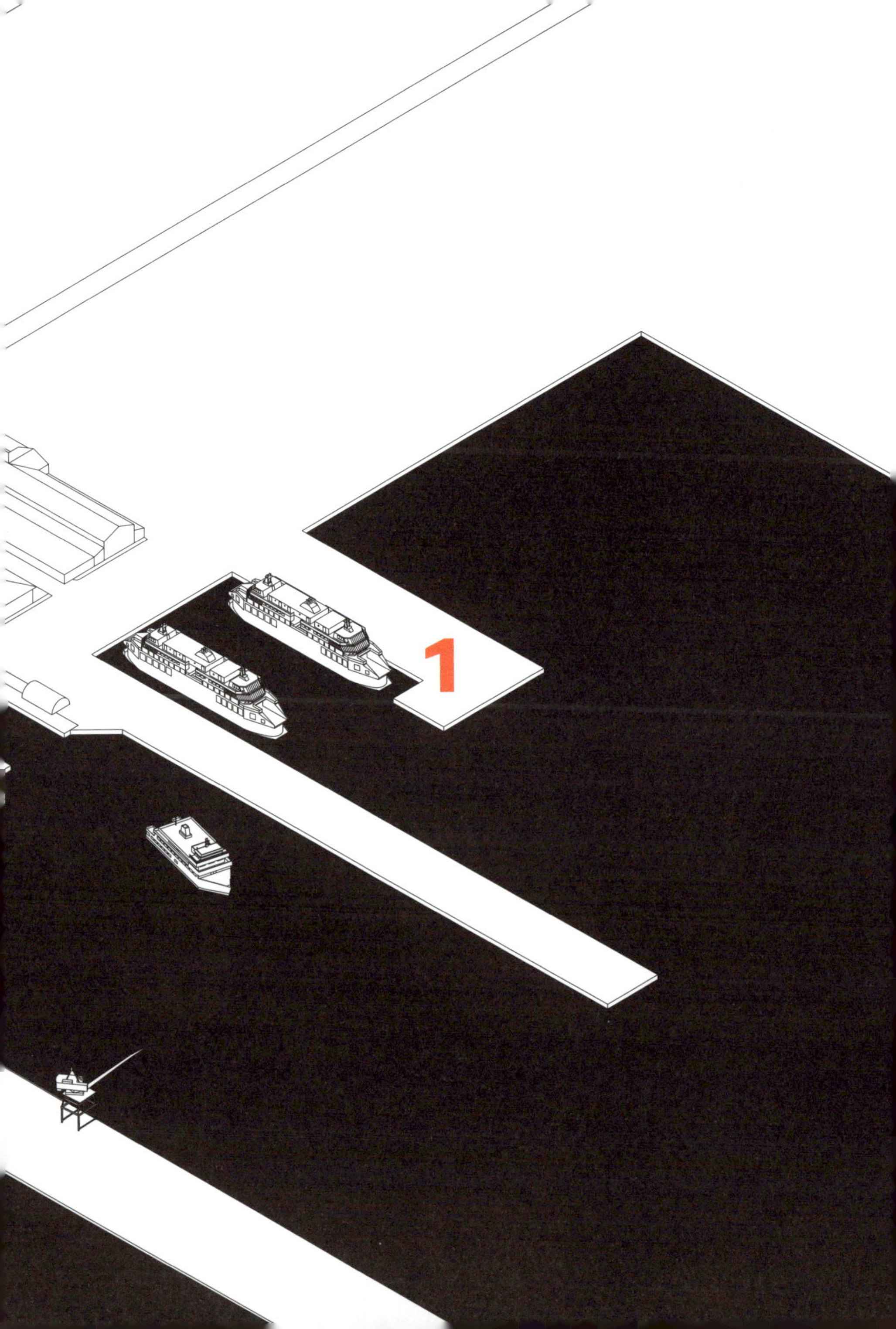
1

If any place can tell the story of 20th century US superpower, it is the Philadelphia Navy Yard, the place were American seapower was built over nearly two centuries. The last ship to leave its docks was the JFK aircraft carrier on September 12, 1995. Workers saluted it —and their jobs—goodbye. Their number had already shrunk in a few years from 12,000 to 2,000. The City of Philadelphia tried numerous legal and political actions to prevent the Navy, the economy, and the jobs from leaving. They failed.

Today the Navy Yard is a vibrant and lively place where high tech research both private, as GSK's brand new headquarter and public, with Penn State and Carnegie Mellon Universities joining forces on a shared energy innovation hub, meets lifestyle and fashion. The startling adaptation of the Dry Docks area for Urban Outfitters' main world platform by MSR Design, landscaped by D.I.R.T. Studio by reusing demolition materials and industrial infrastructure, created a campus to research, design, produce, and communicate.

If the idea of making this far away southern end of Philadelphia's Broadway into a site that attracts businesses and people, counteracts delocalization and suburbanization, and keeps taxes within city boundaries sounded daring if not crazy twenty years ago, today it is sound reality: more than 11,000 employees and about 145 companies have signed on to date. Of the total 13 million square feet of the area, 6.5 have already been redeveloped. Success.

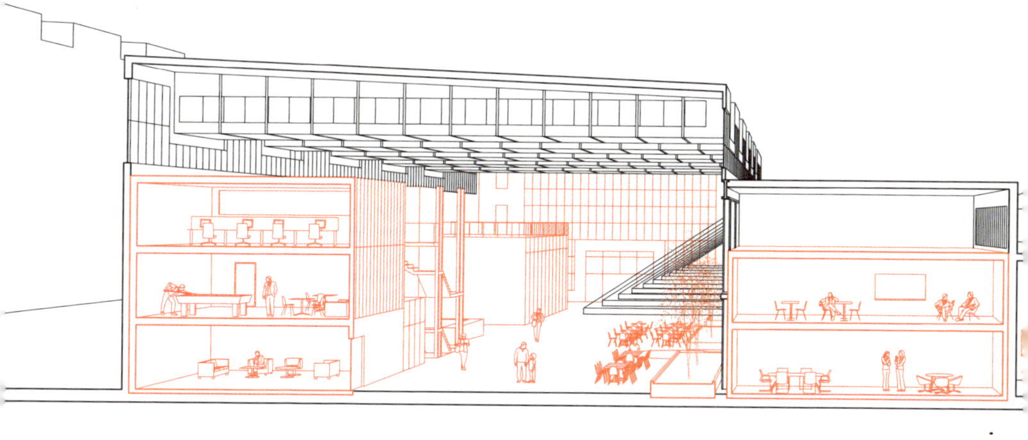

Driving through the area, you meet recently completed areas and buildings, reused historical sheds skillfully adapted for new businesses, set-aside areas that will be developed only as they reach their full potential, sites being prepared for development —building roads, planting trees, opening parks—and you can still see Navy-related industry at work.

The first masterplan from 2004 was reviewed in 2013 to extend the reuse area. The so-called "Historic Core" has become so attractive that PIDC—the private-public partnership developing the whole area—will create housing here, targeting urban loft-lovers and reuse early adopters.

You already meet them on the indoor street of the URBN Campus Commons: millennials that no longer long for the suburban American dream, appreciate the possibility to reconnect in a less time-consuming and more sustainable way of life, work, and leisure, and explore new forms of city living.

1

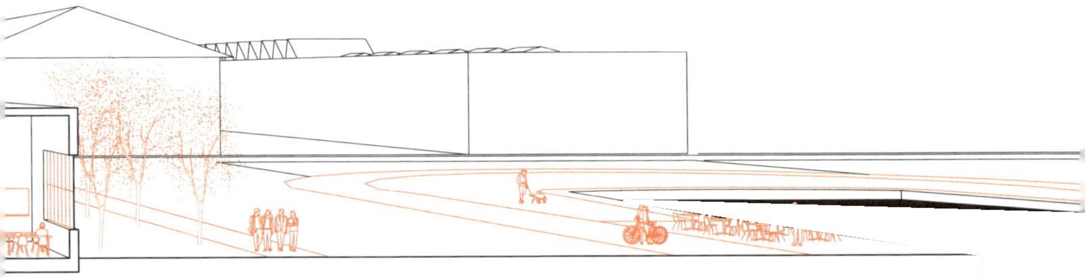

101

58

UNIGLORY

Urban acupuncture in Fishtown

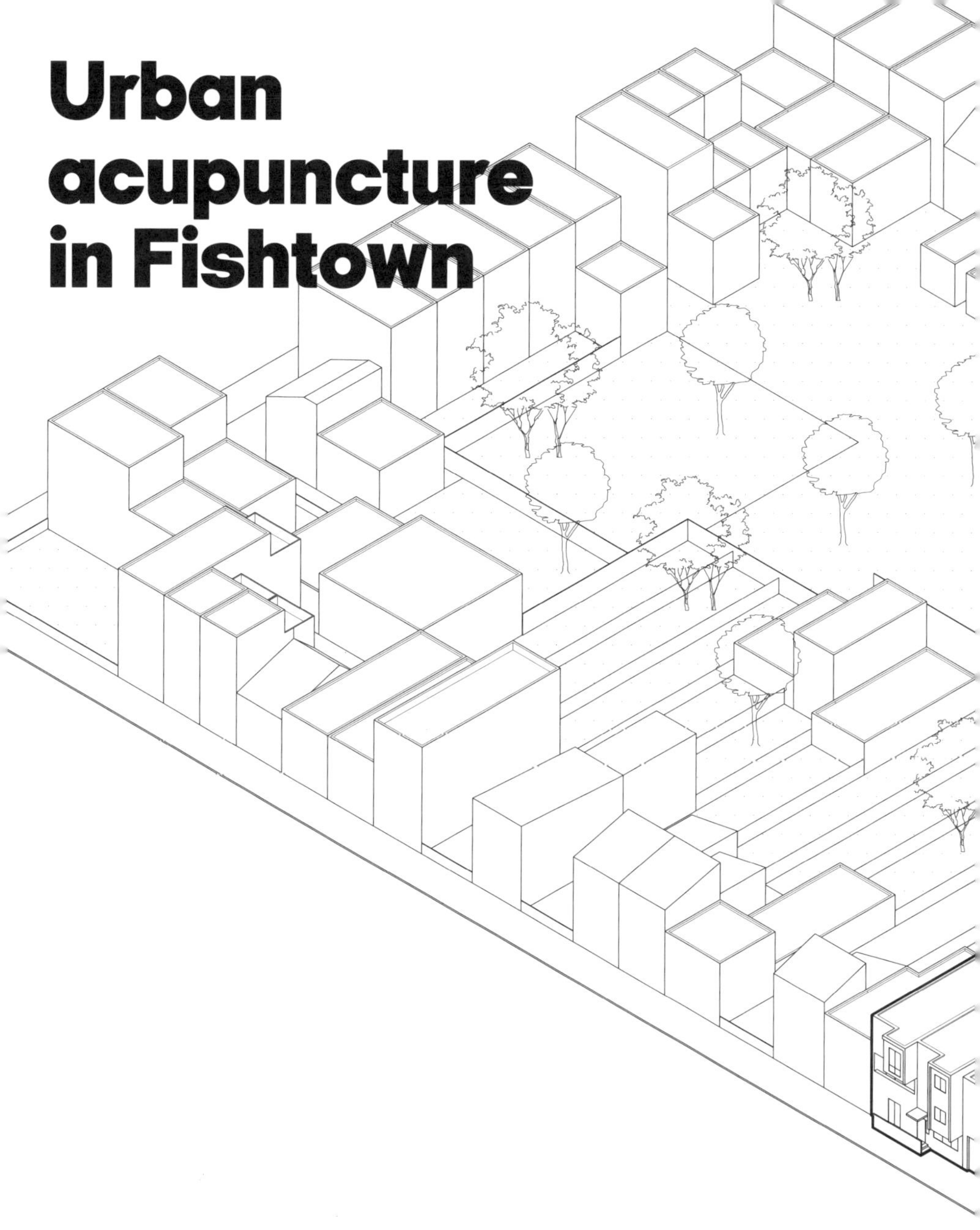

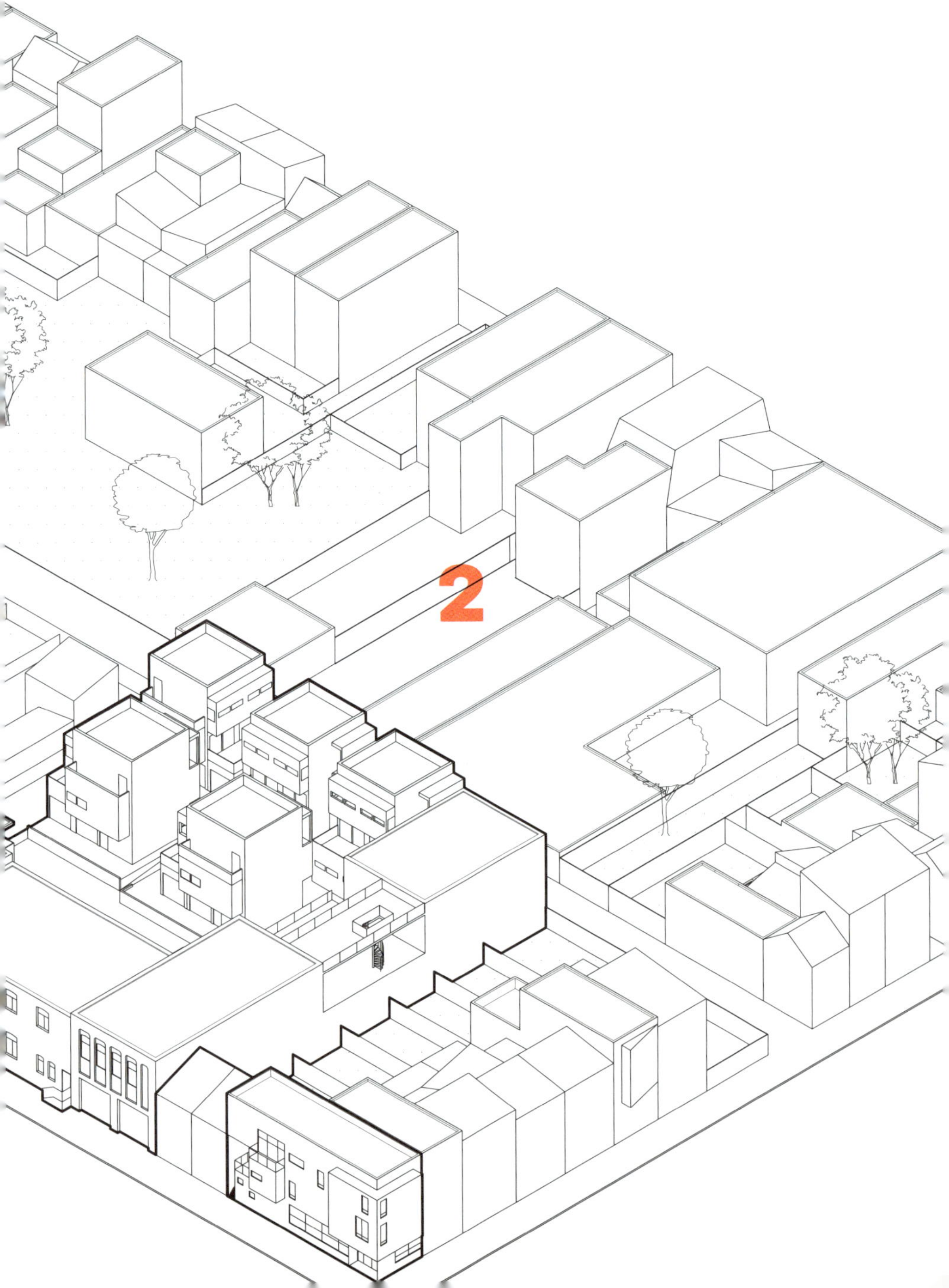
2

Located a few miles up the Delaware, Fishtown is a working class neighborhood that owes its name to the fishing concessions obtained here by the first German settlers in the early 19th century. This was the landing point for successive waves of European immigrants from Sweden, Britain, Germany, Poland, and Ireland for more than two centuries. They settled in an irregular dense urban fabric mixing row houses, factories, warehouses, workshops, and convenience stores in heterogeneous and lively blocks. In the 1960s, the construction of the Delaware expressway cut Fishtown off from its waters. The decade after, deindustrialization hit the jobs and revenues of its residents and local businesses hard.

In 1989, Capital Meats, a meatpacking firm that had operated in the neighborhood for more than eighty years, closed. For ten years, its facilities became the blighted playground of vandalism and a sore remainder of decline. In 1999, the property was purchased by a very special developer named Onionflats. The small industrial building was adapted to host eight brilliantly designed loftish flats. For Onionflats, it was the beginning of a dogged commitment to the area and its community. It was also the first sign of a comeback for Fishtown.

Today, this is the coolest place in Philly: a unique blend of industrial vernacular, gastronomy, art, and music makes it a destination for curious urbanites and new settlers—and maybe soon gentrification.
Onionflats is the creation of Tim and Pat McDonald, the two sons of a craftsman who in 1997 decided that the ancient trade of the architect builder needed to be revived. They started by buying a 5-story, 200-year-old building in Old City and making it into their office, their house, their architecture gallery, and their first development. Onionflats is now a successful business that develops, designs, builds, and promotes sustainability in architecture and construction.

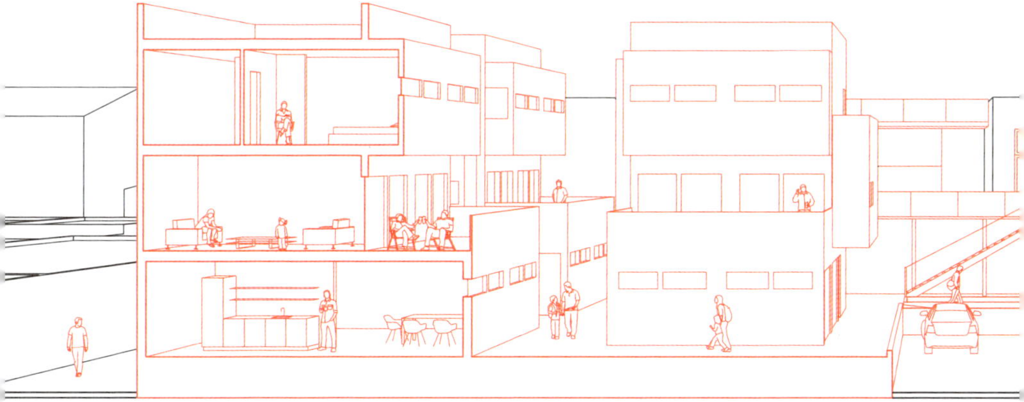

The McDonalds believe that each existing building has potential. They are able to intuit it, carve it out, and make it real and marketable. Capital Flats were followed in 2005 by the Ragflats. An abandoned rag factory was transformed into a typological microcosm of Fishtowns. Along East Berks Street, the factory was reused as lofts with an added pavillon on the roof; two row houses by Minus Studio architects, friends of the McDonalds, were added. Inside, the courtyard was filled with revised trinities that prove the ability of this old layout to answer new demands and join density with privacy.

In total, twenty units were created, which now host a small community of residents who were active in the design process. A few yards west, at the corner with Belgrade, you find their most recent project, "Jackhammer." A local convenience store originally stood here. Abandoned, it became a hot spot for drug dealing; residents were happy that a fire put an end to decay in 2005. In 2009, Onionflats stepped in and turned the tiny plot into a brilliant exercise in distribution, with commerce on ground floor and two floors of residential space above.
A few blocks south, their "Thin Flats" are again an exercise in typology: superposed duplexes with internal light wells, and roof and back gardens which infill the vacant plots of an existing block of four-story row homes.

The project became Philadelphia's first LEED platinum project.
And the story continues: north at the corner of Norris and Front street, Onionflats purchased two vacant bank buildings in 2016—gorgeous American classicist buildings in the McKim, Mead & White line. Condemned to demolition, these local landmarks were rescued by local activists, and will become another point in the McDonalds' urban acupuncture cure for Fishtown. Proof that decline needs bold ideas rather than big money, and that the industrial urban fabric still holds enormous potential for contemporary urban life.

2

Washington, D.C.

3
3

The capital's new food chain

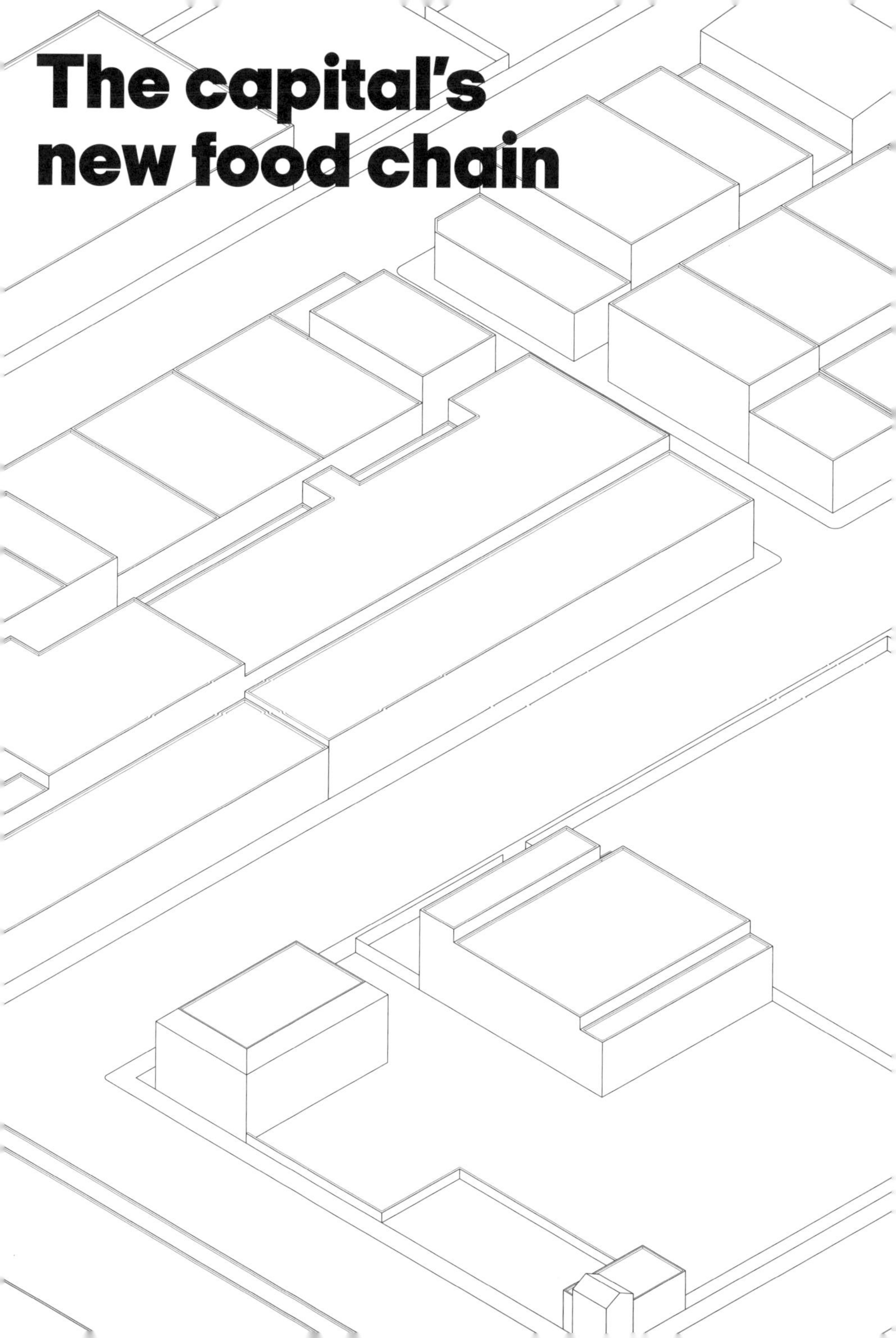

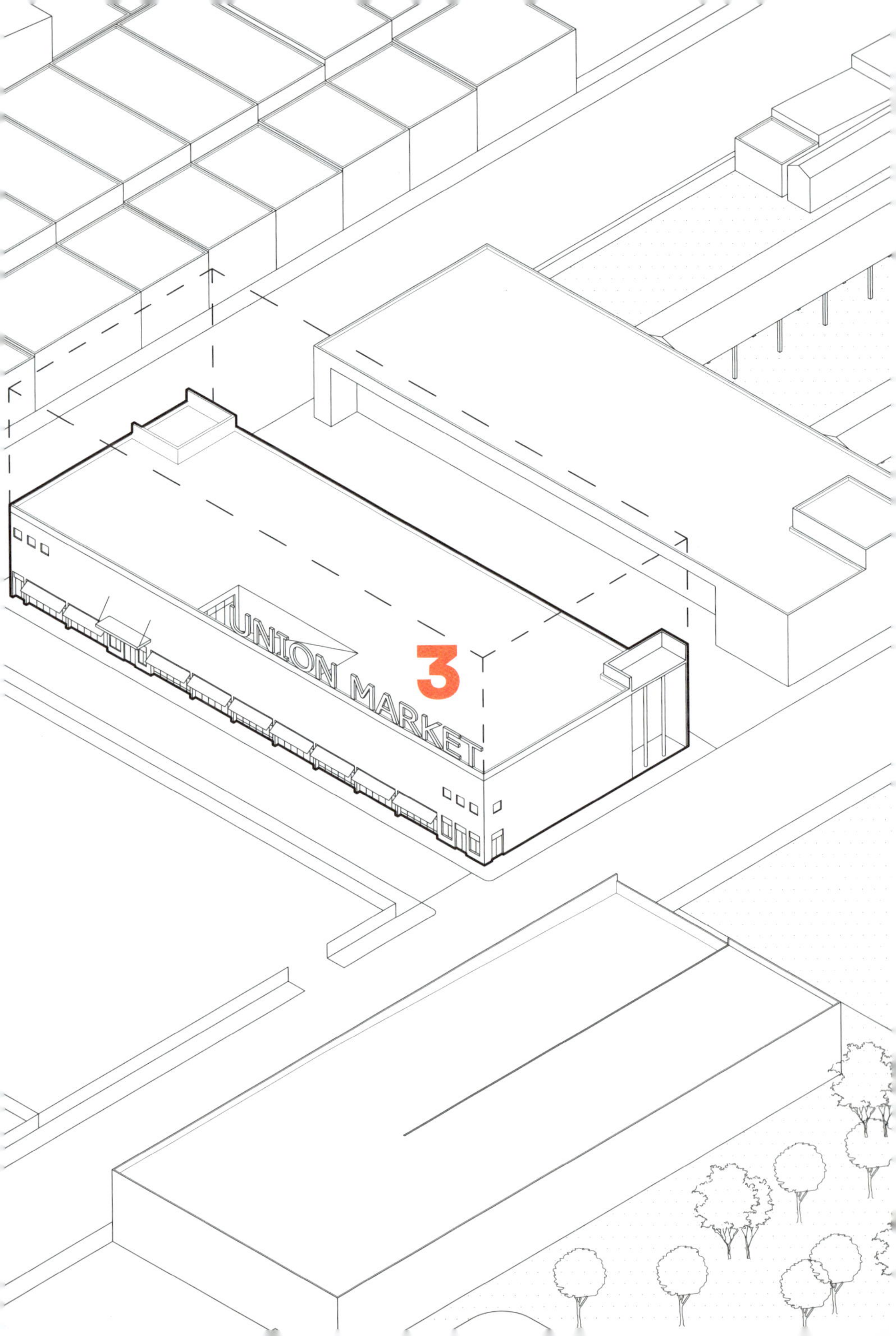
UNION MARKET
3

An old warehouse in Brookland is the heart of the capital's new gastro food scene. With a 10,000 square feet production and catering platform, including a 2,000 square feet event hall, the Mess Hall is a new concept established in 2014 as a "launchpad" for local producers, caterers, food trucks, and bakers. It is also part of a network that links Mess Hall's food start-up to Dupont Circle's farmers market, restaurants, and suppliers. Launchpad is also a contest that brings new culinary talents into the spotlight at Union Market, the place to be if you want to be a star and grow your business in the D.C. food scene.

Located one mile from the Capitol, Union Market has a long history. A key link in the capital's food chain was moved here in 1931, when Centre Market, open since 1871 in the Federal Triangle area, was torn down to make space for the National Archives. Merchants associated to buy forty acres of land near the railway but also close to suburban farms. The new Union Terminal Market offered indoor stalls for 700 vendors selling meat, fish, dairy, and produce six days a week, plus cold storage vaults, elevators, and a public café.

For more than thirty years, this was the gateway through which D.C.'s local and global food passed. In 1962, the city banned the outdoor sale of meats and eggs, killing the farmer's market's foot traffic. People were supposed to buy packaged food in suburban supermarkets. The city food chain was broken.
The current Union Market was built in 1967. In 1989, it lost its role again: once delocalized to the suburbs, distribution no longer needed a central hub.

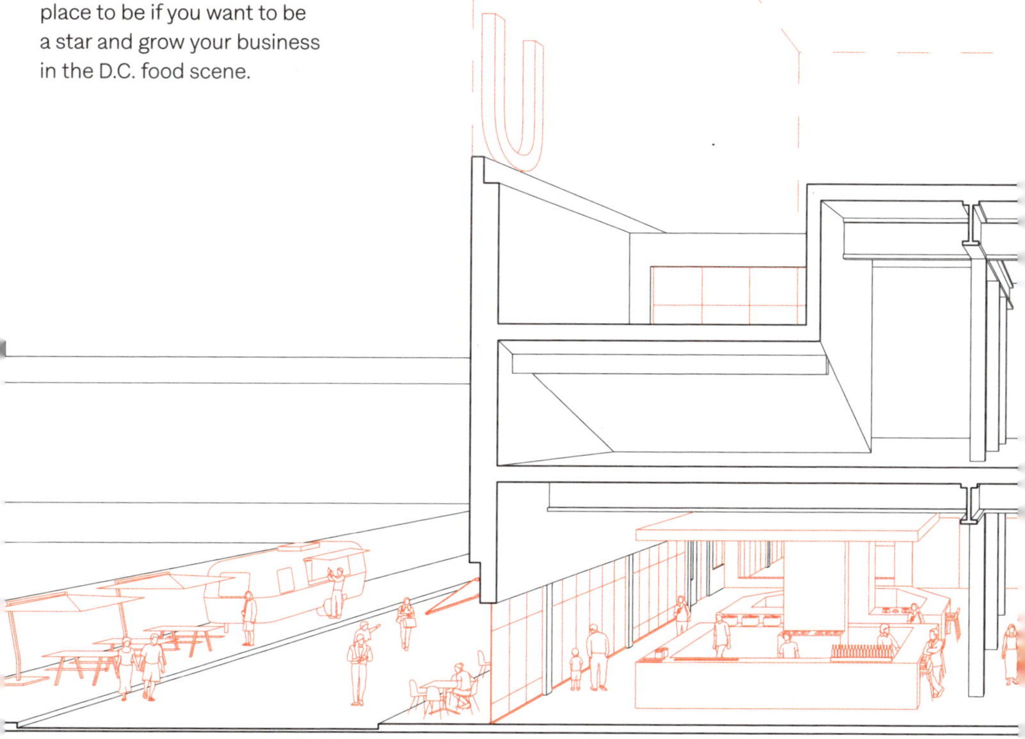

A few independent wholesalers, selling mostly produce, meat, and ethnic foods resisted on site in the midst of decay. In 2012, the developer Edens bought and reopened Union Market. It was the first step in a placemaking strategy with the final goal of transforming the whole urban corridor between Florida and New York to repeat and extend the NoMa boom. They brought back direct sale to final clients in the form of forty food stalls.

It wasn't long before millennials and suburbanites alike were making weekend culinary trips to a part of town they'd previously ignored or even considered desolate and dangerous. Many stalls display the unmistakable orange "Launchpad" sign: this is the stage for the Mess Hall's talent and labor.

Union Market is now the core of a reborn district where abandoned warehouses have become star restaurants, rum distilleries, maker's spaces, tech start-up incubators, pop-up independent movie theaters, and event spaces, while independent whole salers still run their businesses. The market district currently has more than 100 businesses, employing 1,500 people in food production and distribution; the final forecast foresees 20,000 permanent new jobs in the area.

Plans being filed around and over Union Market have been multiplying as Edens is joined by other developers. At the end of 2016, the Union Market area was officially designated a historic district. The first construction sites opened in early 2017. The zoning commission recommends that new buildings have an "industrial aesthetic."

3

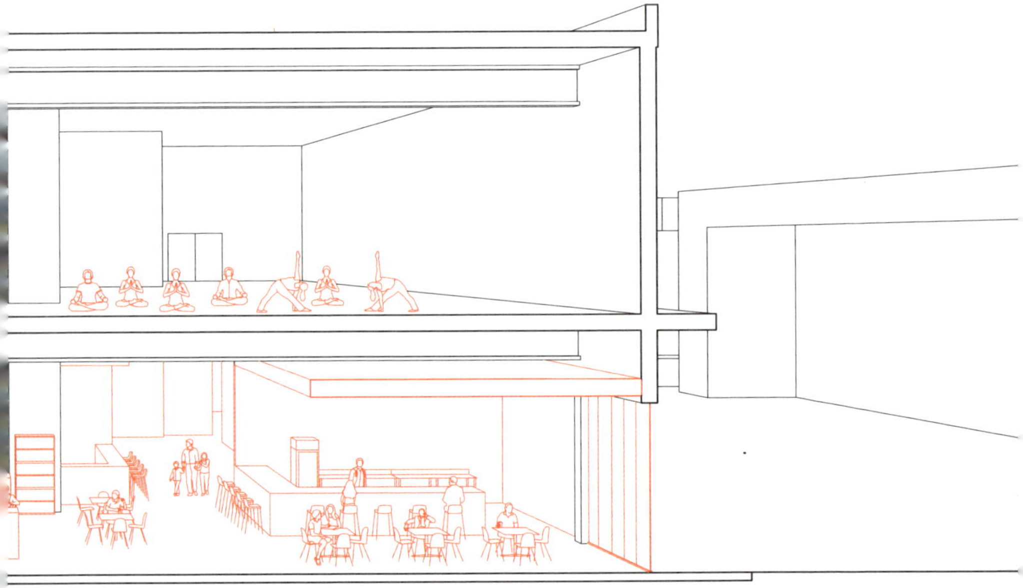

MESS
HALL
FOOD
COMM
UNITY

LAUNCHPAD
LAUNCHPAD
ris
MESS
HALL

BUFFALO
BERGEN
LAUNCHPAD

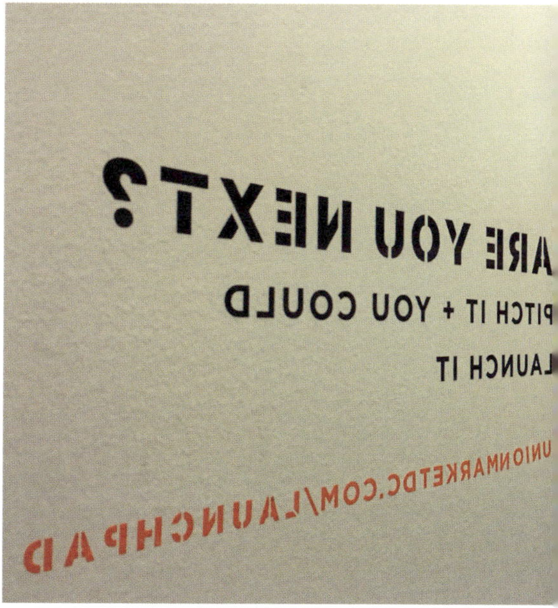
ARE YOU NEXT?
PITCH IT + YOU COULD
LAUNCH IT
UNIONMARKETDC.COM/LAUNCHPAD

UNION MARKET

3

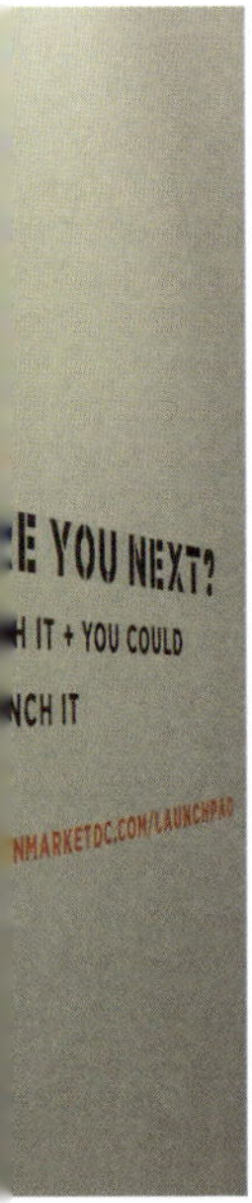
E YOU NEXT?
H IT + YOU COULD
NCH IT
NMARKETDC.COM/LAUNCHPAD

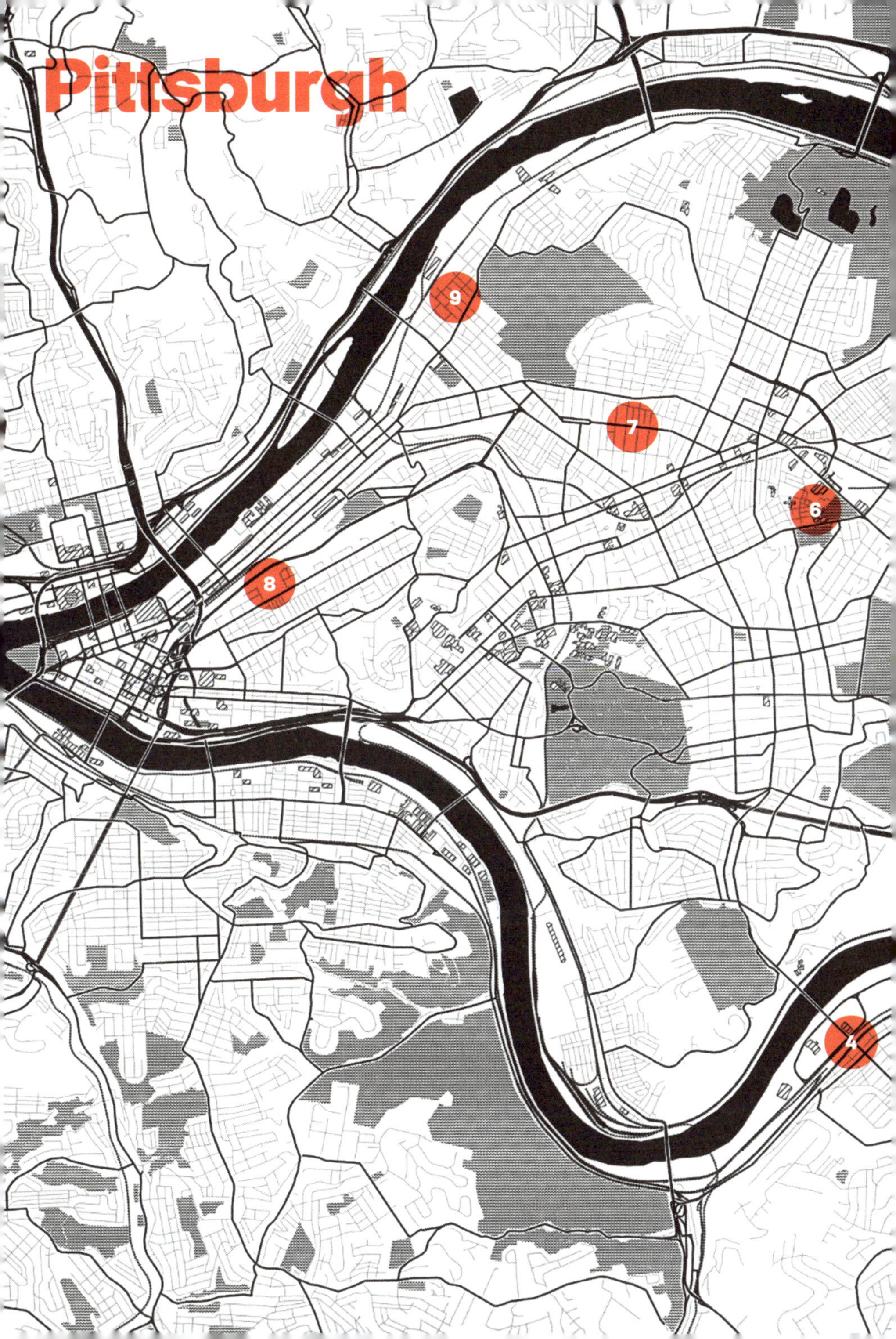
Pittsburgh
9
7
6
8
4

4
5
4

Rust and hope in the Mon Valley

4

The Native American word Monongahela means "falling banks." The name refers to the instability of the river's banks—some take it as a grim forecast of the present. If the Steel Belt ever had a heart, it was pounding in the blast furnaces and steel mills of the thirty-seven-mile continuous plant tied together by the Monongahela hot metal bridges and towboats that tycoon Andrew Carnegie grew around the first steel mill he built. This mill, located in Braddock and constructed in 1872 is still operated by US Steel: it's the only one left in the valley. It was this network of suburban plants that made Pittsburgh an industrial powerhouse.

Immigrants filled jobs in the mills where steel was forged for the guns, aircraft, and battleships that won one civil and two world wars. Between 1955 and 1957, W. Eugene Smith shaped its pictorial epic. Commissioned by the Allegheny Conference of Community Development supported by Richard King Mellon, heir of the family's steel fortune, Smith's 17,000 frames shot in sleepless wanders are allegory, not documentary. Instead of celebrating the rebirth of the city on its 200th anniversary, Smith portrays sweat, greed, smoke, segregation, and faith. Eventually sued by the client for not completing the assigned task, he nevertheless produced one of the most powerful tales of modern America.

Mon's rust towns did not participate in the rebirth of Pittsburgh. They account today for seventy-nine percent of the poverty in the metro-politan area. In neighboring Fayette County, which once provided the coal burning in Mon's furnaces, the poverty rate is over twenty percent, nearing the most deprived urban areas of Philadelphia. Braddock peaked with 20,000 residents in the 1960s, ninety percent of them were gone by the 2000s. All of the Mon Valley towns show similar figures. Today, the eye of Mon Valley is photographer Pete Marovich. His ongoing photographic mission portrays the result of twenty-five years of decline, decay, and despair—together with tiny signs of hope.

John Fetterman's struggle to revive Braddock gained general attention when, in 2011, *The New York Times* named him "mayor of rust"—later featured in *The Guardian* as "coolest mayor" and in *Rolling Stone* as "mayor of hell." Fetterman first came here in 2001 with Americorps to start a program for reducing youth violence. He decided to settle, squatted an abandoned church, then purchased the derelict warehouse next door for 2,000 dollars and turned it into a loft, topped by two remodeled shipping containers for additional

living space. In 2015, he ran for mayor and won.
His decision to have skin in the game gives credibility and powers his multiple initiatives to sustain locals and attract new "DIY homesteaders" from artistic and creative communities—with some results. He runs the non-profit Braddock Redux, which he and his relatives fund. His wife Gisele opened a "free shop" where residents can get clothing on a pay-as-you-can basis. His sister Kristin turned the 17,000-square-foot former Chevy dealership into a furniture workshop, loft, greenhouse, and textile studio. Braddock is now home to art events, an art gallery, an urban farming area, a farmers market, and green roofs; the abandoned church is a community center.
Fetterman's fame attracted support from donors and made Braddock the location of Levi's 2009 advertising campaign. His protagonism also attracts inevitable criticism. However, when he decided to run for Senate in 2016, supporting Bernie Sanders, he scored an unexpected twenty percent in Democratic primaries.
Other signs of hope are more controversial. The 2002 Waterfront redevelopment in neighboring Homestead —where the strike of 1892 ended with nine strikers killed, broken unions, reduced wages, and new production means allowing the use of unskilled workers, marking a turning point in industrial organization—brought three hundred million dollars of private investment. It also generates a yearly income of six million dollars, which brought the town out of bankruptcy—but also a dull suburban layout and lifestyle that, in spite of its name, failed to reclaim the riverside.
Industrial landmarks and heritage sites managed by the Rivers of Steel Heritage Corporation such as the Carrie Furnace attract some tourists—but will they ever be enough to make a new economy? Maybe the answer can be found by following the waters of the Mon and its tributary Youghiogheny upstream along the popular Great Allegheny Passage. Completed in 2013, after thirty-five years of work, the Passage connects Washington D.C. with Pittsburgh. It reuses Carnegie's Union Railroad bed as a trail for hikers and bikers. The railroad, laid out along the Mon from 1894 on, reaches places such as the most popular whitewater destination on the East coast, Ohiopyle, not far from Frank Lloyd Wright's Fallingwater. Here it's easy to understand to what degree nature and industry have shaped the geography of place, which extends well beyond the rusting furnaces downhill. And the future might lie in reconnecting the different destinies of the places along those waters, which once were united by one of history's most powerful tales.

The cathedral of electrics

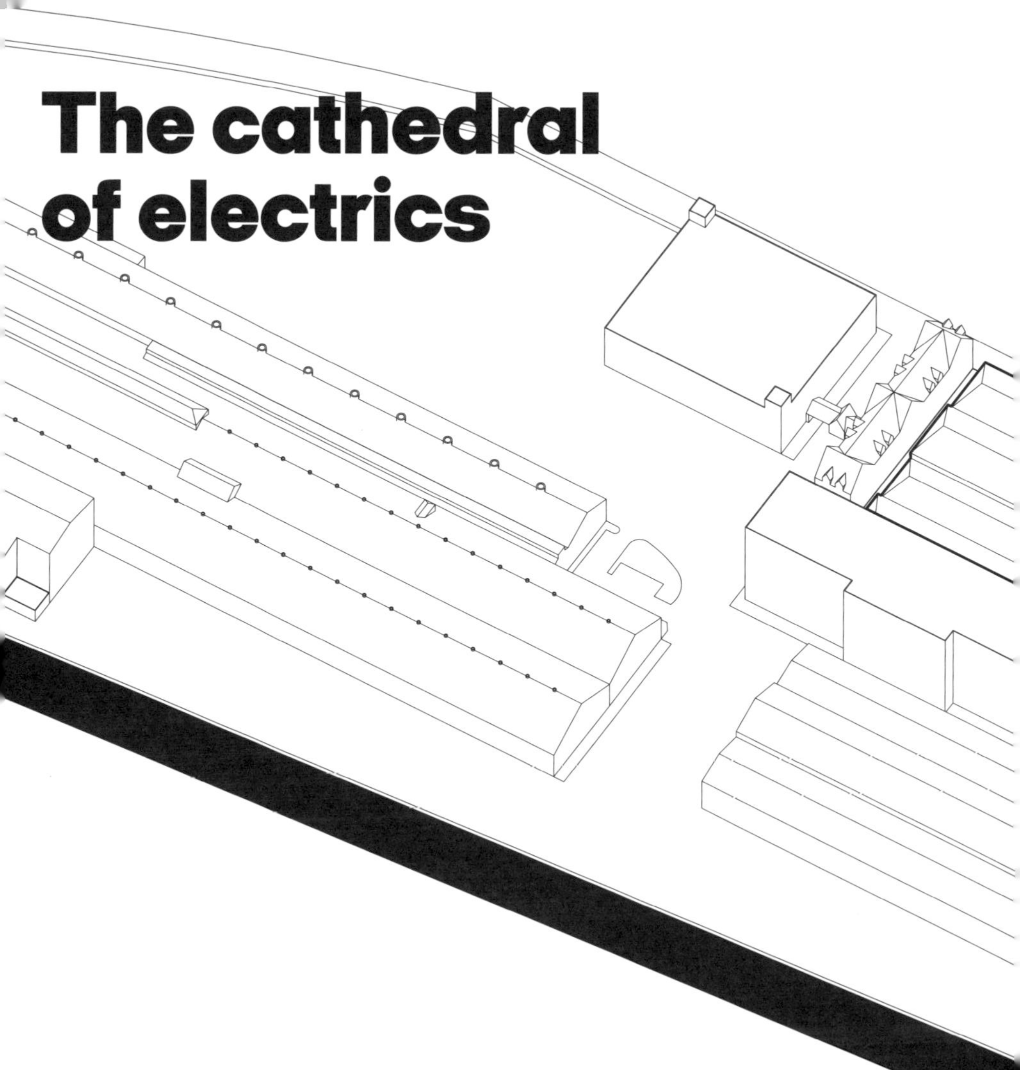

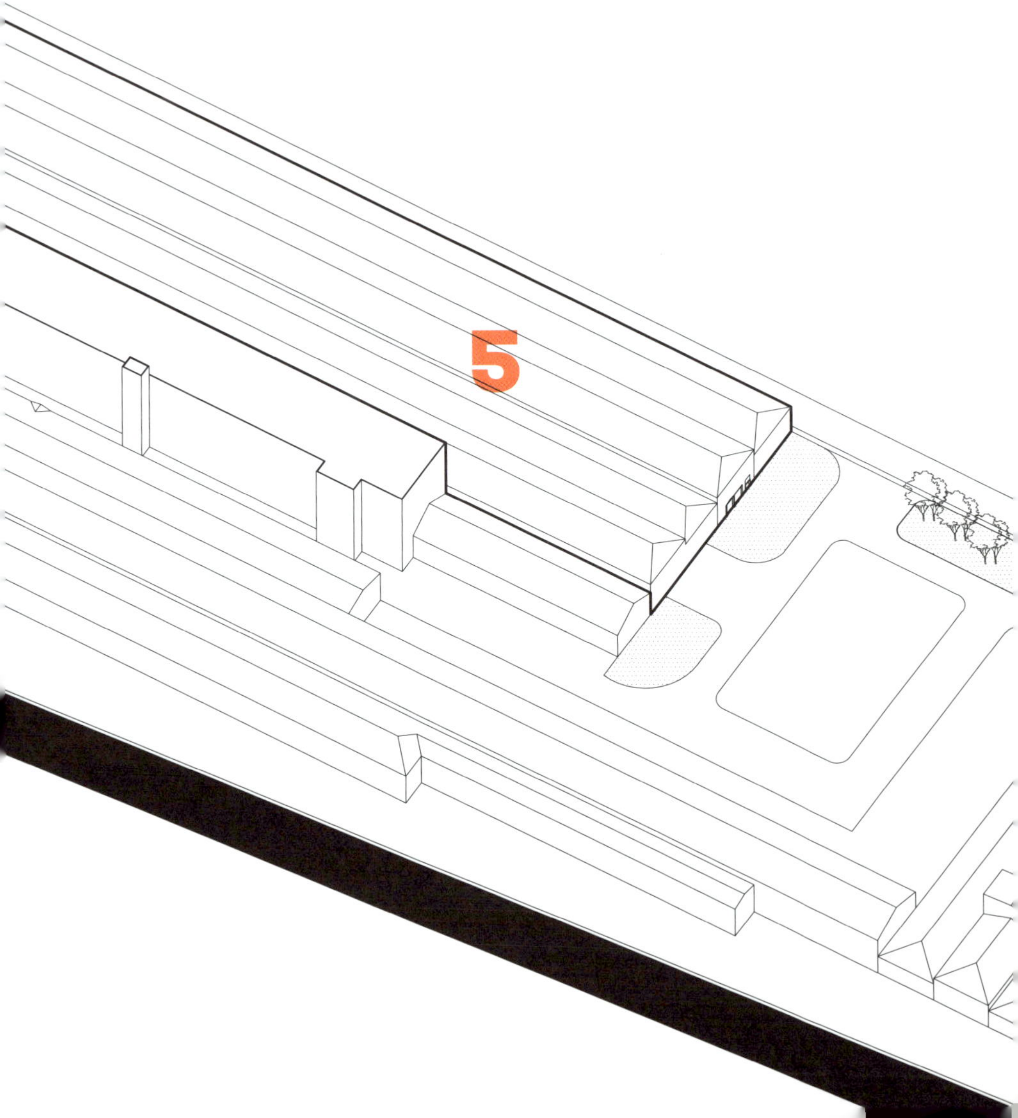
5

The Westinghouse Electric Corporation plant in East Pittsburgh was built in February 1894 when the company purchased forty acres of land and started construction. Production began in September. The plant grew all throughout the 20th century to become the core of the American electric industry. This was due in part to Westinghouse's early leadership in alternating current technologies.

Westinghouse won the "war of the currents" with the alternating current electrical lighting at the 1892 Columbian Exposition in Chicago and went on to beat General Electric in the 1893 tendering process to supply energy power turbines to the Niagara Falls Power Company in 1895. Westinghouse's considerable production line extended to trains and tramways for public transport, radios, and domestic electrical equipment for the booming post-war market. A century of generators was built here. At its peak, the East Pittsburgh facility employed 20,000 workers.

When this story came to an end in 1988, only 800 of them were left. Westinghouse had transferred its generator production to his TECO joint venture in Taiwan and sold its transport division to the German AEG.
Talks with RIDC—the Regional Industrial Development Corporation of Southwestern Pennsylvania, the privately funded non-profit created as early as 1955 to support the diversification of the Allegheny area industrial economy—had already started in 1986. The site was not left to rust. When Westinghouse left on the 1st of January, 1989, RIDC stepped in to deal with the 4.2-million-square-foot facilities.

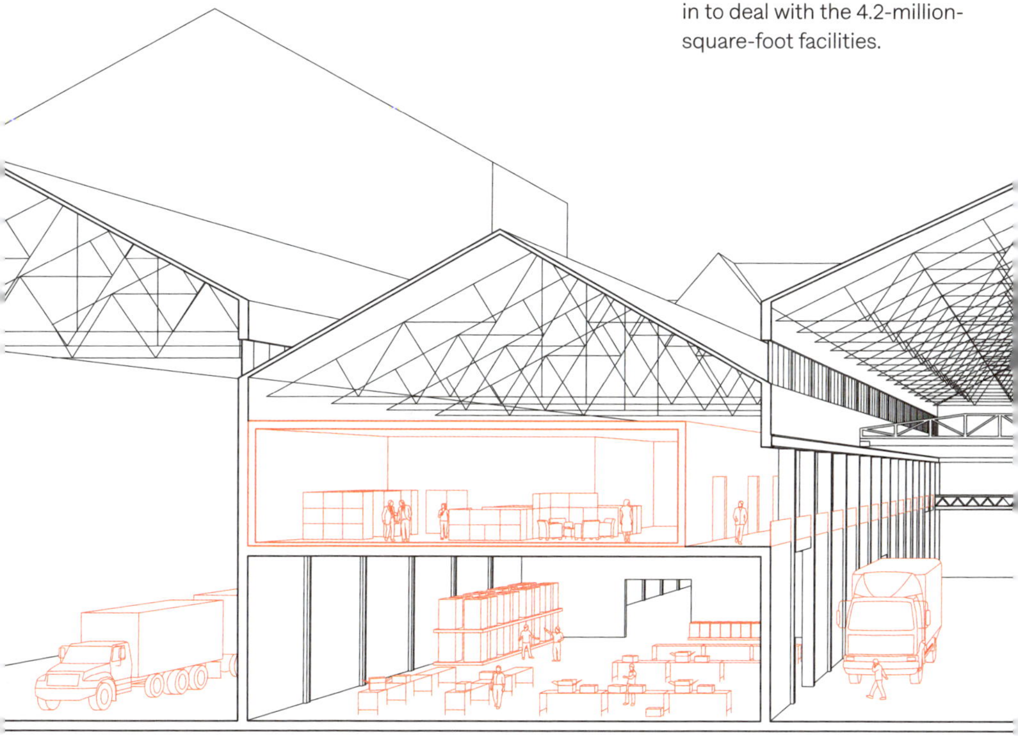

RIDC President Frank B. Robinson was aware of the potential of the site. Production had left a less poisoned legacy here than it had in steel and coal sites. The buildings were in good shape. He saw the cross-section of a cathedral with two-story side aisles fit for the small businesses he had in mind in the long naves of the West Shop. Simple, rough, flexible, iconic. This could be the right incubator for the social and economic experiment he had in mind: to replace—if not in quantity, at least in quality—the lost jobs with small enterprises, to turn the skills of local industrial workers into a redevelopment asset, to reuse the industrial infrastructure of the past for a new breed of suburban industrial park. The new name he gave to the site embodies this vision: Keystone Commons. The keystone referred both to the Pennsylvania state nickname and to the idea of reconstruction. Commons meant that the age of superpowers had ended. Within a few years, Keystone Commons was home to 48 tenants with 650 employees. Today, there are 40 companies with 1,100 employees here. Reuse is still ongoing in the huge plant. Some parts have already undergone a second cycle of refurbishing and diversification of activities. Local actors, fearing the definitive loss of their industrial identity, fought against this change over a long period of time. However, slowly but surely, law offices, gyms, and chocolate manufacturers have moved into the area. History was somehow revived in 2016 as well, when tenant Brush Aftermarket invested nine and a half million dollars to restore the original cranes and deep pit infrastructure—filled when Westinghouse left—and reuse it for its core business: the repairing, balancing, and testing of fifty-five-ton plant generators. Electricity has come back home to East Pittsburgh.

5

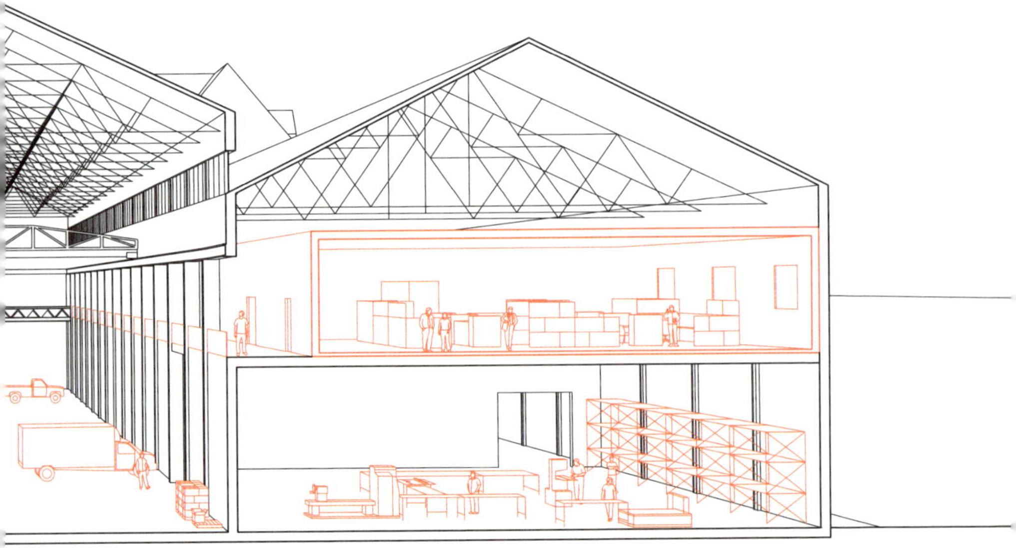

geotechnics
SAMPLE
RECEIVING
PRIVATE
PROPERTY
NO PUBLIC
PARKING
C24

5

From biscuits to bits at Bakery Square

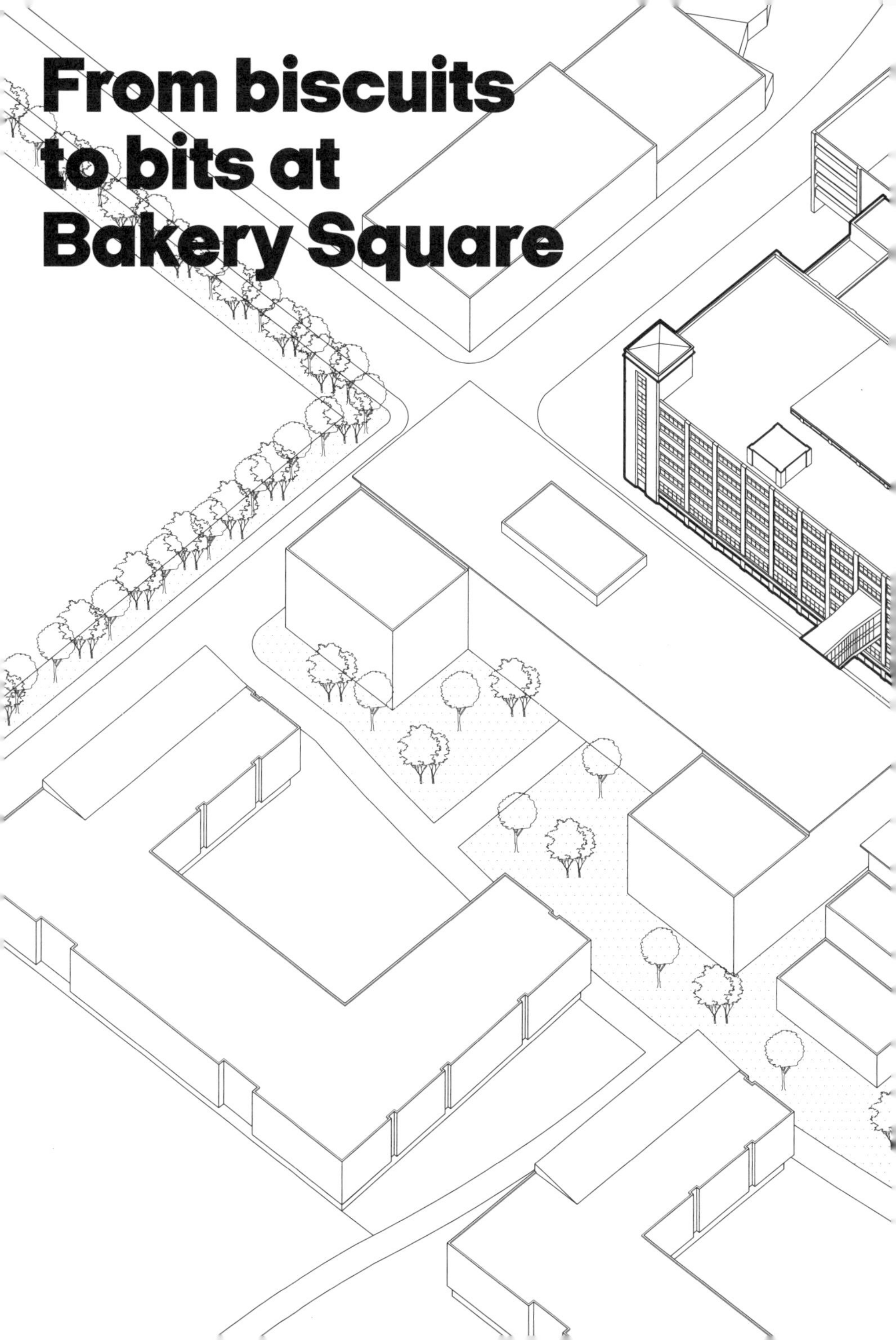

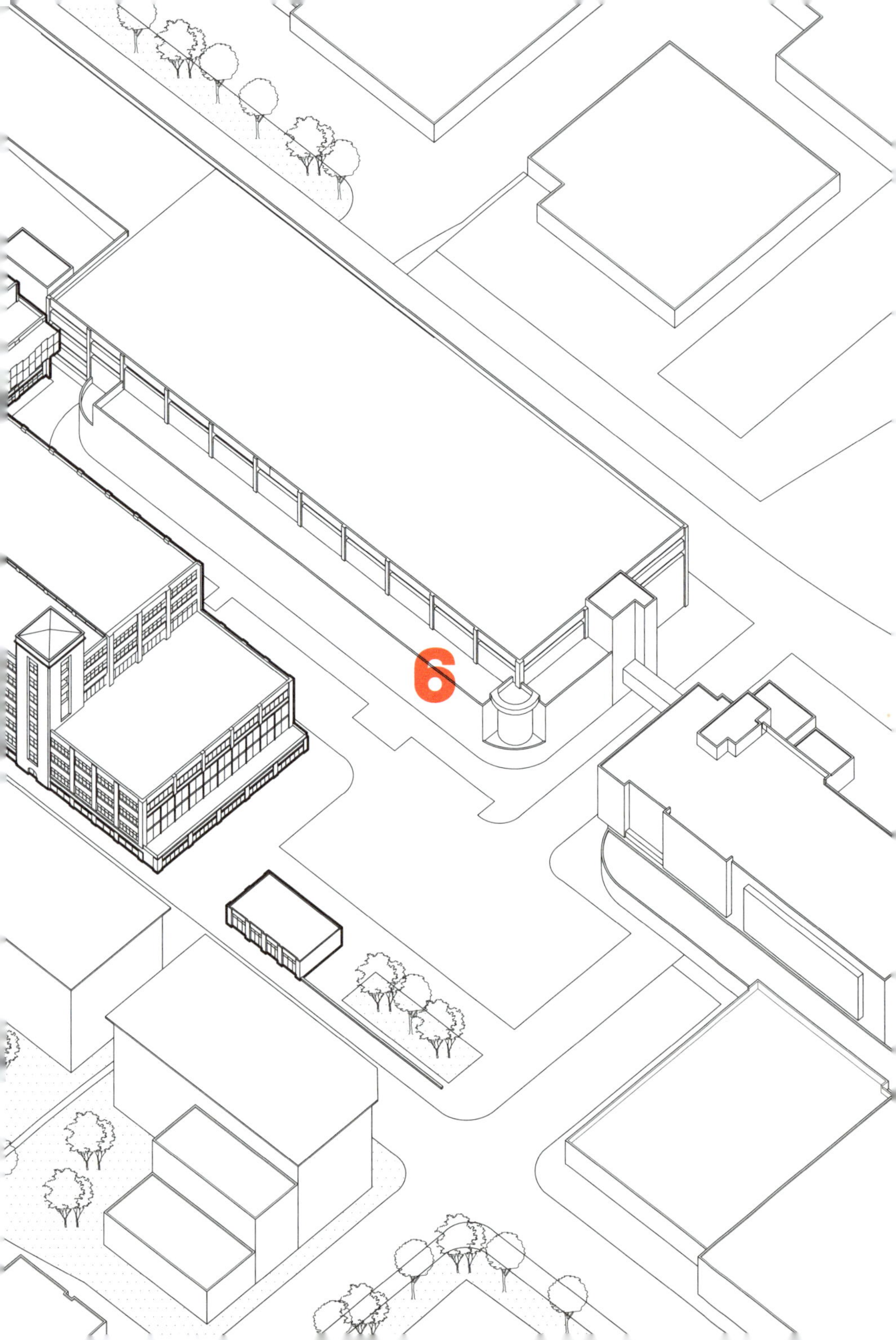
6

The National Biscuit Company (Nabisco) factory on Penn Avenue, built in 1918, was part of a nationwide expansion plan. In-house architect Albert G. Zimmermann designed the new seven-story plant in compliance with the company's values of style and worker dignity. Its large windows for natural lightning, showers and locker rooms for employees, and fireproof stairways made it a point of reference even before construction—it was already written about in 1912 and 1916. Other bakeries opened around Nabisco along and near Penn Avenue in the 1920s and 30s. In 1998, Nabisco abruptly closed the Pittsburgh plant and fired its 350 employees. The decision came unexpectedly, although a first attempt to close the plant had been made as early as 1982. Vertical production had become obsolete and could not be streamlined in the historical seven-story factory on Penn Avenue. Other, more efficient plants had what the Penn Avenue plant lacked. The urban location was poorly accessible by highway, rail, and air distribution networks. Cash was needed for advertising and marketing. In 1999, RIDC bought the six and a half acre area. After a false start, in 2007, a redevelopment plan was proposed by Walnut Capital in partnership with Pittsburgh's Urban Redevelopment Agency (URA) and the East Liberty Development, a non-profit community organization. The initial scheme was concentrated on the old main factory building and its immediate surroundings. The factory reopened in 2010 after a LEED standard renovation by the architecture firm Astorino, and currently hosts the Google Pittsburgh campus, the Human Engineering and Human Movement Research Laboratories of the University of Pittsburgh, and the UPMC Technology Development Center, making it one of the city's hubs for research and

technology transfer. Google's 115,000-square-foot campus, designed by local architecture firm Strada, reuses the double-height penthouse space for a collaborative work environment completed by relaxation areas, services, and an outdoor terrace. The original concrete trusses and exposed walls add the rough industrial look to the informal layout and eclectic interior design typical for Google. Around the old biscuit factory, new buildings on Bakery Square host a tech shop, a gym with swimming pool, a hotel, restaurants, coffee shops, and retail, making the site a new destination and an attractive place for the affluent, educated, and young residents—the new East Enders. Business attraction was so successful that Bakery 2.0 is already under construction. An abandoned public school on the opposite site of Penn Avenue that will host the expansion of the Google campus, directly connected to the existing location by a footbridge over Penn Avenue. The development of a new residential area with apartments and townhouses will complete the area's urban mix. Green spaces, walkways, and local roads designed to maintain soil permeability and water retention will connect Bakery Square with neighborhoods that were on the other side of a factory wall for a century.

In total, Bakery Square will be worth three hundred and fifty million dollars of investment leveraged by initial public support in the form of tax credits, tax increment financing, and public grants amounting to sixteen percent of the total. This reuse project will produce an estimated total of nearly 3,000 high-quality new jobs in the area. The obsolete factory on Penn Avenue had more potential than one might have expected when, in August 1998, a furious Mayor Tom Murphy came back from a meeting with Nabisco corporate officials in New York which he described to local press as "insulting." The "gifts" that Nabisco had refused were later better used for attracting and creating new businesses and jobs to the city.

BAKERY
SQUARE

OFFICES AT BAKERY SQUARE

STOP

WHO'S ON DUTY
Alex- OFF DUTY
GABE COTTRELL
Amanda - OFF DUTY
Janeka - OFF DUTY
Jordan- OFF DUTY
Robert- OFF DUTY
Ash - OFF DUTY
JUSTIN GEORGE
Ollie- OFF DUTY
J.- OFF DUTY
TechShop

6

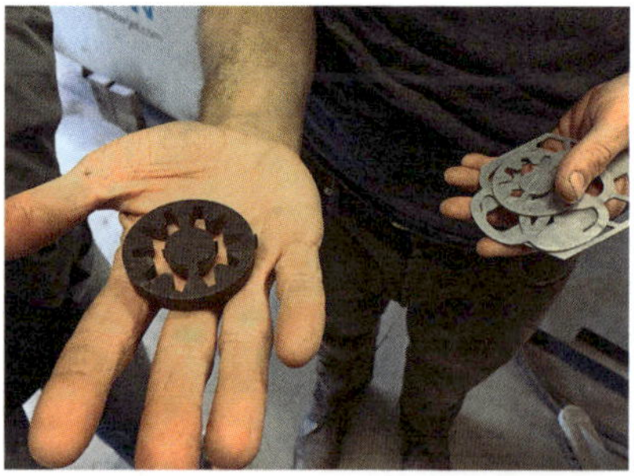

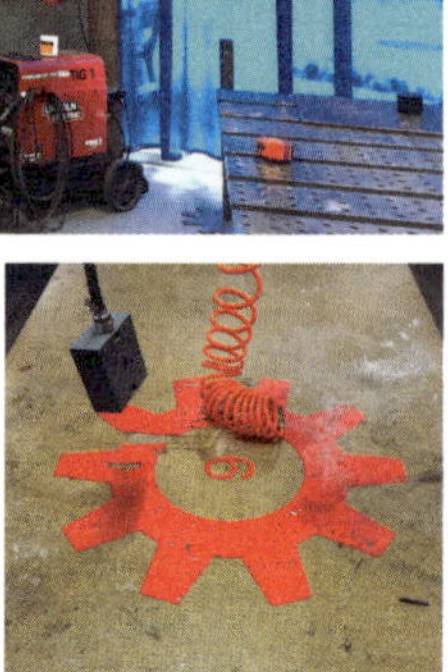

Penn Avenue, one plot at a time

7

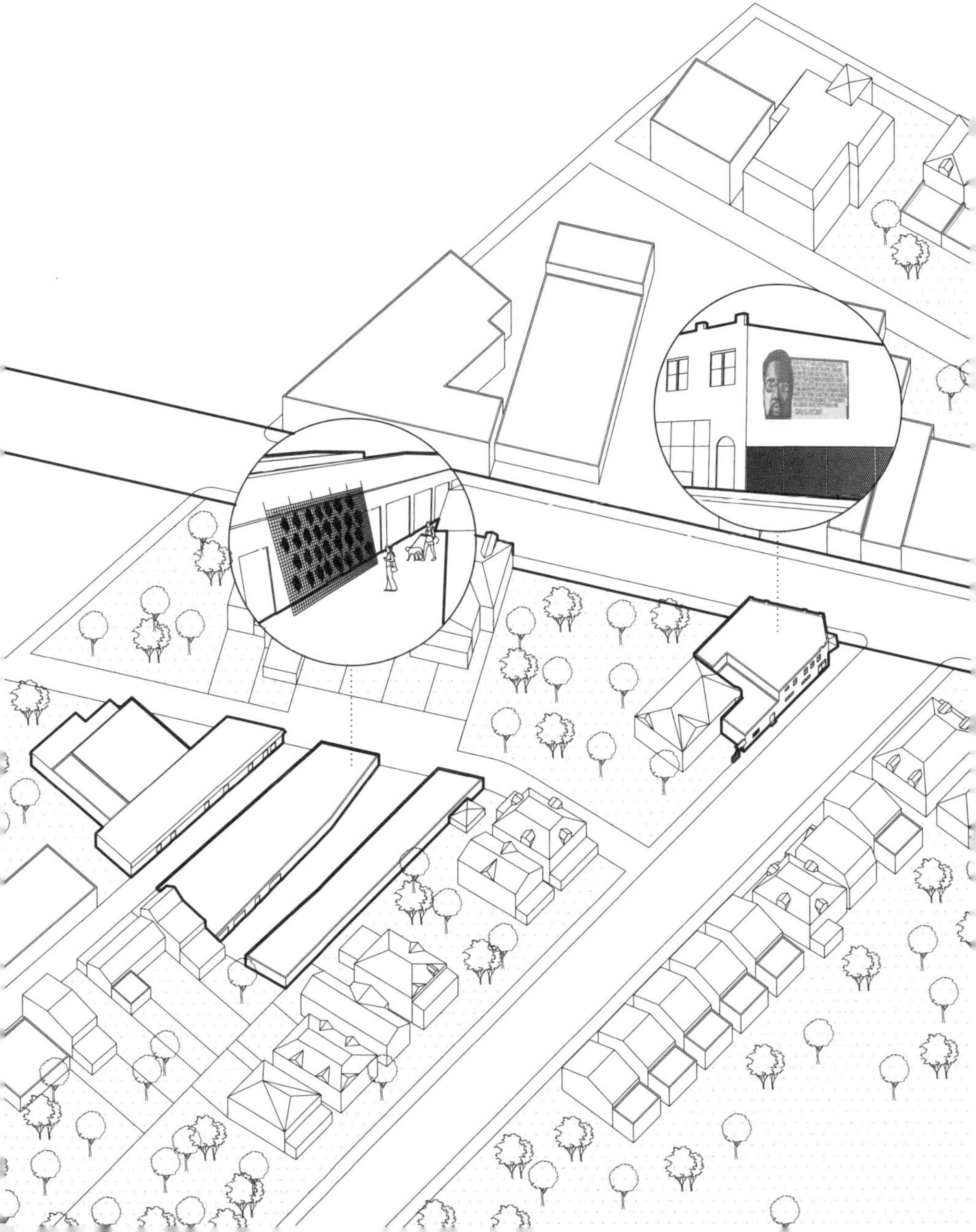

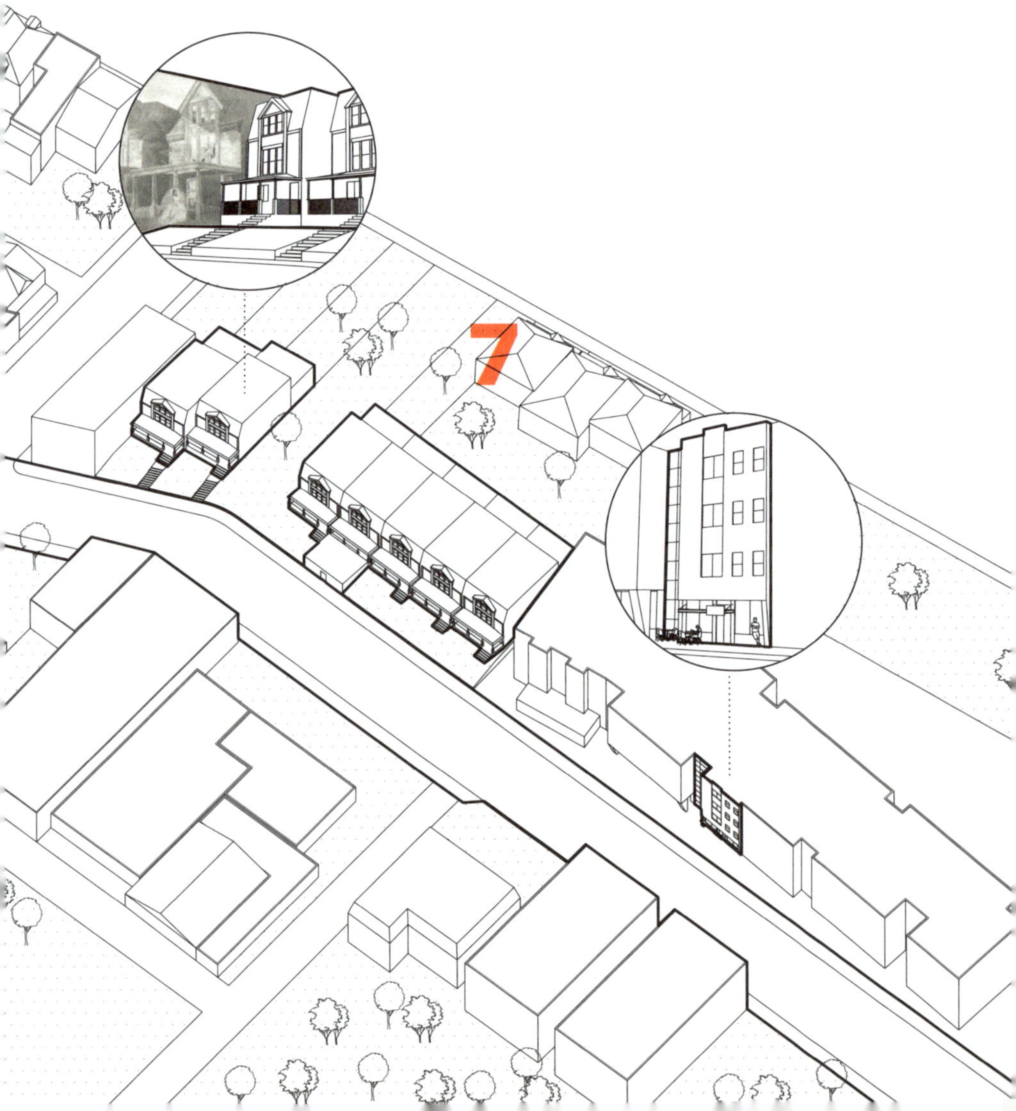
7

A few blocks up Penn Avenue downtown from Bakery Square, the vacant plots of East Liberty are finally under redevelopment. A renewed station of the East Busway fast public transport corridor, built in the 1980s on the abandoned rails of 1930s Pittsburgh Railways streetcars, will be the core of a mixed, transit-oriented development masterplan with office, retail, service, and residential spaces. It is praised as renewal and revitalisation. It is criticised as "black removal." Skepticism is understandable. Here blight was not the result of industrial foreclosures. It was the result of planned urban renewal. The history of Penn Avenue contains a lesson on the undesired consequences of big projects, the stubborn efficacy of small ones, and the need to balance the two modes.

As the oldest access way to the place where the waters of the Monongahela and the Allegheny blend to form the Ohio River, the street also traces the invisible line between wealthier neighborhoods on its south side and predominatly working class neighborhoods on its north side. Along Penn Avenue, the tale of two cities is palpable. As the main access to downtown Pittsburgh, Penn Avenue was a commercial street for decades until suburbanization challenged its primacy in the 1960s. In an ill-fated yet well-meaning strategy applying the suburban ingredients of rapid transit and pedestrian malls to the inner city, the Urban Redevelopment Agency razed 1,200 homes, reduced the size of the shopping district by one million square feet, and routed cars away from Penn Avenue to distribute traffic on the newly built Penn Circle.

The project failed to attract retail and public, but succeeded in disrupting the area. Hundreds of small businesses closed and, in the four decades that followed, more than 4,500 residents left. On November 1, 1975, the Rev. Leo Henry gathered his parishioners at St. Lawrence O'Toole Church on Penn Avenue. He wanted to take some action against decline and blight. Two months later, the Bloomfield-Garfield Corporation was born. Residents could become shareholders by purchasing a five dollar membership, and volunteering to help drive a program of advocacy planning for the revitalization of the Penn Avenue commercial district and the surrounding neighborhoods. They wanted to reconquer Penn Avenue, plot by plot. Progressively, BCG committed two and a half million dollars of deposit to convince a bank to reopen an office on Penn Avenue; succeeded in getting federal and local support, gathered a staff, and started building new, decent and affordable housing in vacant lots. In 1984, a family medical center opened in a vacant storefront. In 1986, BCG invested one million dollars to transform an abandoned laundry into Champion Commons, a first-class office location.

In 1996, BGC celebrated twenty years of struggle by commissioning the mural "The Bride on Penn Avenue," by artist Judy Penzer.
The following year, the Penn Avenue Arts Initiative (PAAI) was founded to promote art as a placemaking tool—and a creative way of occupying vacant plots. It later became the Penn Avenue Arts District. In the 2000s, the size of investments grew and housing projects of fifty to sixty units were launched. In 2006, Penn Ave joined the "Main Streets Program" by the National Trust for Historic Preservation. In 2008, BCG joined forces with Lawrenceville Corporation, Friendship Development Associates, and East Liberty Development Inc. to launch the East End Partnership for the revitalization of the four diverse communities. In the 2010s, City Hall invested five million dollars in the refurbishment of the Penn Corridor infrastructure. The first bike lane opened in 2014. In 2013, the Penn Avenue Corridor Strategic Plan 2014–2019 was drawn up by local actors.
As change slowly continued, external forces joined the process. In 2015 a group of designers and social scientists from CMU started the "Latham Street Commons" initiative. They wanted to fight blight and promoted self-help through urban agriculture—reuse instead of demolition. The immediate goal was to grow fresh vegetables in what is still a food desert—at least for those who cannot afford to shop at Whole Foods. Community workshops and cooking retreats promote food culture and, at the same time, grow awareness and social capital. These ingredients are still needed along Penn Avenue in order to avoid the mistakes of the past.

Latham St
STOP
3-WAY

Latham St.
commons
Imagine
with
us...

FRESH EGGS
FARM FRESH
EGGS
FOR SALE
East End
Community
Thrift

Food drives reuse on the Strip

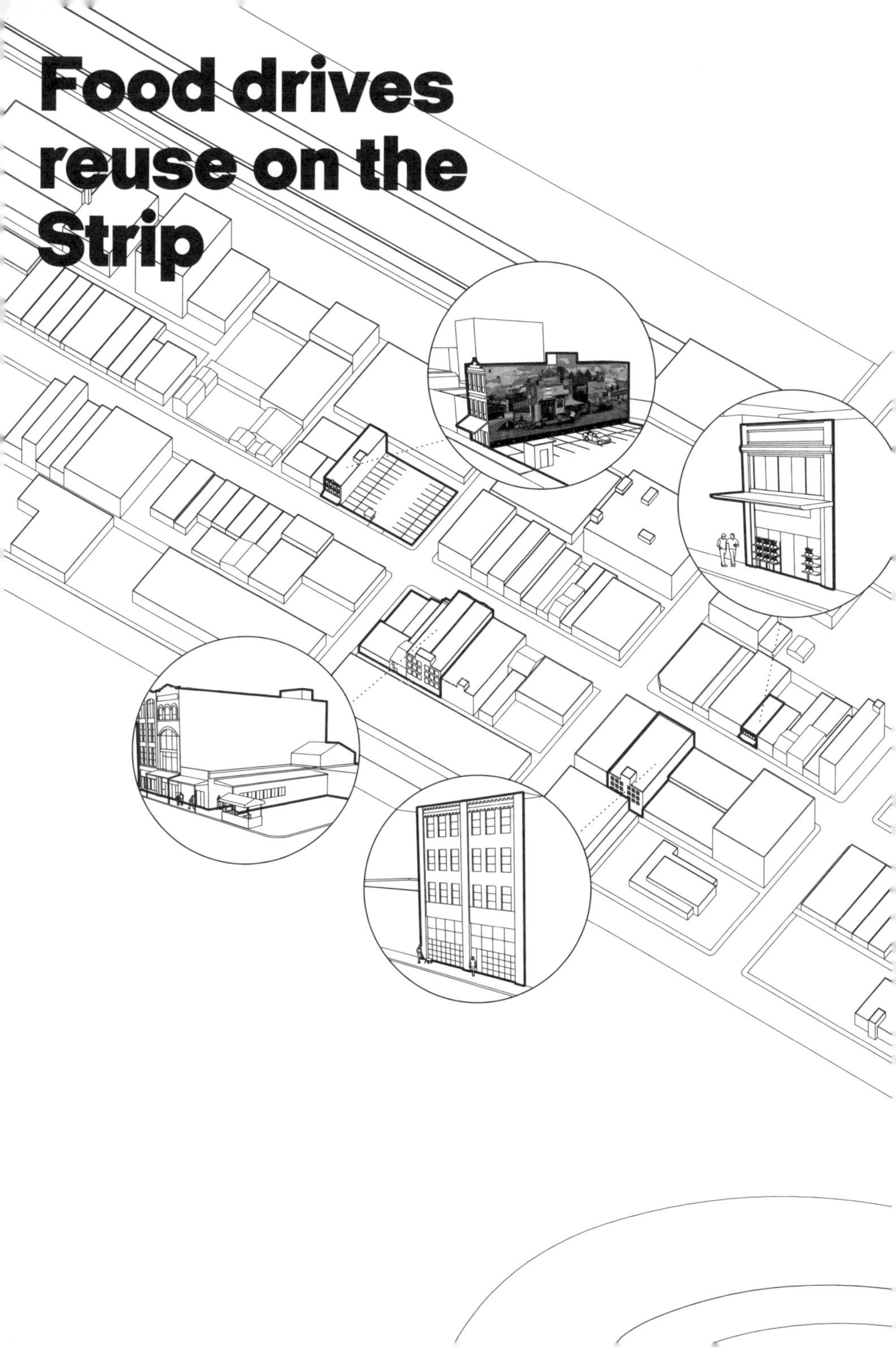

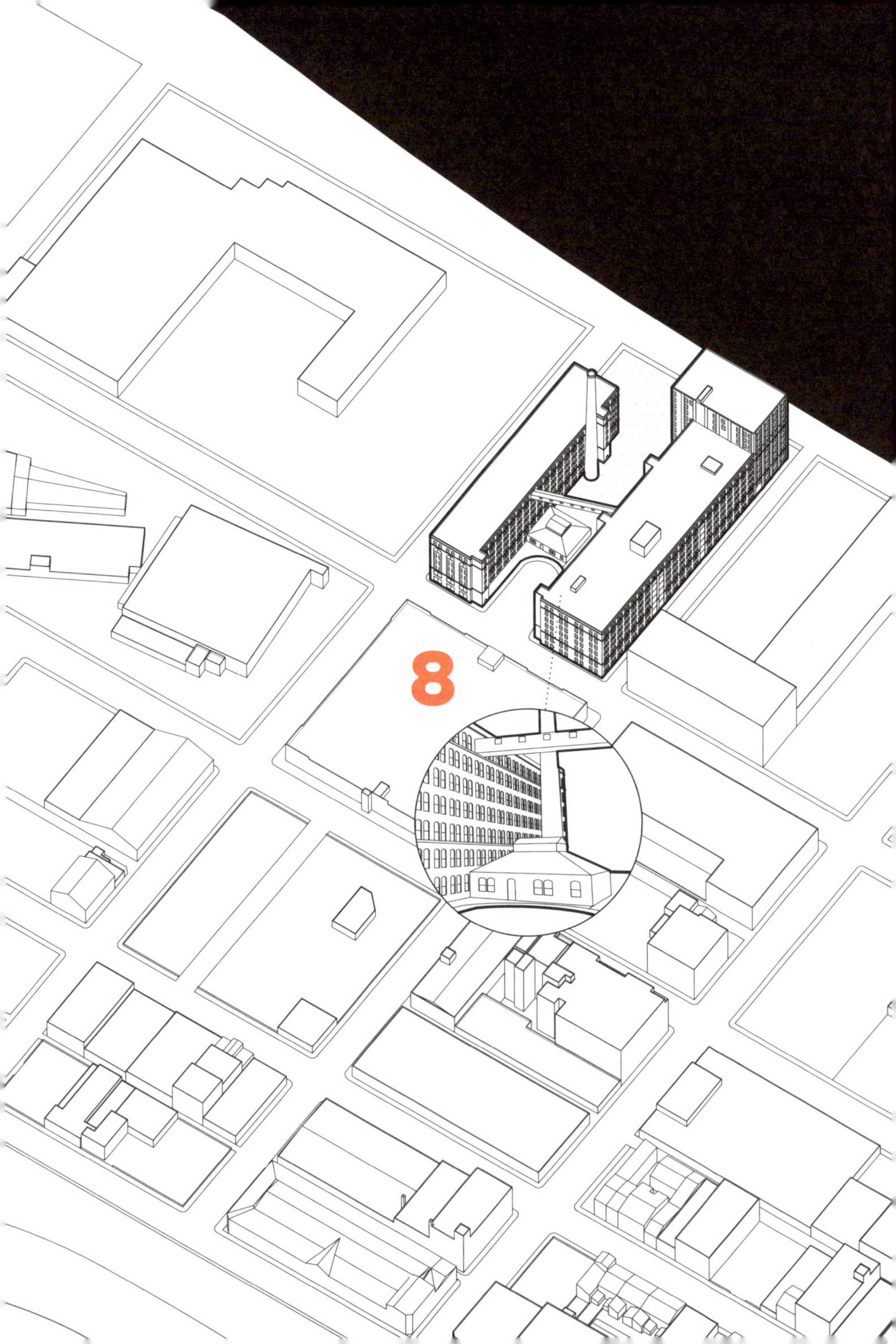
8

The last tract of Penn Avenue descends from the hills to align with the Allegheny. With Liberty, Smallman, and Railroad streets it makes the Strip District, one of the places in Pittsburgh where you can see the effects of two hundred years of urban change—and understand where the city is heading. The first industry opened here in 1814. In the 1830s, the Strip District hosted iron mills, foundries, and glass factories. The Civil War gave great impulse; industries expanded and multiplied along the Allegheny. Here Carnegie Steel, ALCOA, and Westinghouse had their premiere. As they grew, they had to relocate. The new plants were constructed outside of town: we met them in East Pittsburgh and along the Monongahela. Smaller industries in the same sectors followed them. Their place was taken by food wholesalers expelled from downtown as the railroad tracks were removed from Liberty Lane. Here they benefited from accessibility by road, rail, and the river, while remaining near downtown markets. Factory sheds and small worker's houses were replaced by multi-story offices and warehouses. Between the wars, the Strip District prospered by feeding the city. From the 1950s on, truck deliveries and suburbanization transformed the logistics of produce. More and more wholesalers were cut out by supermarkets buying directly from producers. In 1950, the Strip District had more than seventy operating firms, in 1970 two dozen were left. Empty buildings and vacant plots marked the end of prosperity. But the potential of location and infrastructure remained intact. Downtown is still there, accessibility has not changed, buildings can be reused. New communities

joined the city as Pittsburgh attracted new settlers from a global world. They brought their food chains with them and located their terminals where previously European settlers had: in the Strip District. New and old wholesalers started to revive a distribution mode they had stopped after the Depression: the direct sale of raw and processed food. Downtowners can come here for lunches and dinners like steelworkers did between the wars for a cheap meal. There is no masterplan behind this viral incremental transformation that has reversed the organization of place and revived roads as the warehouses have moved their main entrances to the street front and opened ground floor shops, restaurants, groceries, and coffee houses. Vacant plots have been reused as parking or for temporary markets. The transformation has taken advantage of the trend for good and local food and at the same satisfied the curiosity for world kitchens, making Penn and Liberty into an open air natural culinary mall with a taste of history and a variety a planned scheme could not have achieved.

The Strip District is a destination again. The liveliness and urban quality of the district has started to attract new residents, further enhancing its diversity. Reused industrial buildings like the 1901 Armstrong Cork Factory profit from the renewed beauty of riverfront locations—"working rivers" are being cleaned after decades of industrial pollution—and are transformed into loft condos. Remaining working class row houses achieve unexpected prices—an unrenovated row house on Penn Avenue can sell for over 350,000 dollars—as developers start to promote townhouse schemes in industrial precincts, partially reusing existing structures, with names evoking foundries and yards.

Eastwards along the Allegheny, industries reuse the empty shells of steel mills and depots. They make movies, robots, and driverless cars. Their highly skilled employees love the buzz of the Strip more than the quiet dullness of suburban technology parks as well. The five hundred engineers at Uber's new Advanced Technologies Center are located just a few blocks from here in a 100,000-square-foot reused restaurant depot redesigned by San Francisco firm Assembly Design Studio together with Pittsburgher Strada in 2016.

HERMANOWSKI
City of Champions
20
19
17

Strip
14

TOTTI
10

PENNSYLVANIA MACARONI CO.
EST 1902
INTERNATIONAL CHEESE SHOP
A Family Tradition

Robots in the steel mill

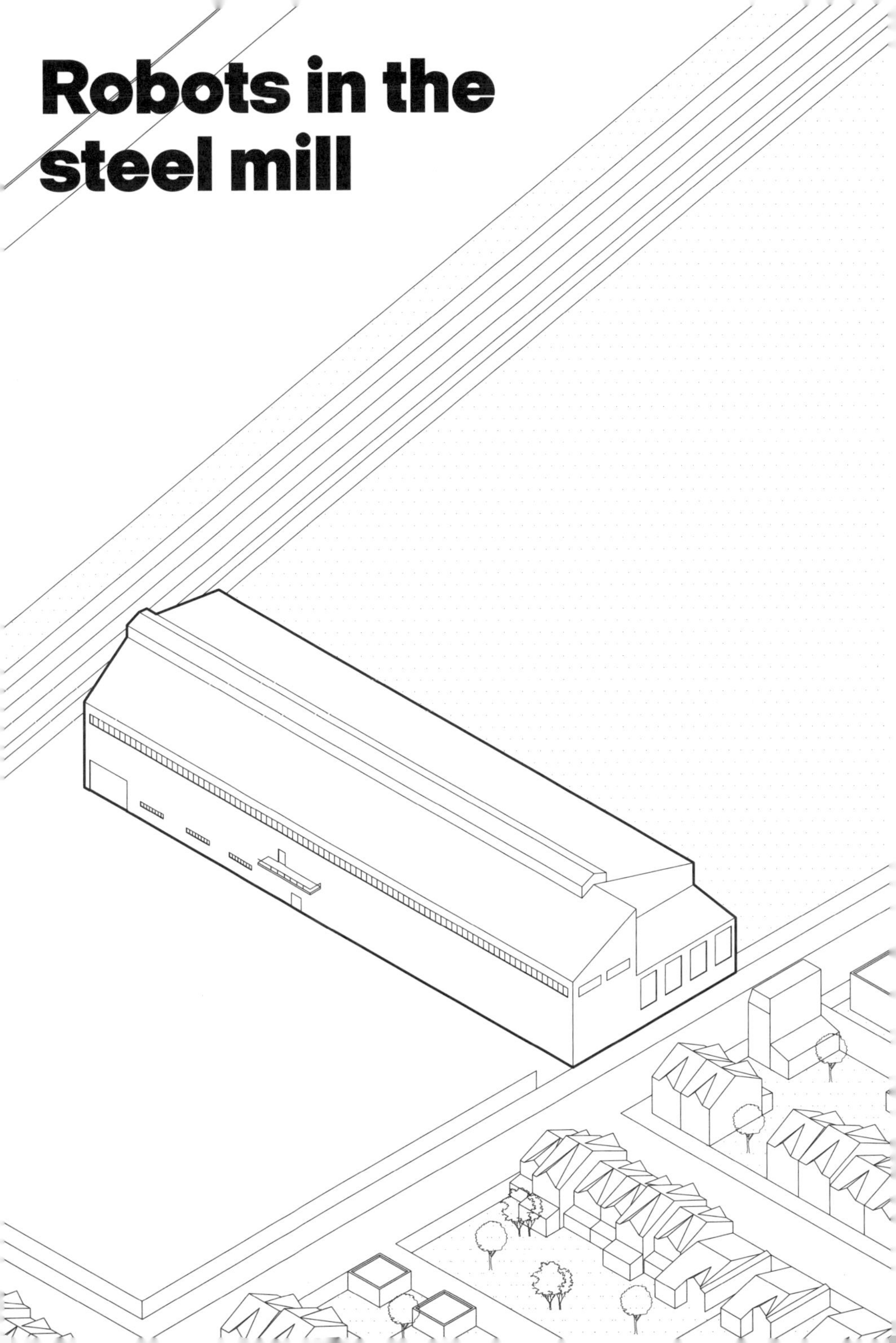

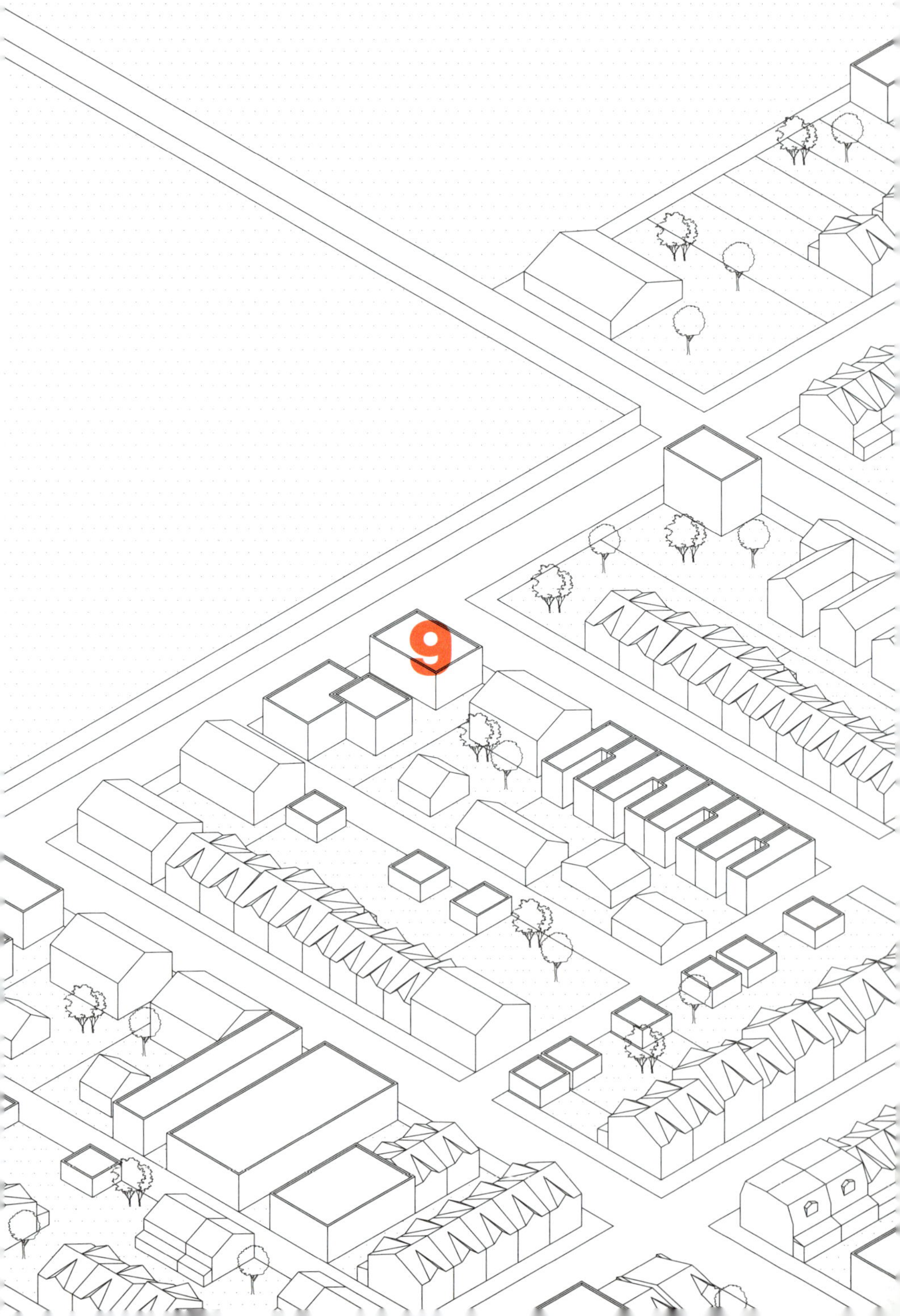
9

What is the image of innovation? For the 19th century tycoons, it was the power of their production plants. They displayed and distributed this image through prints and photographs. Sometimes they wanted them to have a specific style, more frequently size and capacity were enough. The smoke from the chimneys meant feverish activity—and corresponding profits. Their workers agreed. In spite of perpetual conflict for better wages and shorter shifts, they shared their bosses' pride for production and they too loved both the rough beauty of furnaces and cranes and the mathematical precision of mechanics.

When crisis came in the 1970s, this pride was somehow lost. Factories had to be razed as if even their memory had to be damned to oblivion. Deindustrialization was not only an economic process, but also the active removal of the traces of the recent past. Innovation was in services and research. High technology was better represented by the curtain glass cladding of new offices and laboratories, pavilions floating in the suburban greenery.

This is what you can see at Pittsburgh Technology Center, a 1990s project by URA and RIDC in partnership with CMU and the University of Pittsburgh on the site of the former Jones and Laughlin Company, Carnegie's main competitor employing almost 22,000 people. No trace of the grand halls and bays of the steelworks is left, just the renovated hot metal bridge over the Monongahela remains.

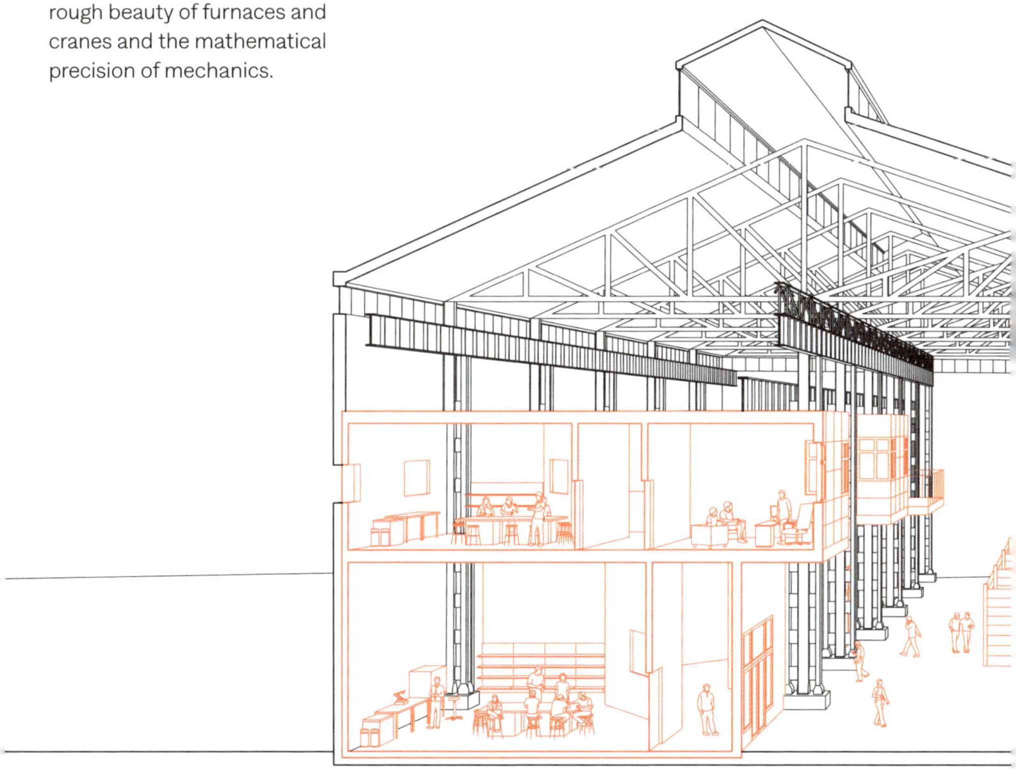

In spite of the proximity to downtown, the project has a suburban density and layout and no connection to neighboring areas. The futuristic imagery of science and technology parks rapidly went obsolete. Twenty years later, the taste is back to industrial aesthetics. Frank B. Robinson's intuition for Keystone Commons was right. A new breed of researchers, engineers, and makers praises and seems to love the rusted and smoked halls.

From the outside, it would be hard to notice that the content of the 30,000-square-foot Heppenstall Steel building—the sole building deemed reusable by RIDC when they purchased the twelve and a half acres site in 2002 after a thirty year vacancy—has changed. The iconic shed is the same. Only some new windows and a balcony were added to the light blue metal cladding. Inside, the high bay has been split in two by Desmone Architects to meet the requirements of Carnegie Robotics, a research and production spin-off of CMU's National Robotics Engineering Center, established a few blocks from here in 2009. On one side, a three-story "building within the building" adds 8,500 square feet of floorspace housing new clean room assembly labs, two new research and development labs, office space, and team building and conference spaces. The upper floor and side areas were set aside for future development. The driveway bay has been kept free as "tinker space" where temporary boxes hosting specific projects can be easily built and dismantled. Each project can be assembled and tested in a dedicated environment meeting specific requirements while granting secrecy if needed. The result is something between a makerspace, a high-tech lab, and a container stack enveloped by a historical factory. RIDC spent ten dollars per square foot to buy the site and forty dollars per square foot for infrastructure and remediation. After the 2013 lease, tenant Carnegie Robotics adapted the building with less than one hundred dollars per square foot and less than one year of construction. Cheap, fast, evolutive, iconic: adaptive.

9

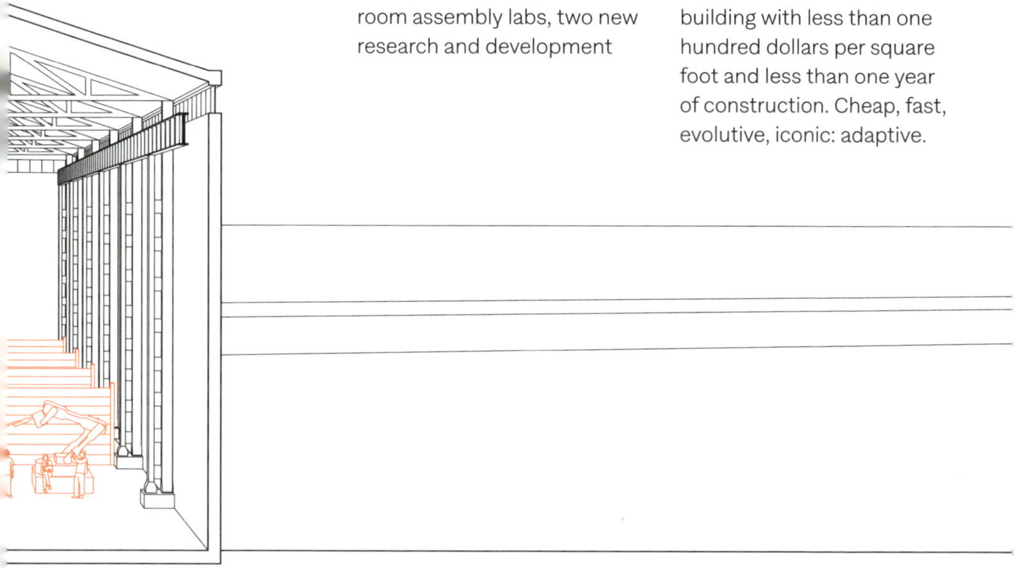

GENERAL

Carnegie Robotics
9

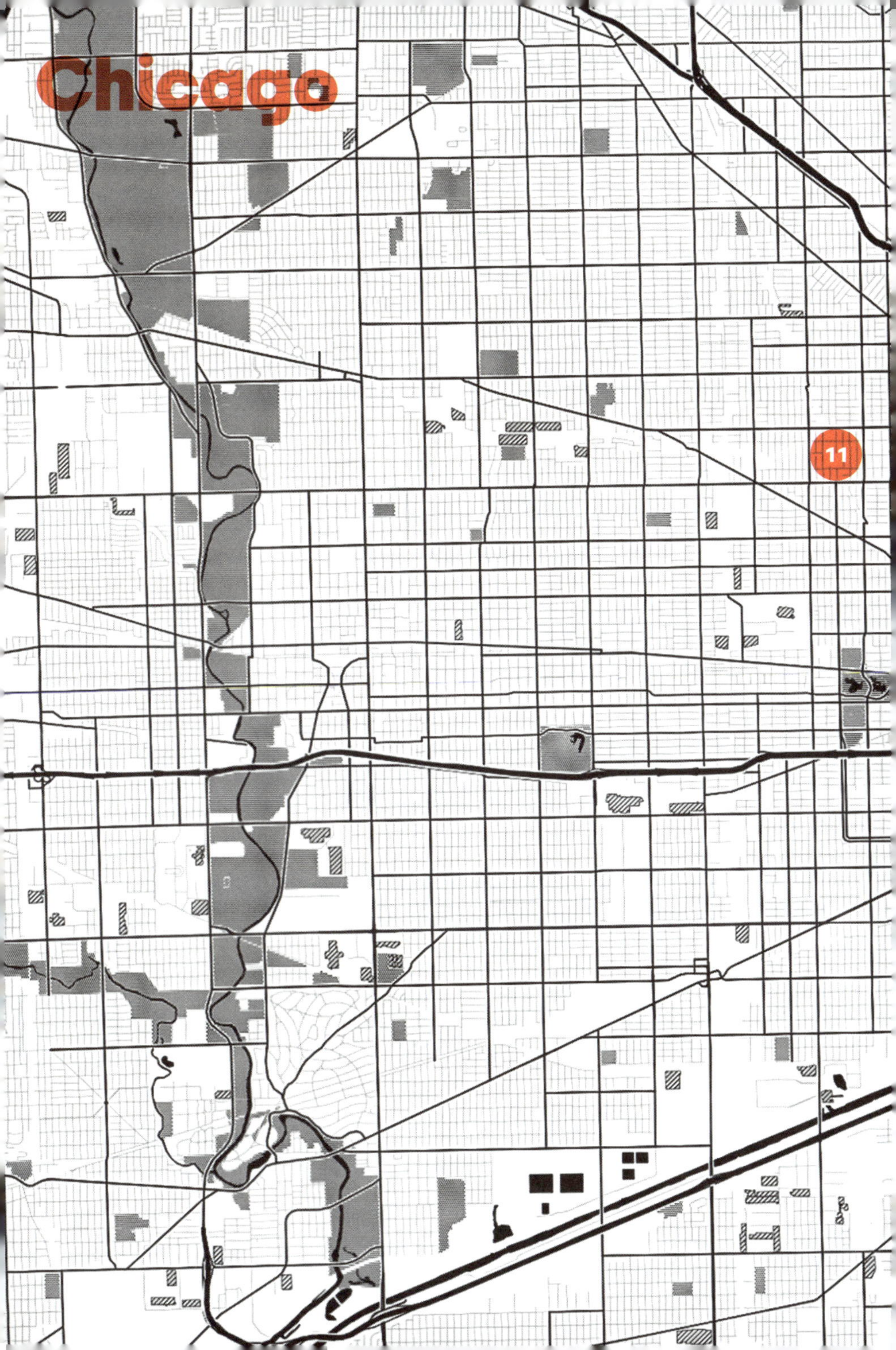
Chicago
11

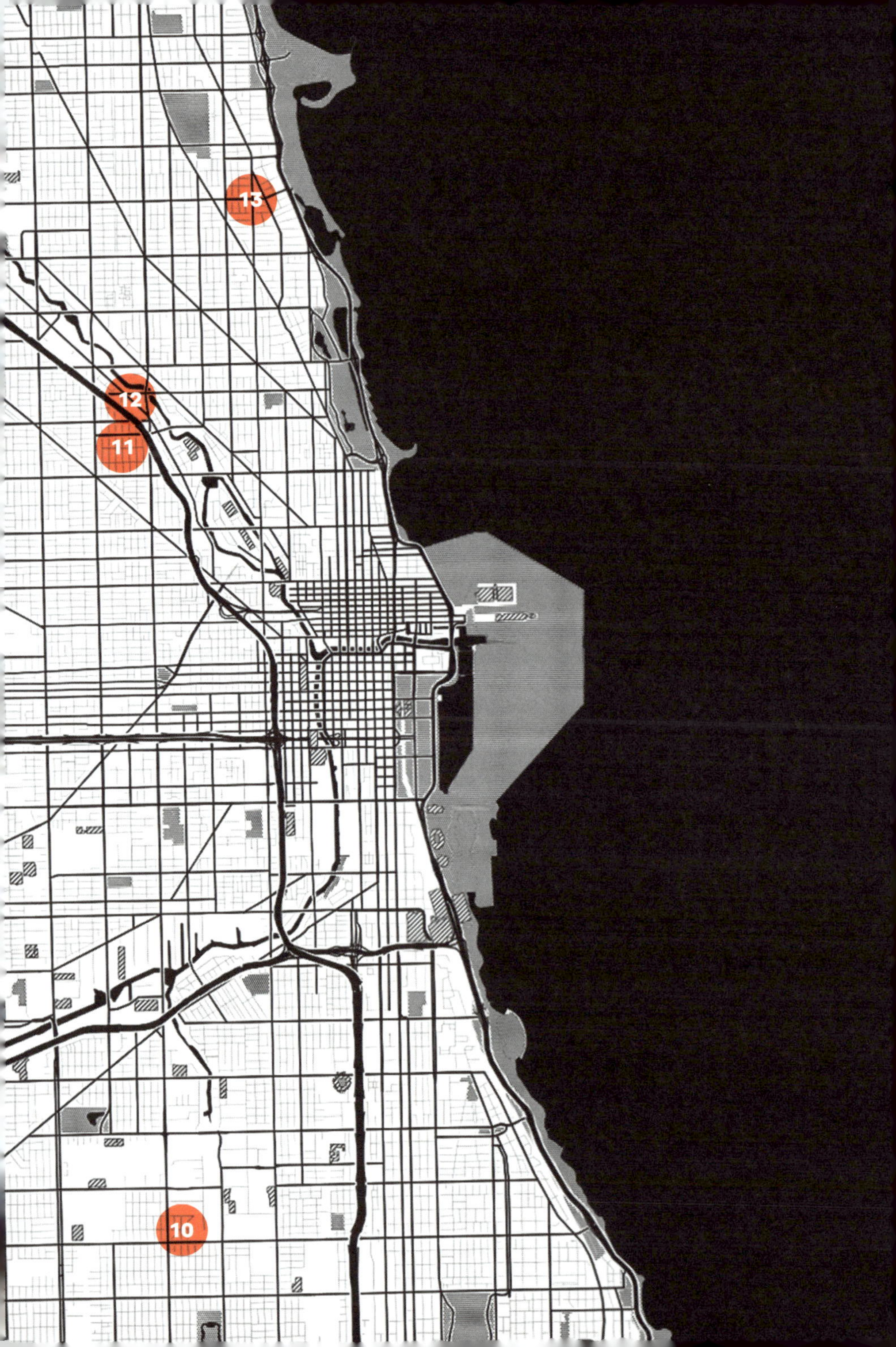
13
12
11
10

The Plan(t) to feed the city

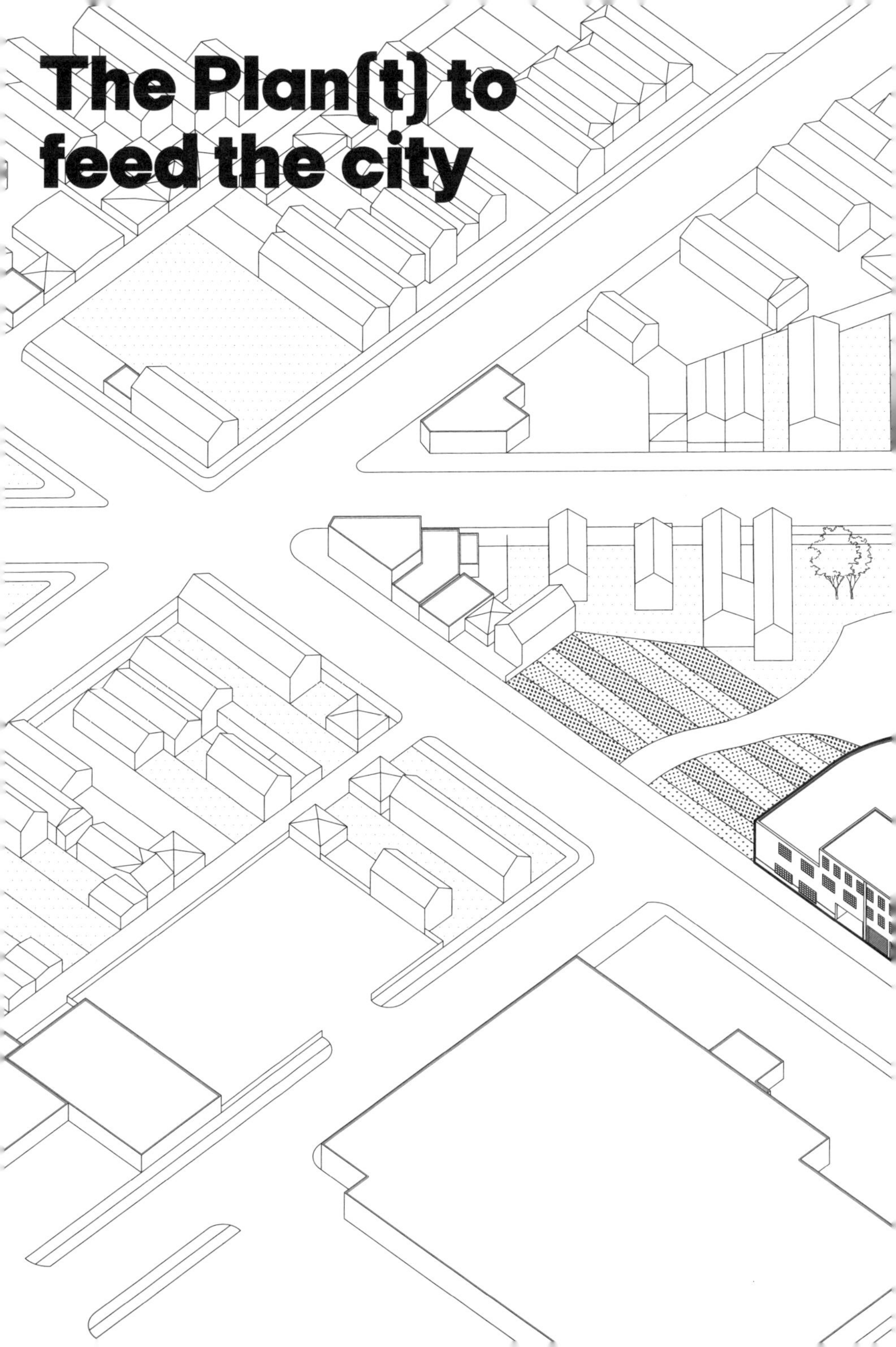

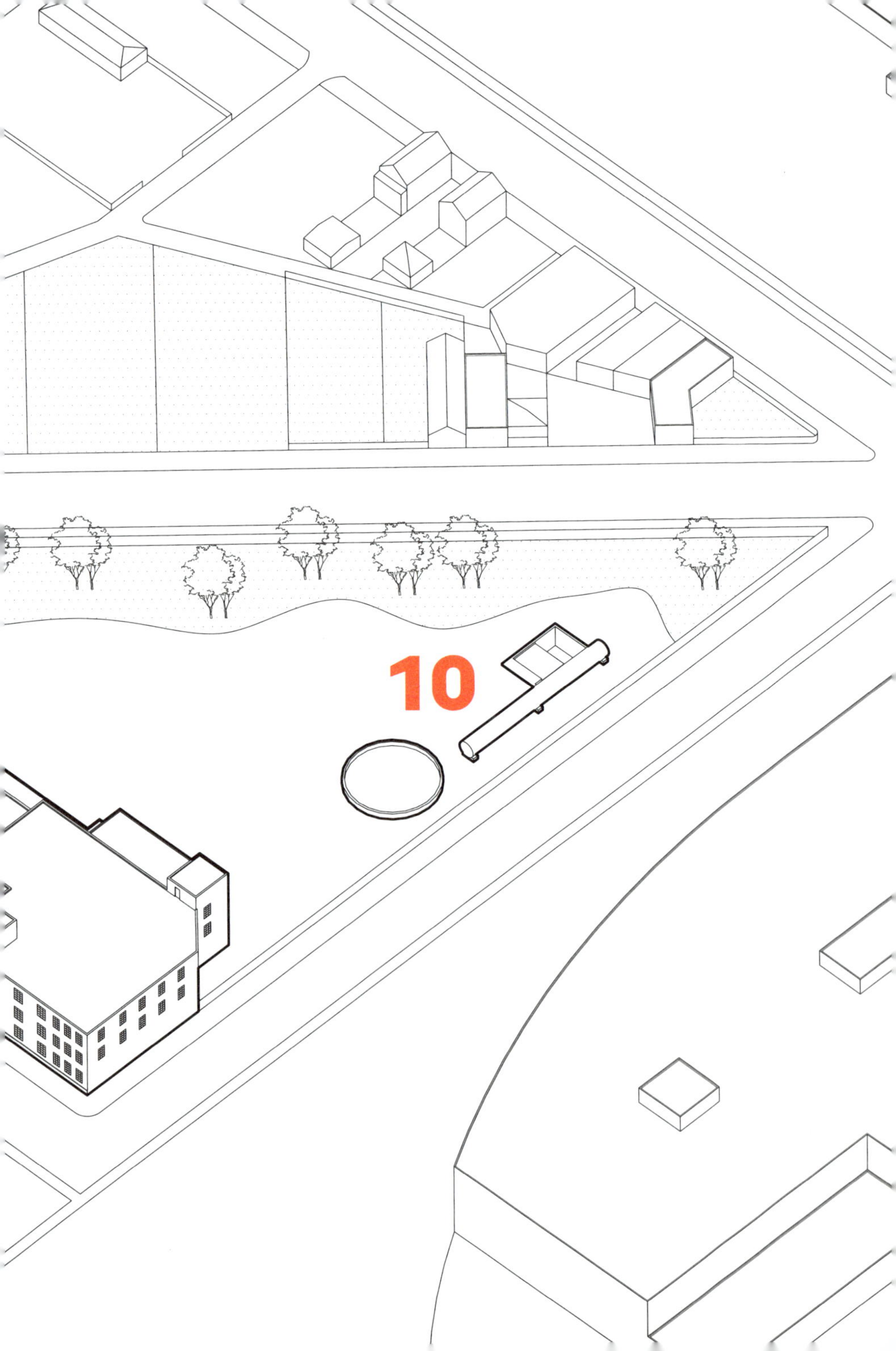
10

The conveyor rails once used to move slaughtered hogs are still hanging from the ceiling in the former Peer Foods factory—one of the last meatpacking plants to close in Chicago. It shut its doors in 2007. It was by observing something similar that Henry Ford—as he states in his 1922 autobiography *My Life and Work*—understood the potential of employing a moving conveyor system and fixed work stations in manufactoring. If you could disassemble a hog this way, you could reverse the process and assemble a car.

The meatpacking district was one of the cradles of modern production. The US railways brought cattle from all over the nation to the Union Stockyards, which had 1,000 employees and could handle up to 400,000 animals at the same time. Before being disrupted by decentered logistics after WWII, this site spelled death for an estimated four hundred million animals. It was the "hog butcher for the world." It was also a cradle of innovation in food handling: modern packaging and safety standards were first developed and applied here.

When visionary John Edel —owner and developer of the Chicago Sustainable Manufacturing Center (CSMC), a green business incubator a few blocks away housed in an old industrial building he acquired in 2002, adapted in 2007, and is now fully occupied and profitable—bought the 93,500-square-foot plant in 2010 for 525,000 dollars, the building was described by the real estate broker as a "strip and rip." The price was the supposed value of the metals you could strip before ripping down the building.

Edel saw much more than scrap metal in it. The building complied to USDA standards with food-grade features like floor drains, aseptic surfaces, and heavy floor loadings. Thanks to his work and his one-of-a-kind five person team, the building was re-designed, deconstructed, and adaptively reused as a new kind of food production and tranformation hub with the final goal of moving food production to the place where food is consumed: the city. The Plant, as it is known, is today a complex production system for raising tilapia, growing mushrooms, and nurturing aquaponic vegetable gardens, which combine aqua-culture (fish farming) and hydroponics, or growing plants in water rather than soil. It is a hub for small artisanal food businesses like an organic bakery, a kombucha tea maker, a beer brewery, a cheese distributor, a coffee roaster, and other emerging food producers and distributors.
It is surrounded by community gardens and organizes regular dissemination events, training sessions, and farmers and vegan markets in an area that is known as a food desert.
It runs solely on green energy, thanks to an anaerobic digester that transforms thirty tons of food waste every day—both from within The Plant and from businesses in the surrounding community—into biogas powering a turbine generator. Paired with a combined heat and power system, it can take the facility entirely off the grid.
As of early 2017, there are approximately eighty full-time employee equivalent positions based at the facility. The Plant is still under construction and is approximately sixty percent leased; the full build-out should be completed in 2019 and add a total estimate of 125 green jobs in the economically distressed neighborhood known as Back of the Yards. Innovation is back on the South Side, in a new, circular, and local mode.

10

10

Inclusion and leisure along the 606

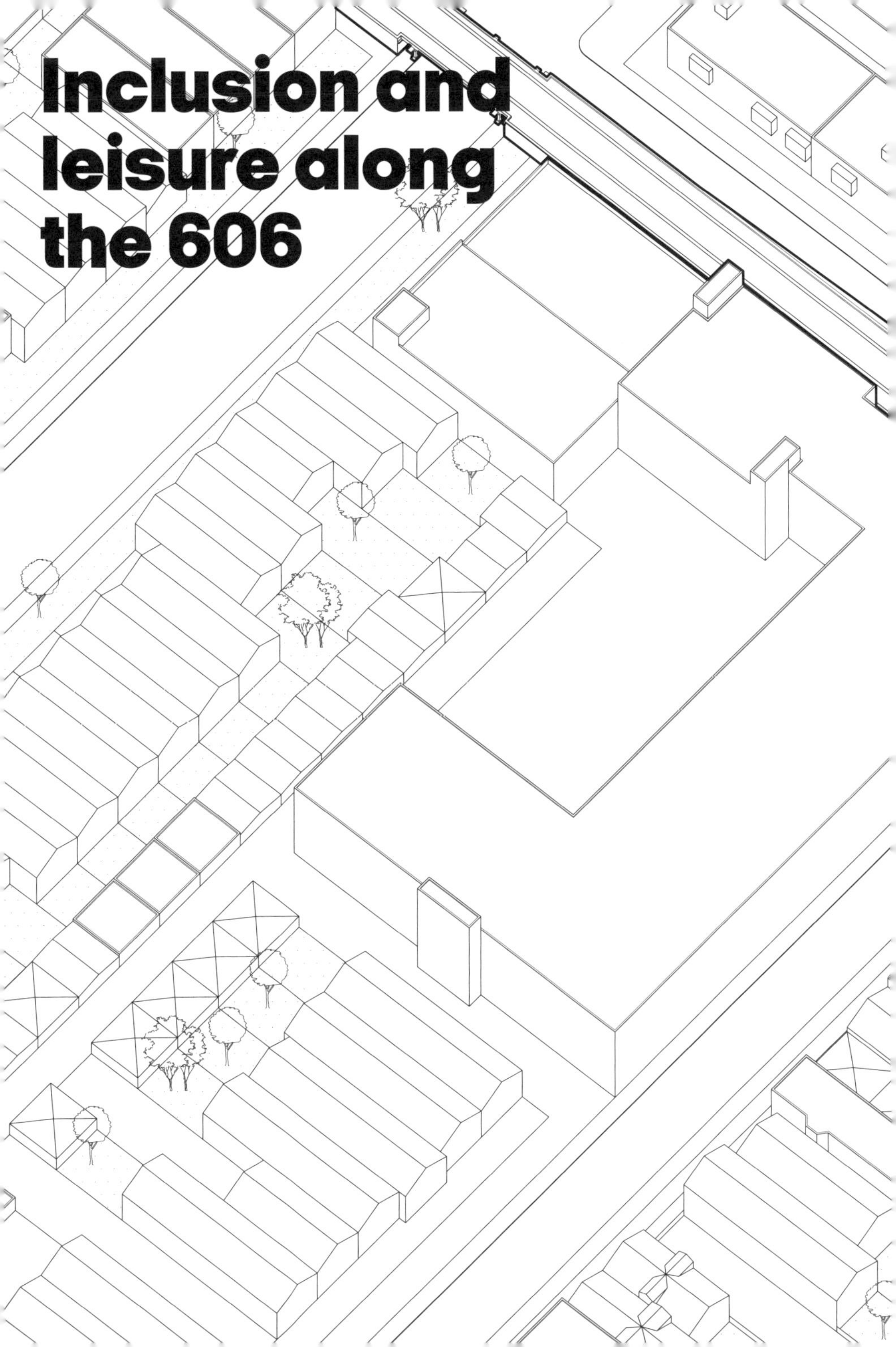

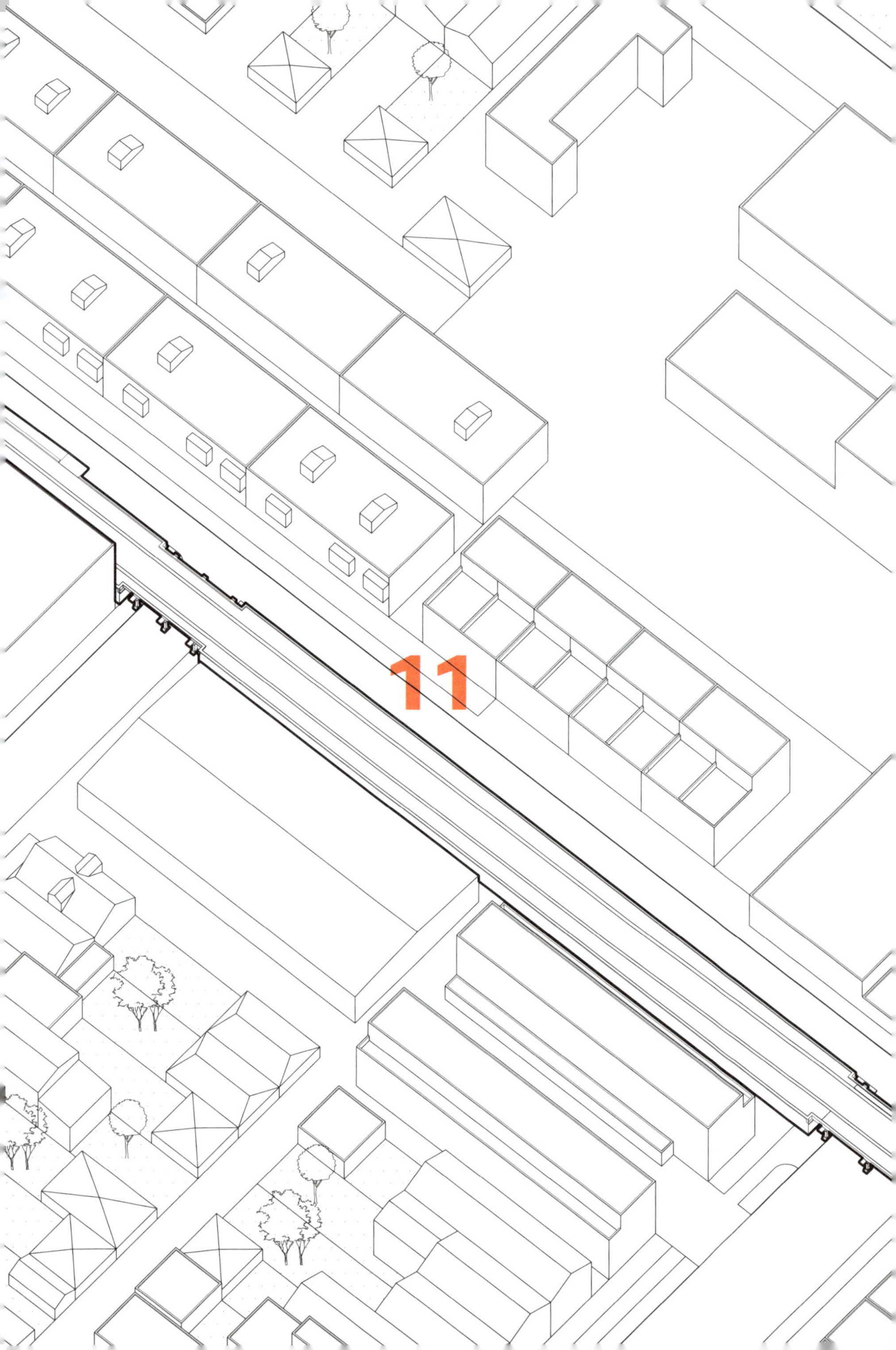
11

Few cities in the world have their history so tightly linked to railways as Chicago. A look at any US rail transportation map—no matter which year was it drafted—will show a web of lines converging here from all over the United States. And, zooming in, all of the histories of this "city of neighborhoods" are crossed by rail lines, connecting and dividing.
One of these lines was the Bloomingdale, which hauled freight for the Chicago, Milwaukee, St. Paul & Pacific Railroad from 1872 onwards from the north side of Chicago to the rest of the country via the company's nationwide rail network. Its rails crossed a dense urban area at grade, causing frequent accidents at crossings and raising protests by residents. Eventually, in 1910, the city required the St. Paul to elevate the urban tract of the Bloomingdale. Raising rails inside the city without interrupting traffic was a planning and engineering feat, possible thanks to one of the first extensive applications of reinforced concrete to railway construction.
Consequently, all of the factories and warehouses that had settled either side of the line in the meantime, forming an "industrial corridor," had to elevate their rail connections. The vital link between industry and infrastructure was now materialized in space: a whole layer of the city had been raised to the first floor.
But what made connections easier and safer also brought separation. A massive concrete wall now separated the neighborhoods of Logan Square and Bucktown from Humboldt Park and Wicker Park.
From the 1960s onwards, trucks outcompeted rails. The Canadian Pacific, which had taken over the line from the bankrupted St. Paul's in 1977, ended all freight traffic on it in 2001.
As soon as 2003, a group of neighbors had already joined to form the "Friends of the Bloomingdale Trail," calling for the trail to be converted to a "Bloomingdale Linear Park." The "Logan Square Neighborhood" association included the proposal in their 2004 Open Space Plan. Momentum was growing.
The city of Chicago recognized the trail's potential. In 2011, Mayor Rahm Emanuel's administration began to pursue the new design for the 2.7-mile-long viaduct. Neighbors and community members were actively involved in the planning of the park and trail system's design and layout which was headed by Brooklyn-based landscape architecture firm Michael Van Valkenburgh Associates (MVVA). An estimated 50,000 people participated in the opening day celebration on June 6, 2015. The name came from the opening date—6.06. Some call it "the anti High Line" for its restrained design and extended usability.
The 606 is more than an amenity, it is an alternate urban commuting path—this is how the 606 could nab fifty million dollars of US

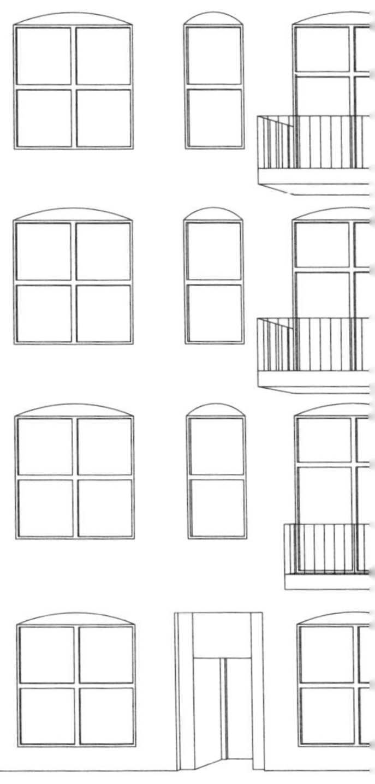

Department of Transportation funds for the project's total ninety-five million dollar budget. The Bloomingdale now connects what it once divided: 80,000 residents within a ten-minute walk share its space, coming from neighborhoods with diverse racial, ethnic, and economic populations. And just like the Bloomingdale once attracted industrial facilities, its refurbishment now stimulated their reuse even before its opening.

The Churchill Cabinet Company building was converted for residential use, and the developers retained the original painted signage. Samuel Olson and Co.'s factory of conveying machines is used as an art gallery. Majestic Wood Carving Company's furniture factory on Maplewood Avenue is used for residential living. According to a report from the Institute of Housing Studies at DePaul University, since its groundbreaking and even more after its opening, the 606 is having a great impact on housing prices within half a mile from the track, with price increases nearing fifty percent west of Western Avenue and an average one hundred thousand dollars "606 premium" on sales prices. In 2015, the year the trail opened, the figure approached twenty-one percent, and in the first quarter of 2016, it was almost thirty-one percent. Since then, housing prices west of Western Avenue have increased by 48.2 percent. Longtime residents say diversity is on the wane while property values—and property taxes—are on the rise, stirring fears that homeowners as well as renters will be priced out those neighborhoods. A battle over gentrification erupted in Summer 2017. Residents, housing activists, and developers will square off over two aldermens' plan to introduce a "demolition fee" to curb new speculative projects near the 606 and finance affordable housing for local residents. The idea to extend the 606 eastward over the Chicago River to Lincoln Park has gained nearly universal support.

11

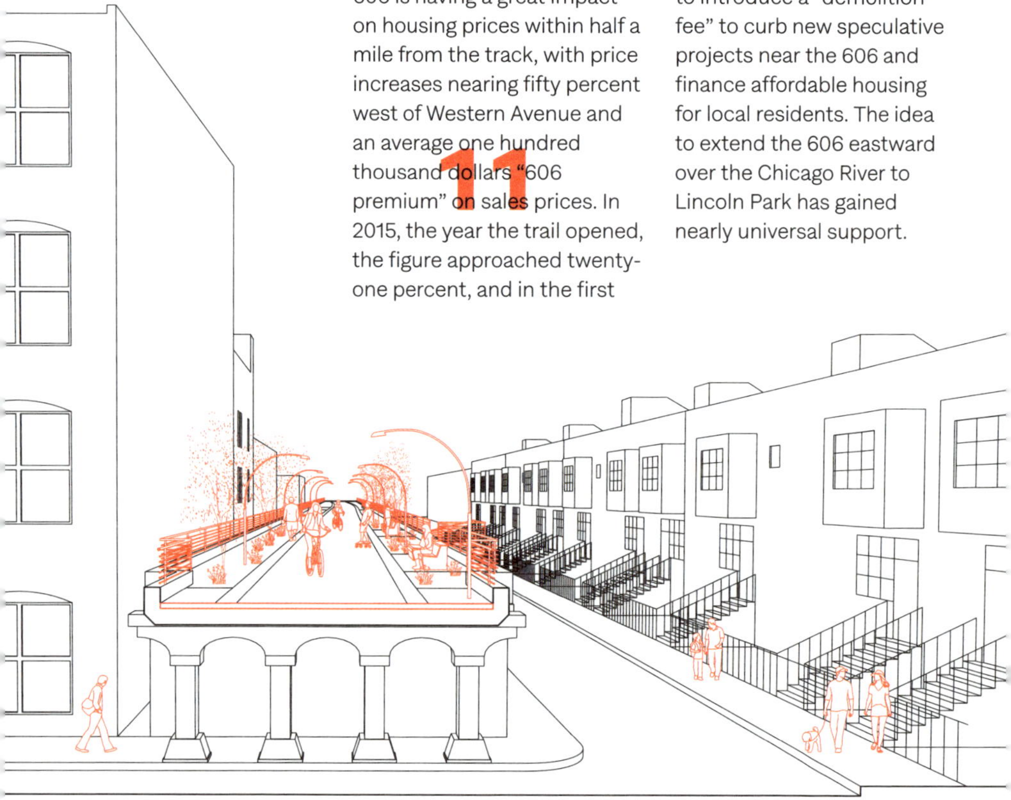

SPEED
LIMIT
25
COME ON UPWARD
003691
2208166

0.3

11

Stuff to reuse at Rebuilding Exchange

12

Deconstruction is not the name of an intellectual device from French critical theory, as you might learn in your architecture school. It is the deepest form of adaptive reuse. When a whole building cannot be reused, there is still a way: its components can. Deconstruction is the alternative to the wrecking ball—and you do not need a demolition permit. If you cannot adapt the building, adapt its parts.

Deconstruction is the manual, accurate dismantling of a building into its parts, so that they can be classified, evaluated, inventoried, and stored. This preparation for a second life begins in places like this 24,000-square-foot warehouse in Bucktown. Countless layers of construction culture and the history of Chicago are carefully stored under its roof: windows, fireplaces, sinks, floors, plumbing fixtures, cabinets, lumber, lighting beams, stairs, doors, steps, tiles, bricks, pipes, handles, chimneys, columns, and more.

Disconnected from their original context, they become available for creative reuse. The original use of a piece might not be recognizable anymore. You can travel through time and incorporate both 200-year-old wooden parts and 1950s aluminium components into your new house. I was taught that pine is a soft and clear wood. I learned here that it can be hard and dark—at least in old planks that were cut by the first pioneers from primeval American forests.

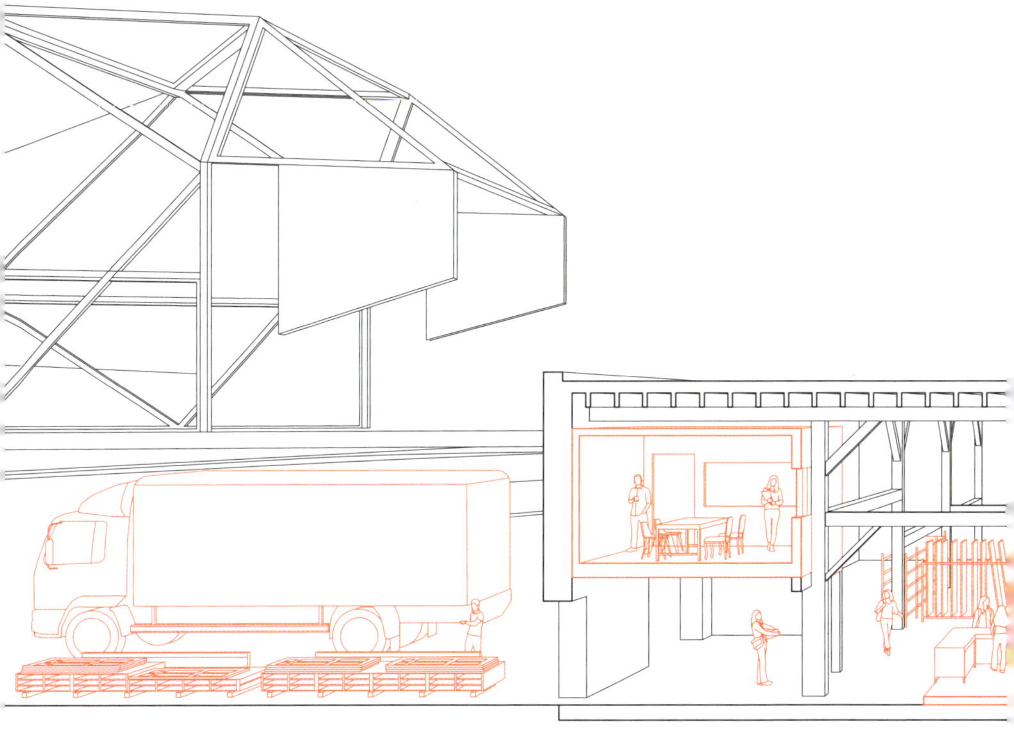

The building itself is a case of reuse. In its many prior lives it already served as the operations for a synthetic lawn company, a U-Haul office and, long ago, a sheep shearing facility. Most recently a plastics recycling plant, it's been partitioned into smaller offices that were carefully dismantled. All of the removed material was either used to refurbish the space —a rough, non-heated depot and a more comfortable training and teaching area hosted in customized low tech self-built "boxes"—or sold to sustain the different programs offered by its workshop. For here material does more than wait: it generates a market for itself by actively stimulating possible users.

At Rebuilding Exchange, people can get inspired by other users' work, exchange ideas, learn new skills, and share equipment, tools and experience. The building serves about 16,000 customers a year, is the local distribution platform for an expanding urban market of reused building material, and additionally organizes workshops and training sessions. Initiated as a marginal practice, deconstruction is now proposed by handbooks and assessedby environmental guidelines as the soundest way to conserve embodied energy and reduce waste. Each reused piece is one less piece in the Chicago landfill—set to close by 2020. Here people with barriers to employment find job training and placement in the growing deconstruction industry, a sector that will always require workmen and craftsmanship. Here DIYers find materials for their dreams, advice to make them feasible, and the skills to make them happen. Here a growing number of designers and architects find ideas and material for projects that hybridize old and new materials and vintage and modern details. Taste and memories can also contribute to environmental goals.

12

TILE/STONE

REBUILDING EXCHANGE
TERRACOTTA
BRICKS
$35-$45

Whole house deconstruction La Grange, IL
Whole house deconstruction La Grange, IL
hole house deconstruction La Grange, IL
Whole house deconstruction La Grange

 Stuff to reuse at Rebuilding Exchange

The proudest home in town

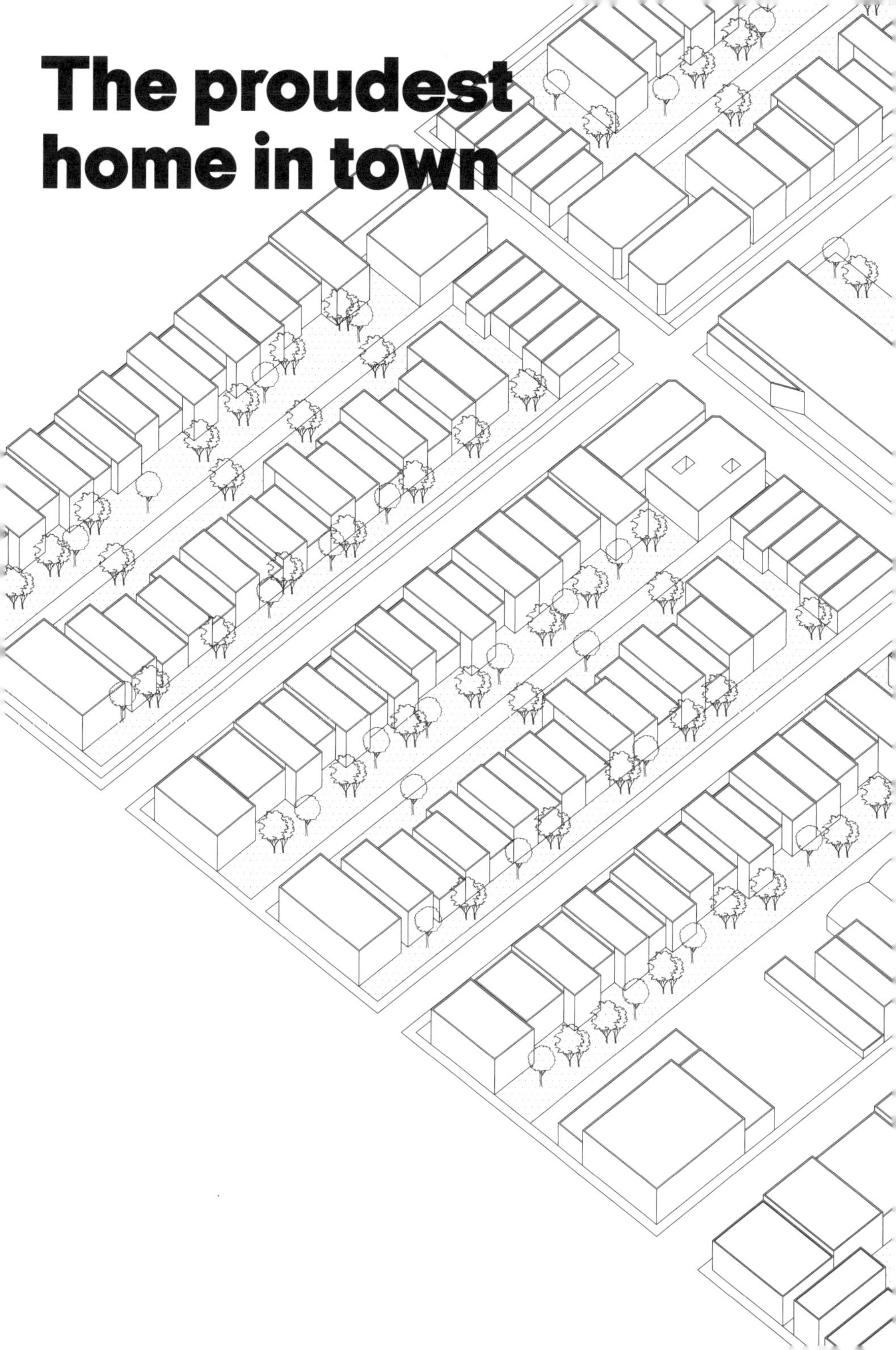

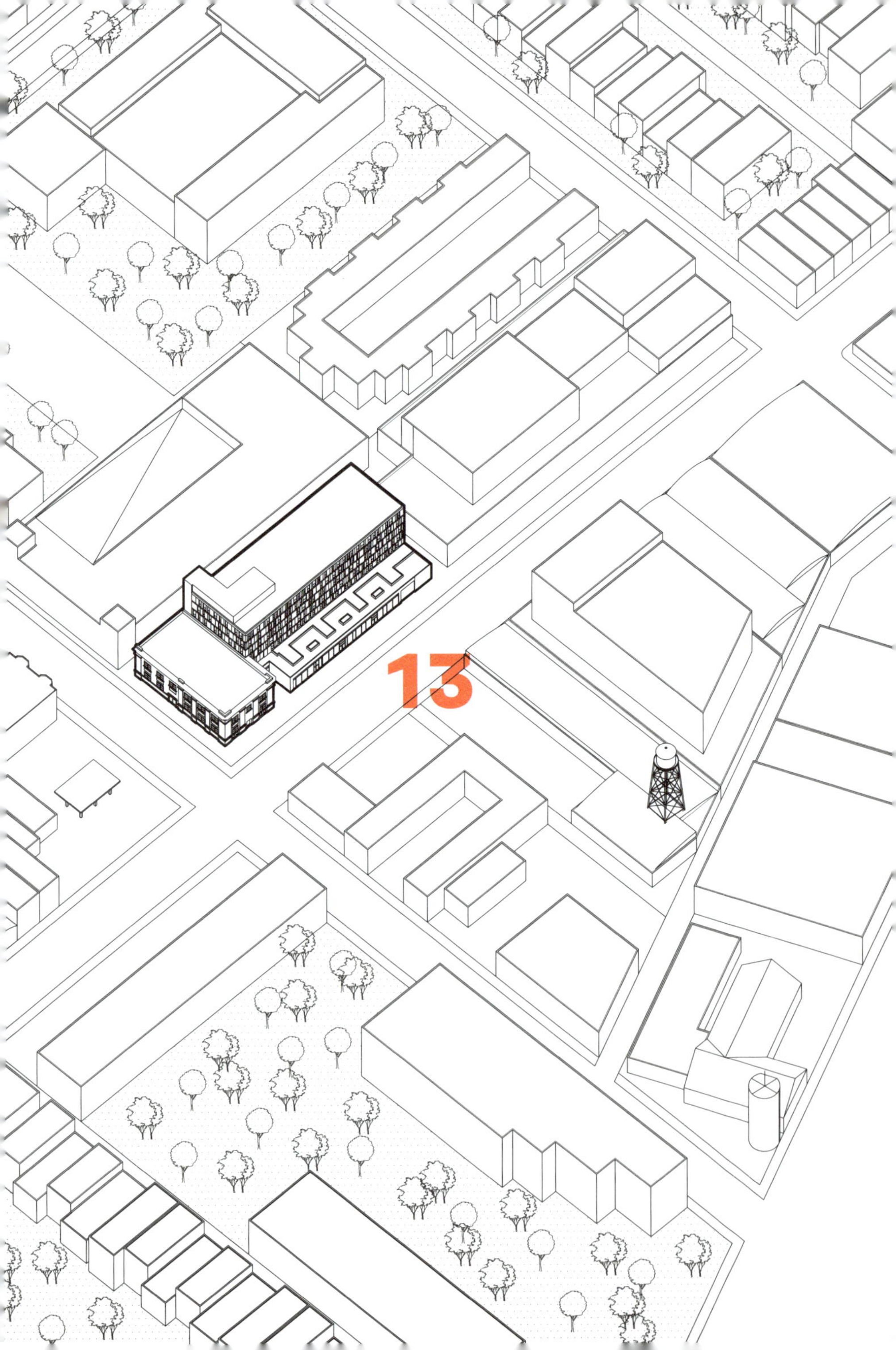
13

The 42nd Precinct Chicago Police Station on Halsted Street was constructed in 1907 on the site of Lake View Township's Town Hall. This is why it has always been referred to as the "Town Hall Police Station." It's a place of mixed feelings for Boystown's flourishing LGBTQI community, since the area is also the world's first officially recognised "gayborhood." Many from the LGBTQI community remember spending the night in the police station because of bar raids and other run-ins with law enforcement or after being arrested during protests. Others recall that Commander Joseph DeLopez founded the police liaison to the gay and lesbian community here in the Town Hall District Precinct in the 1990s. The police left Town Hall in 2010, when a larger and more modern station was built nearby.

In 2014, the severe Classic Revival building began its second public life as the "Center on Addison," a senior home promoted by the social service provider Center on Halsted. But the vision went beyond the old walls of the former police station: it is the first senior home expressly addressing the social needs of aging LGBTQI community members. Heartland Alliance—the anti-poverty group that developed and manages the property with Center on Halsted—estimates that Chicago is home to 40,000 of the US's 1.5 million elderly LGBTQI, and that one-fifth of these residents are living in poverty.

The Center on Addison therefore targets LGBTQI seniors—although applications are open to all, thanks to anti-discrimination laws—earning between fifty and eighty percent of the area median income; this means on average 30,000 dollars. Subsidies by the Chicago Housing Authority's Property Rental Assistance program help to keep rents below thirty percent of each resident's income. The total development cost was 23.7 million dollars.

The project was made possible due to a five million dollar loan from the city and one and a half million dollars in low income housing tax credits that generated fourteen and a half million dollars in equity, integrated by state and federal grants. The adaptive reuse of the historical building is amended by a new six-story residential wing on Halsted Street with thirty studios and forty-nine one-bedroom apartments, designed by the architecture and planning firm Gensler.

Amenities include a landscaped terrace facing Halsted Street, a fitness room, a computer lab, a family dining room for small gatherings, and bike parking, as well as laundry on each floor. Heartland Alliance and the Center on Halsted provide on-site property management and social service staff. The ground floor and first floor are accessible to the public. Each week, more than 150 seniors attend workshops, take classes, share a meal, or make new friends in the new facilities.

This makes the Center on Addison much more than a place to live: it is a physical hub for social and recreational services addressing the whole community.
On the 25th of June 2015, the first residents watched the 48th annual annual Chicago Gay Pride Parade—attended by more than one million participants— from the first floor terrace. The parade snaked down Halsted Street, also the location of the legacy walk that honors national historical LGBTQI icons.

13

EXIT

GREEN FEATURE

E LEGACY WAL
JANE ADDAMS
HEARTLAND ALLIANCE

SEXUALITY
LIFE
HEALING
SUNLIGHT
NATURE
ART
HARMONY
SPIRIT
TRUE COLORS FLY HERE

WHOLE FOODS

13

Detroit

14
18
15
16

Russell's creative outlaws

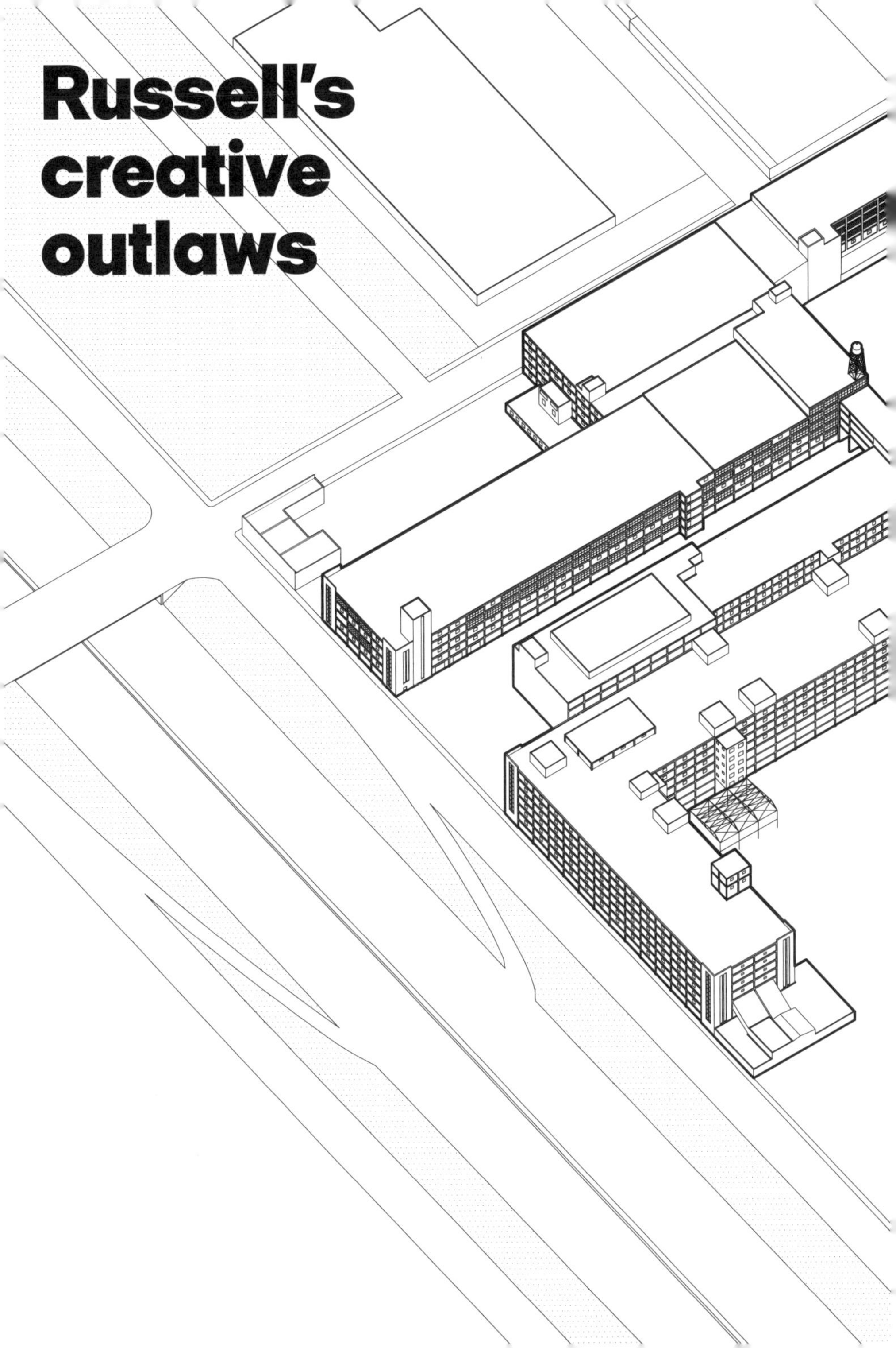

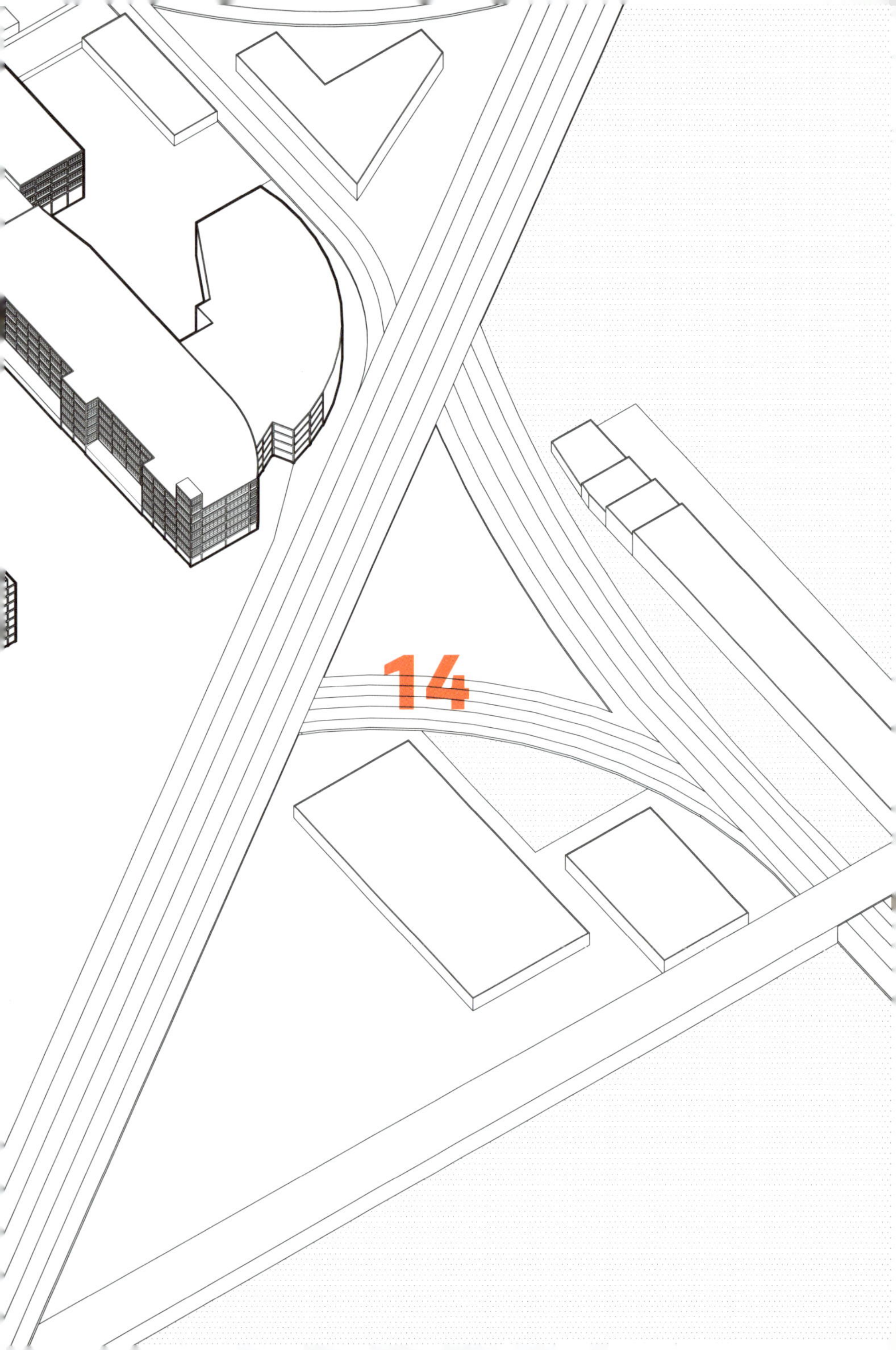
14

Around seventy people were listening to a house music concert in the main hall of the Ghost Ship in Oakland, California on the evening of December 2nd, 2016. The old warehouse, converted into a DIY performance space with living and working units, and famous for its baroque wooden vintage interiors, was a reference for the local creative scene and a rare haven in the Bay Area's gentrifying landscape of skyrocketing rents and disappearing artist spaces. At 11:20 pm, fire broke out, rapidly extending to the whole building.

At sunrise, firemen counted thirty-six bodies. It was the deadliest fire in California since 1906. It was probably also the end of the age of innocence for DIY adaptive reuse. Authorities opened files they had ignored for decades. On February 21st, 2017, the Russel Industrial Center in Detroit was ordered vacated by the city due to safety violations. The 150 tenants had one week to move out of the buildings. Seventy percent of them did, the others—most of whom owned heavy or large equipment—reached an agreement with city officers: two of the seven buildings were allowed to remain open and had ninety days to submit architectural plans and obtain occupancy certificates, while owner Boydell Development had to comply with a long list of safety prescriptions. Heated discussions on the web and press reports leave the reader with mixed feelings: was this place the next possible Ghost Ship or a marker of Motown's comeback, its "new factory of deams," as Fortune titled in 2010? Was Boydell's boss Dennis Kefallinos a daring innovator exploring new markets or a "bad landlord" renting out substandard space he acquired as ruins and rebranded as creative spaces—but without investing in any improvement? Probably both tales hold some truth.

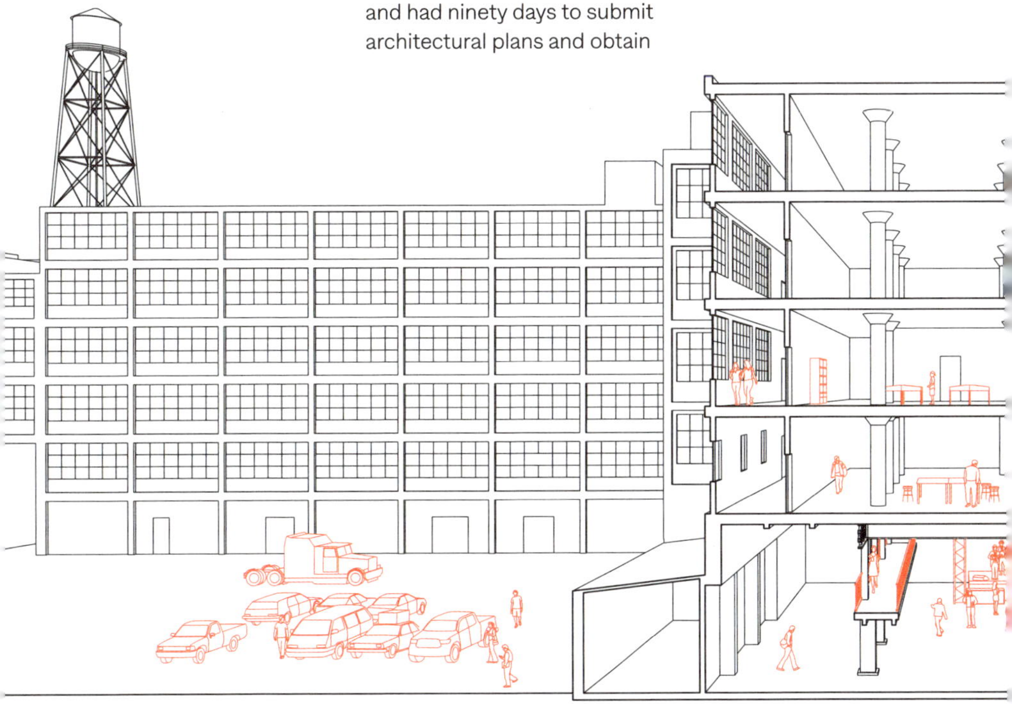

The 2,200,000-square-foot industrial complex in Milwaukee Junction designed by Albert Kahn for Murray Auto Body Corporation in 1915 was converted to a kind of industrial condo in the 1960s when Murray started to lease space to other activities and rebranded the site "Russell Industrial Center." Damaged by a tornado in 1998, RIC had been vacant for five years before being bought by Kefallinos in 2003, reportedly for one million dollars, or just forty-five cents per square foot. His managers were scared, but when, a few months later, artists flocked in, lured by the cheap rents and the quality of space, they changed their minds. Their boss was right: in 2015, studios, workshops, architecture offices, designers, musicians, food stores, shops, printers, and other makers occupied nearly one million square feet, while events ranging from open air markets to porn festivals and film shootings animated the place, making it a destination again in Detroit's blighted map.

In 2015, the place was generating a yearly income close to the purchase price. Facility management rules were summarised in three bullets: "respect the place, respect the people, pay the rent." When rent deals were closed, spaces were summarily made fit for use—partition walls were raised, broken windows replaced—to be later completed by tenants. Investments flexibly followed revenues.

The Detroit Chimera graffiti mural, painted on building number two in 2010 by artist Kobie Solomon, became a landmark of a city's hopes on the Chrysler Freeway. Detroit was even starting to attract young artists from as far away as New York City and London. RIC was one of the places to be. Will it be it again, or is "wild" DIY reuse inherently dangerous? The question is crucial, as much of Detroit's comeback narratives are based on outsiders joining locals to share Motown's new destiny as a creative and productive hub thanks to an extensive, affordable yet powerful industrial legacy. Its easy adaptability is a key attraction factor, and making it compliant to rules originally devised for ordinary commercial developments risks making low cost adaptive reuse unfeasible. Or, as it was able to do in its glorious industrial past and is doing today in many other fields, Detroit will find its way and define new codes which will help innovation be simultaneously safe, accessible, and visionary.

14

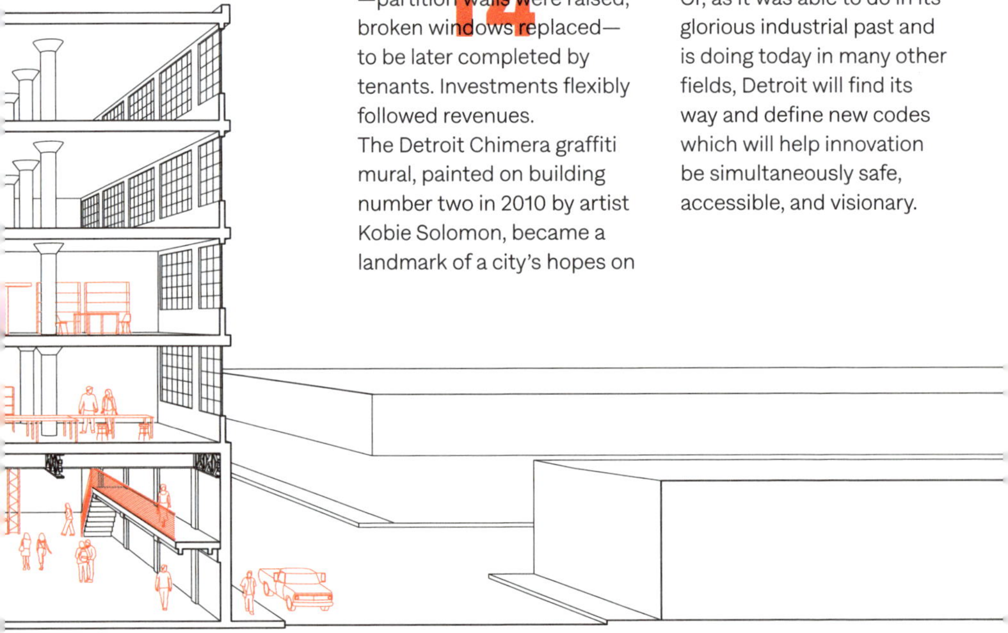

RUSSELL
TRADE
CENTER
972-7009

G0586

The jobs of Shinola

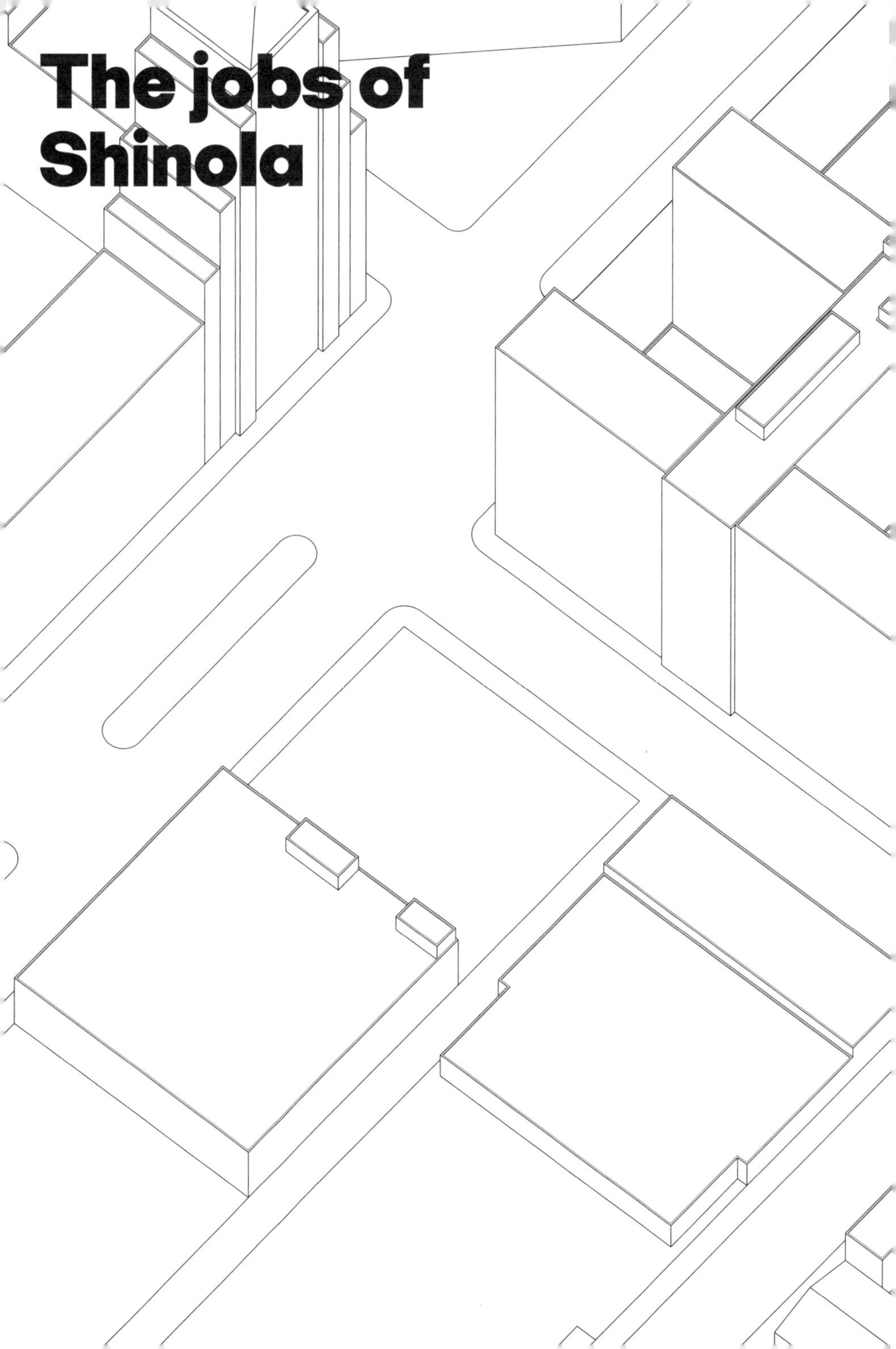

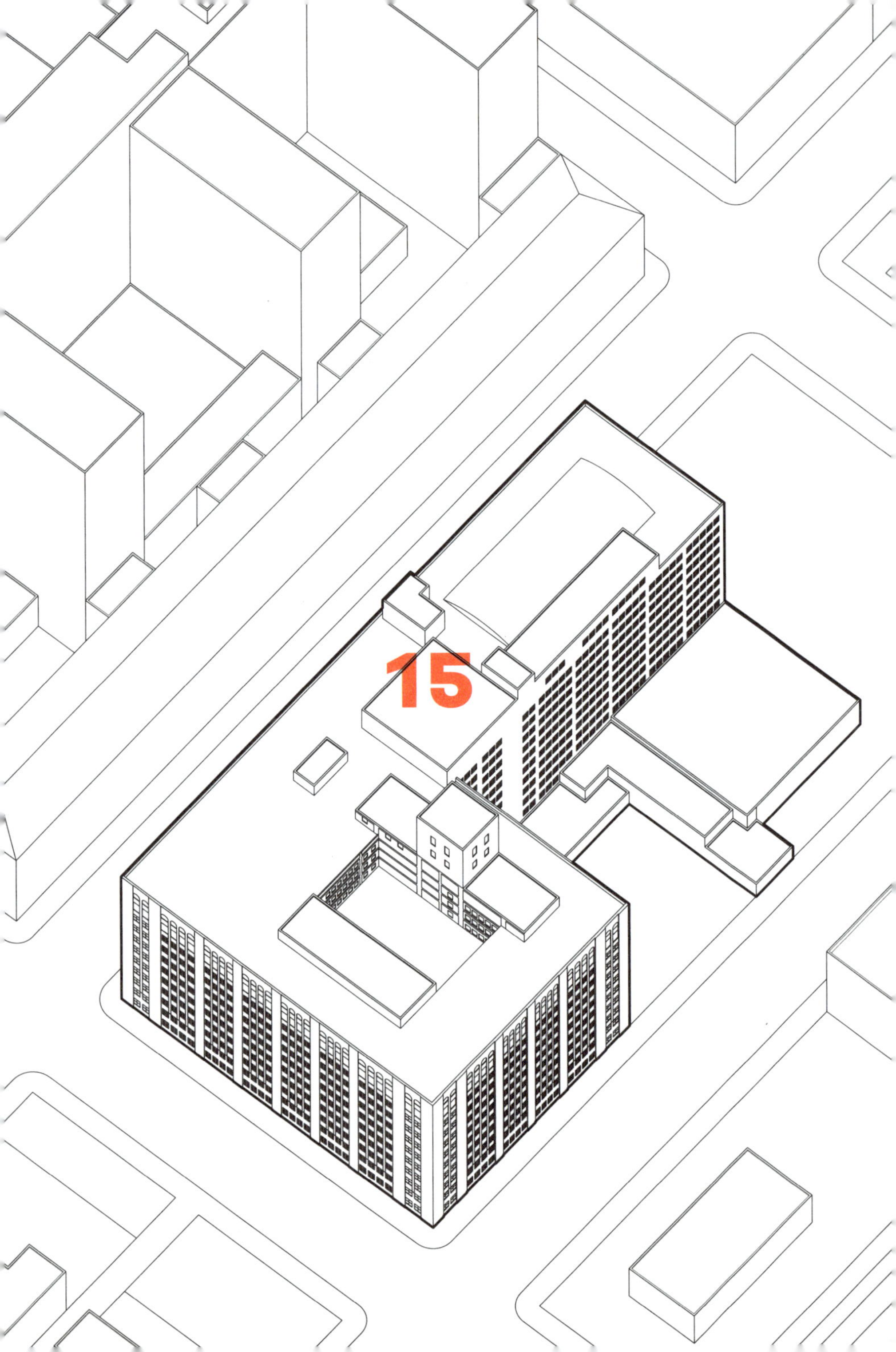
15

The perfect headline of Detroit's comeback is located on the fifth floor of a building in Midtown that was at the heart of its first fortune: the Argonaut. Like so many buildings here, it was designed in 1927 by Albert Kahn for Argonaut Realty Corporation, the real estate division of General Motors. It was the company's research laboratory until 1956. GM eventually left the building in 2000, and in 2007 donated it to the College for Creative Studies, heir to the Detroit Society of Arts and Crafts founded in 1906. The building hosts a charter high school for children, a school named "Henry Ford Academy," CCS's graduate program, and 300 units of student housing. A 145 million dollar renovation was completed in Fall 2009. For the last ninety years, this place has been the epitome of design in the epitome of the American manufacturing town.

After visiting more than 120 possible locations in Detroit —there is no shortage of vacancies here—a new firm whose vision was to bring back well-made and well-designed American products settled here. They could not have landed in a better place. In 2012, Shinola leased and renovated 30,000 square feet on the fifth floor of the Argonaut. Shinola is a new company with an old name. Founded in 1907, for over half a century, Shinola meant shoe shine—Shinola was such a household name that in WWII its name was permanently incorporated into the English colloquialism "you don't know shit from shinola"—or you're not very smart. In 1960, the first life of Shinola was over. In 2011, the brand was bought by Texas-based investment fund Bedrock, after focus groups had suggested that customers were ready to pay a premium price for American-made products, and a even higher one for the Detroit tenacity aura. The name was chosen to address smart customers who know the difference between ordinary stuff and watches, bikes, leather goods, and other accessories proudly "Built in Detroit." Solid, well crafted, robust, with a slightly vintage look and a clear Norman Rockwell aftertaste. Objects that come from the glorious past of a land of makers. Shinola at the Argonaut has both a production plant and a design, marketing, and administration HQ. Here watches are designed and assembled, leather accessories are sewn, and both are packaged to be sent to the brand's growing retail

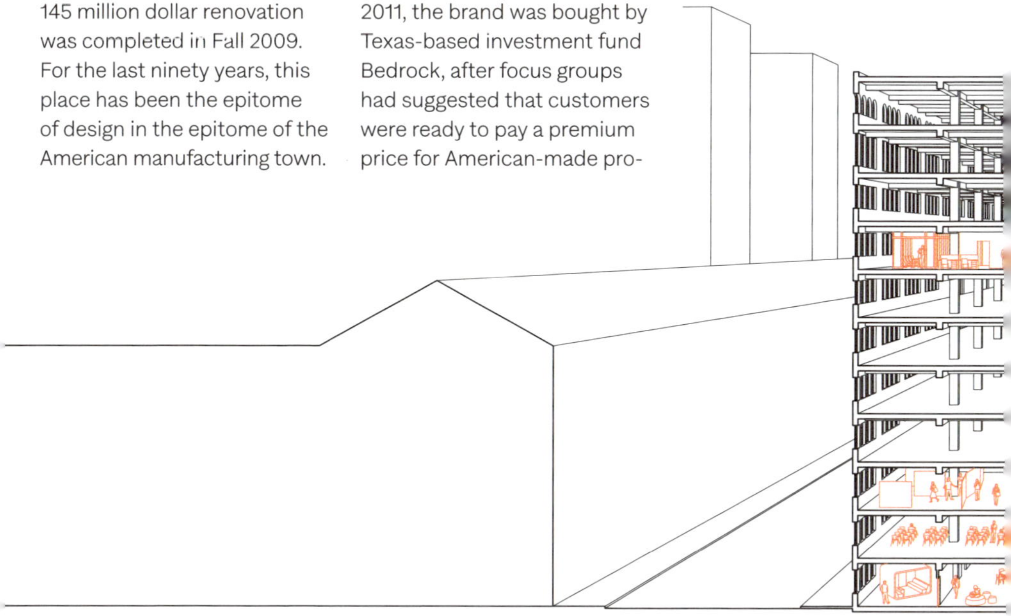

network—one flagship store is here in Detroit, in an old reused warehouse also in Midtown. Creative and factory staff share the same space and services. The interior design reflects brand identity: solid, slightly retro, lean. Hope and self-respect are part of being here, as jobs that pay over the minimum wage and add benefits have long since vanished from this part of the city. The nearly 500 employees—a small number in a city where GM is still the employer of 40,000 people—are important: because they are new, because they are growing—up from just nine in 2011—and because they are in Midtown, back to the center after fifty years of production relocated to suburbs. Some criticize Shinola's "white knight" narrative as opportunistic marketing; others repute its products are overpriced. In 2016, Shinola was ordered by the Federal Trade Commission to stop using the tagline "Where American is Made." Watch parts were imported from East Asia and quartz movements were fabricated in Switzerland by Shinola's partner and shareholder Ronda. The best way to correct the slogan would be "Where American is Assembled"—of course this takes away much of the "maker" flavor. Shinola continues its Detroit affair notwithstanding: a new turntable production unit has been recently started and headphones are on the way. Here again, there is an attempt to reincorporate a lost legacy of the city—today's Motown Records. Shinola recently purchased an abandoned creamery in Midtown to create the audio factory. And a building on Woodward Avenue is currently being renovated and extended to become a Shinola Hotel expected to open in Fall 2018, with 130 rooms on eight floors and 16,000 square feet of food and beverage retail. Real estate and hospitality seem to be a step away from manufacturing. But Shinola, in the words of its founders, is not a watchmaker or a bikemaker: it is "a job-creation vehicle."

15

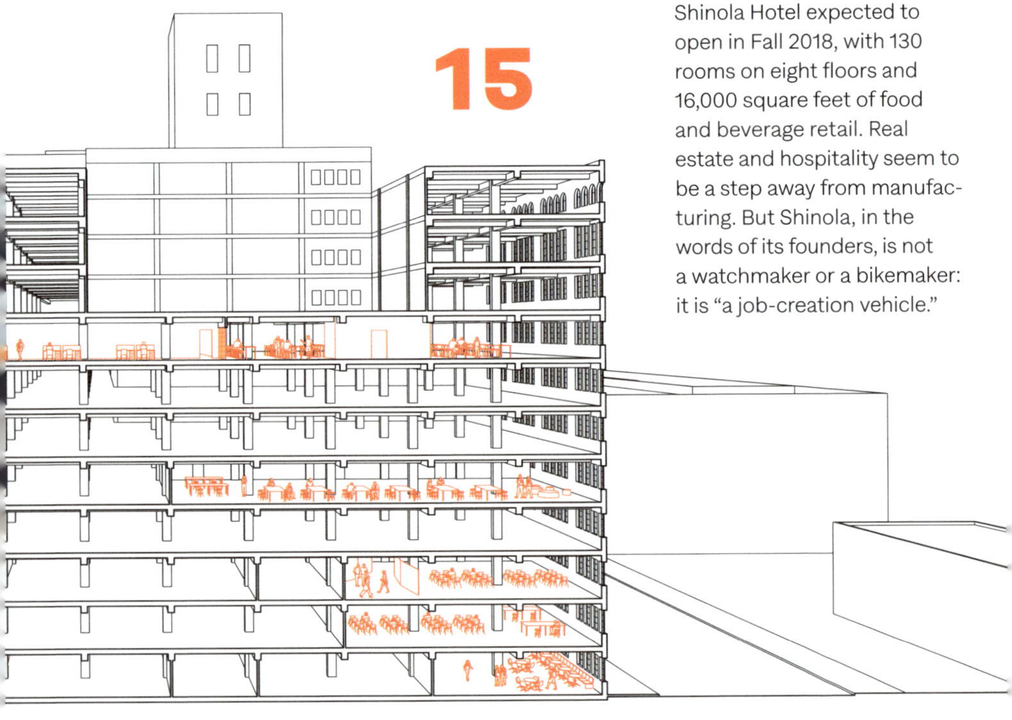

CHAMP

EXIT

BBQ remaking Corktown

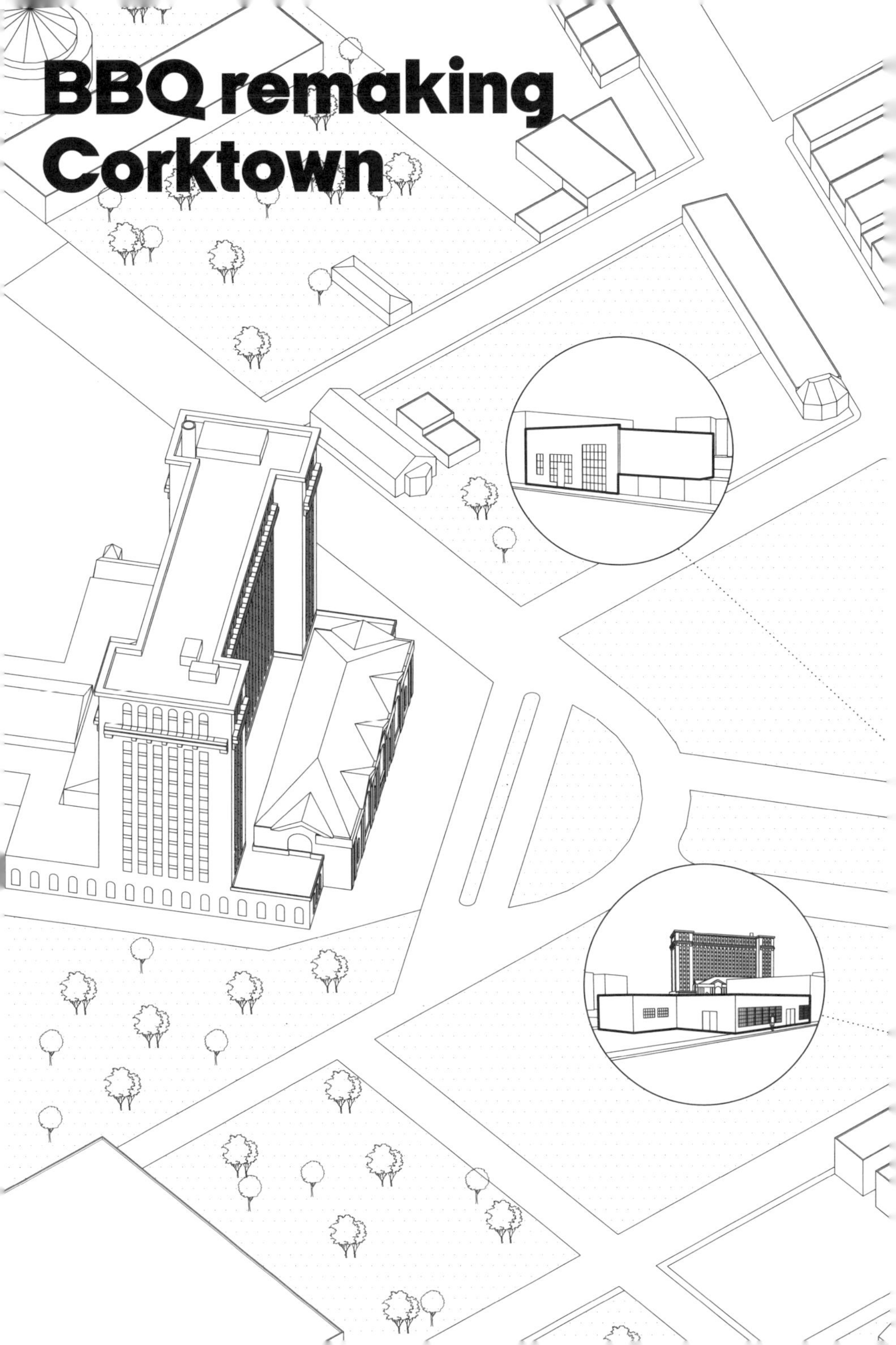

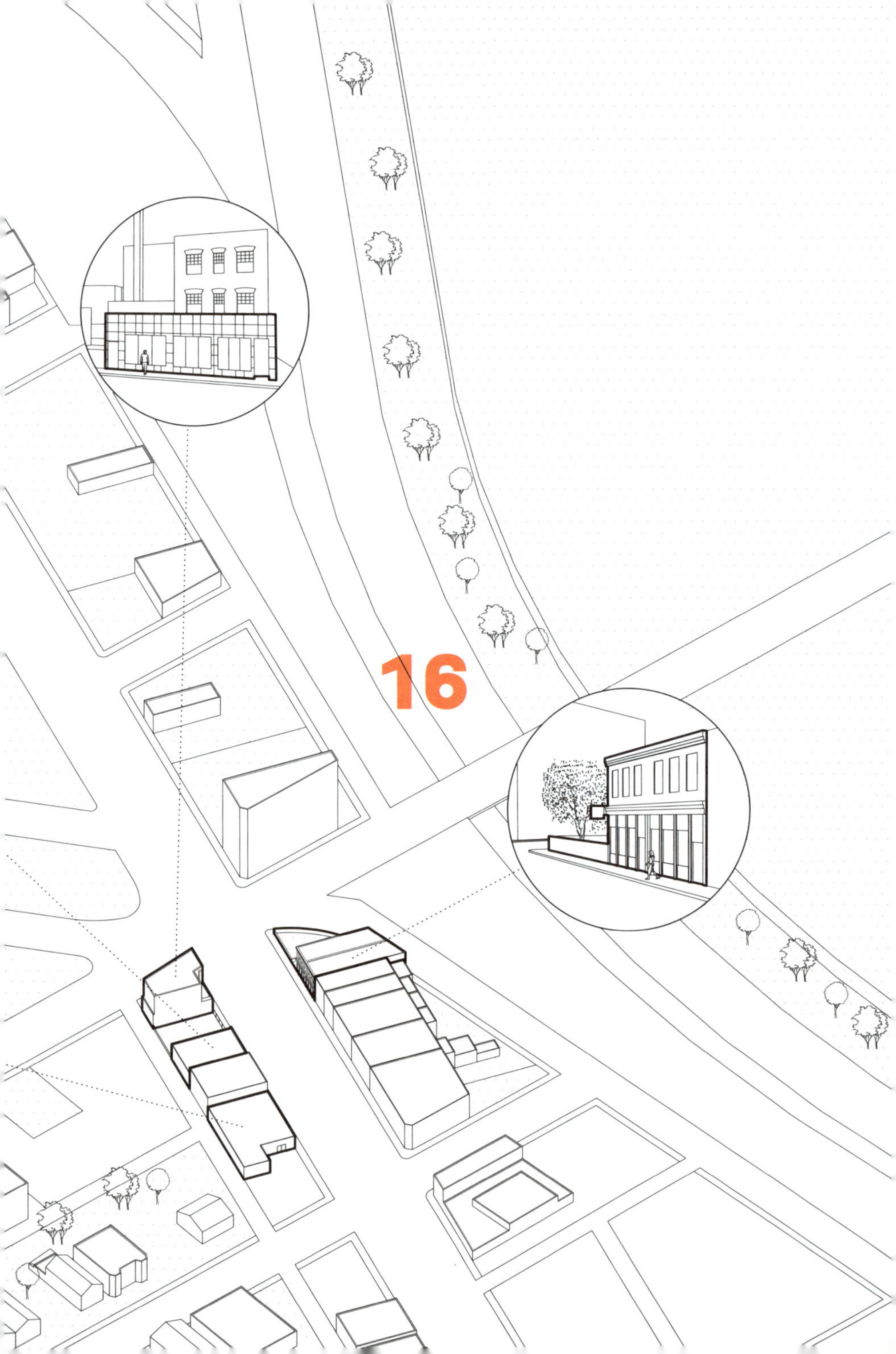
16

For social scientist Robert Putnam, the neighborhood barbecue was a ritual of social networking and a root of civic engagement: its end marked the decline of American community and the rise of individualism. He might be surprised in finding barbecue, although in a new form, at the core of the on-going neighborhood remaking and community-building in Corktown, just under the towering ghost of Michigan Central Station, once the world's tallest station, now the preferred set for "ruin porn" photography. Henry Ford's 1920s plans for developing the area were squelched by the Great Depression, and Corktown maintained the small scale of its original low-rise Federal-style detached houses and row houses with storefronts along Michigan Avenue. This did not spare the area from abandonment and blight. Settling in Detroit at 24 after dropping out of architecture school and a short international career as a fashion model, Philip Cooley had a hard time finding the right place for his barbecue & beer restaurant. He eventually leased two buildings in decent condition at the edge of downtown on Michigan Avenue for 159,000 dollars. He added 900,000 dollars for construction using an advance on his inheritance, with his future chefs as sweat-equity partners. Together, they refurbished the space by themselves. Cooley had a woodworking shop in an abandoned warehouse not far away, where most of the wooden features of Slows were made. "Slows Bar BQ" opened in 2005. Now the brand has four permanent and two temporary locations. In 2011, it doubled its footprint with an addition designed by Laavu architects, using reclaimed wood and steel wrought by Cooley and friends.

On site, Slows is an attractor of activities and Cooley is well aware of the positive effects of clustering. He supports other businesses in locating here with know-how, networking, and work. The 200-yard stretch of reclaimed Michigan Avenue—five miles of blight—is nicknamed "Cooley corridor." His brother Ryan opened a real estate agency next door, and the family is turning two more buildings into lofts, art spaces, a pop-up shop, and, eventually, another restaurant. He promoted the reclamation of the abandoned area in front of Michigan Central Station as a community garden. His woodshop became "Ponyride," a 30,000-square-foot artist and start-up colony offering cheap work space to socially conscious creators, artisanal bean distributors, a metalwork studio, a graphic studio, a denim retailer, and a recording company—and regularly hosting workshops, pop-up dinners, movie nights, and yoga classes. He eventually had to move his workshop elsewhere to make space for tenants. In 2015, he and his wife Kate Bordine bought the local Fire Station, closed in 1982, to settle in and make their home. Their two business partners will open a design studio and a pizzeria on Michigan Avenue. To no surprise, for the media Cooley is "Detroit's Renaissance Man;" he and his wife stand as testimonials to, inspirers of, and active promoters of all kinds of community and entrepreneurial activities. Corktown's renewal is rapidly upscaling. After nineteen years in Brooklyn, Galapagos Art Space bought nine different buildings in the area in 2014, a planned move from New York City to Detroit, with the double goal of escaping unsustainable rents and profiting from art's placemaking potential. Galapagos' partner in the deals was local real estate mogul Dan Gilbert, owner both of the Cleveland Cavaliers and a total of some fourteen million square feet in Motown. In 2015, a new state-of-the-art, 66,000-square-foot technology center opened just in front of Ponyride. In 2016, the redevelopment of the old Tiger Stadium site started: sports facilities plus a 37 million dollar mixed-use development with residential, retail, and commercial space. In May 2017, another developer broke ground on a 150 million dollar, multi-phased, mixed-used development in Elton Park with 420 apartments and 30,000 square feet of retail space. The son of a developer, Cooley has definitely proved to have the placemaker instinct. Hopefully, the savvy balance of business and community that made Corktown a destination again will not be lost in its success.

16

BIKE SHOP
AND REPAIR
Squirt
LIQUOR

SLOWS

934-4628

16

The art of reuse in Klinger Street

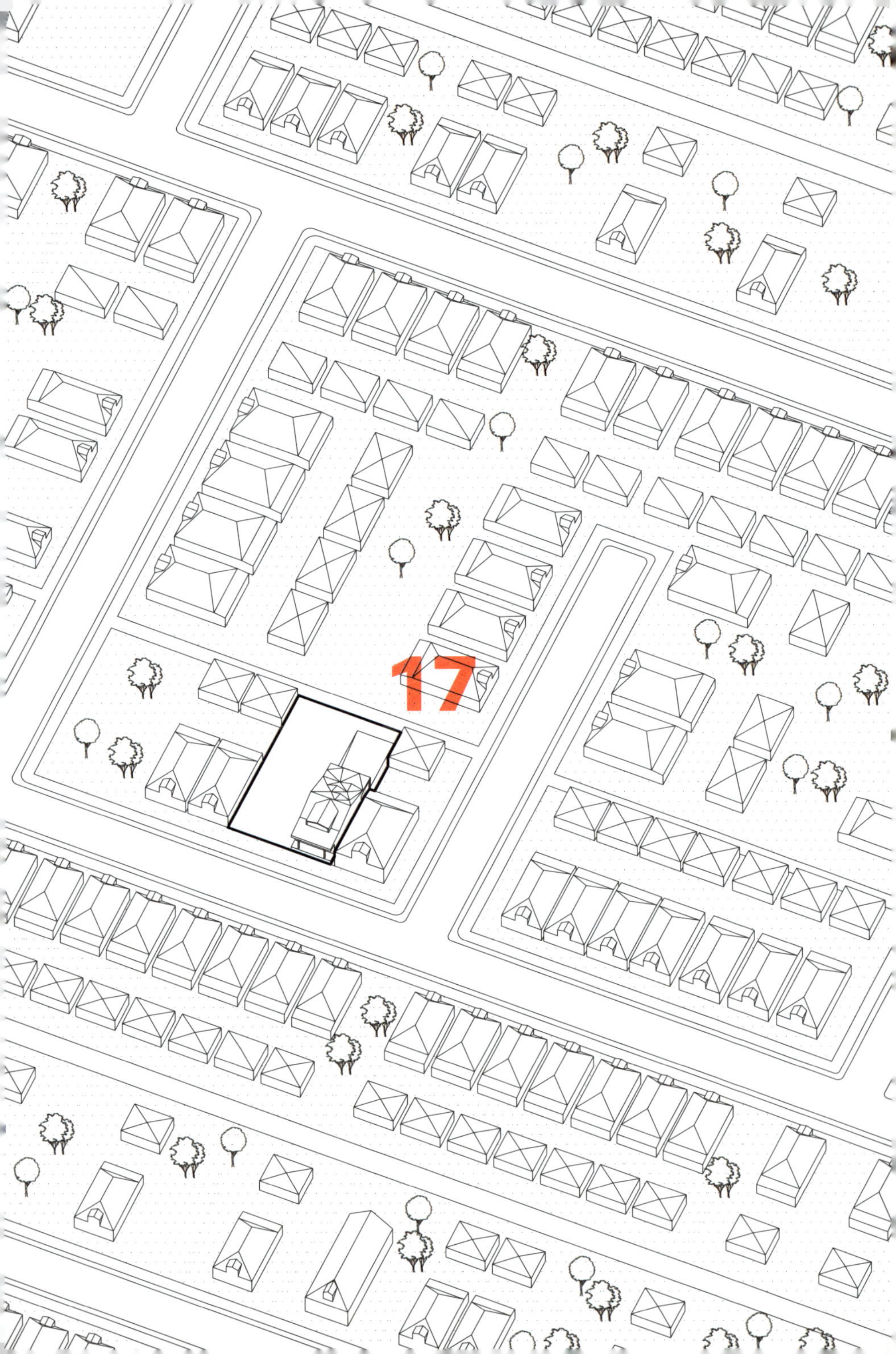
17

When Dmytro Szylak retired from GM in 1992, he did not want to sit on his hands. He started to collect, reuse, and assemble the most incredible variety of objects in a playful evolutive sculpture over the two garages of his detached house on Klinger Street in Hamtramck. He called his artwork the "Hamtramck Disneyland." City code enforcers periodically threatened to tear it down. It became instead a vernacular landmark, attracting visitors from outside to this otherwise unremarkable stand-alone residential neighborhood.

For Europeans, Detroit is the epitome of low density —Paris is twelve times denser. However, despite the fact that it shrank from two million residents in 1950 to 677,000 in 2017, by US standards it is still dense, much denser than the sprawling sun belt cities, like Houston, which is thirty percent less densely built than Detroit.

Our perception of emptiness is due to a great extent to today's vacancies and blight, but if we imagine the "mammoth" factories floating in a carpet of small family houses with tended gardens we can also imagine the liveliness when workers walked to their factory or to the next Department of Street Railways streetcar stop—the city of Detroit operated one of the largest public transportation systems in the world. Thirty years of decline transformed this low-rise high-density urban fabric into a desert with an impossible logistic, where even most basic services are hard to maintain. The city's strategy is to concentrate residents and activities along a north-south corridor: on May 12th, 2017, fifty-one years after the last streetcar was removed from Detroit, the new tramway on Woodward Avenue was inaugurated. What will happen to the city's 139 square miles? Will it be razed, farmed, set aside, or, when some concentration is left, turned into villages? The latter might well be the fate of the first official Banglatown of Wayne County, a neighborhood straddling the Detroit/Hamtramck border.

In the 1920s, Polish workers came here for jobs at nearby car factories. In the 1970s, Bangladeshi immigrants joined. Along with African Americans and European Americans, they form a culturally rich neighborhood with a walkable commercial corridor on Conant Avenue linking ethnic restaurants, markets, and

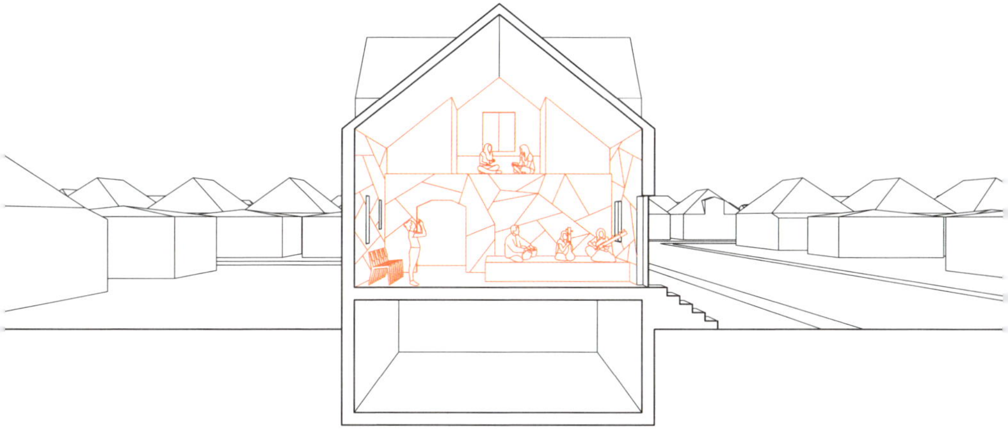

retail shops—one of the rare retail strips in town with virtually no vacancies.
The area is not exempt from crime, vandalism, and poverty. In 2008, a foreclosed drug house on Moran Street was auctioned off. Artists, architects, and residents Mitch Cope and Gina Reichert bought it for just five hundred dollars, and transformed it into the Power House. Power, because it produces electricity for itself and an adjacent house from sun and wind, creating a localized power grid, and because it takes control of public space and gives it back to the community. House, since it is an artist residence and meeting house. Power House became a non-profit, purchasing several more foreclosed properties on Moran and Klinger Streets. Each became a site-specific art project and community facility: the Yellow House, the Jar House, the Squash House, the Sound House, the Play House, and the Skate House, with the Ride it Sculpture Park. Similar independent initiatives sprung up in the neighborhood: Write a House project, Burnside Farm, the Afterhouse greenhouse, the Right Brothers studios, the Zimbabwe Cultural Center of Detroit, and architect Charlie O'Geen's—construction manager for Powerhouse Productions—Floating House. It was not planned, but rather a plot-by-plot opportunistic tactic and an exercise in typological subversion, proving that a monofunctional, residential, low-rise, stand-alone urban tissue could be diversified by transforming vacant houses into artwork wraps for communal facilities such as playgrounds, theaters, sport facilities, galleries, skate-parks, and music halls.
The plan came later: in Summer 2016, Global Detroit and goodgood, an interdisciplinary design firm, drafted a first Vision and Action Plan for Banglatown, developed with input from over 350 residents and stakeholders from the neighborhood. The plan integrates the art initiatives with actions ranging from integration to urban farming, from safety to housing, from economic development to cultural life. And Disneyland? Dmytro Szylak died on May 1st, 2015 at the age of 92. The local group Hatch Art took ownership of his property a year after his death, thanks to a successful crowdfunding campaign; restoration work began immediately. More importantly, his idea of art and reuse as trasformational powers lives on and has reshaped his neighborhood.

17

13133

17

Packard, or the next big thing

18

Of the 500 large-scale industrial buildings totalling 6.1 square miles of vacant industrial property in Detroit, Packard is by far the largest and most famous. Some even say it is the largest abandoned building in the world. For sure, if a place embodies Detroit's past and possible future, it's this one.
The first nine Packard buildings were designed by Albert Kahn for Henry Joy, president of the Packard Automotive Company, when he moved the company's headquarters from Warren, Ohio to Detroit in 1903. Although innovative in distribution and lighting, they were still built with wooden columns and floors like old mills. For the tenth, Kahn hired his brother Julius, who had just patented his Kahn-bar reinforced concrete system. Its innovative construction technique allowed larger spans, floor-to-ceiling windows, more load capacity, and was fireproof. The advance was so significant that the previous nine buildings were remade. By 1910, this was the largest and most modern factory in the US, and the Kahn-bar system had become standard. In the 1920s, Packard introduced the assembly line. At its peak, it employed 40,000 workers producing luxury cars in fifteen buildings totalling four million square feet connected by internal roads, bridges, and underground corridors. The last Packard rolled off the assembly line on June 25th, 1956. Two years later, Packard went out of business. The plant entered a troubled period of subdivisions, renting, progressive abandonment, stripping, vandalism—a severe test for Julius Kahn's system. In 2010, the last tenant left the site. Already in 1993, Wayne County had begun foreclosure proceedings due to tax delinquency and had reclaimed the property. The procedure was settled in 2012 and, in 2013, the property was put up for auction.

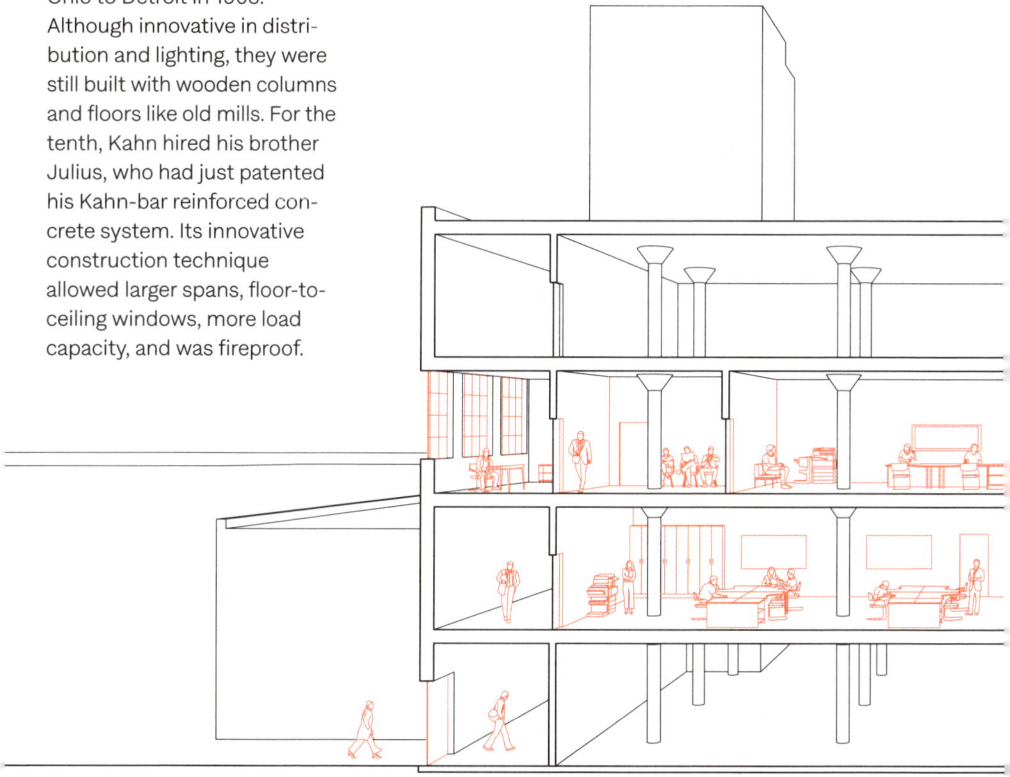

After two failed deals, Fernando Palazuelo, a Spanish developer from Lima, Peru, bought 2,700,000 square feet of the Packard plant for 405,000 dollars—less than half the price of Russell Industrial Center in 2003. He rapidly refurbished two stories of one minor building as the headquarter of his Arte Express development company. He hung a hand drawn concept scheme on the wall envisioning a future of creative industries attracting new settlers. He hired Albert Kahn Associates and announced investments of more than four hundred million dollars. Detroiters nicknamed him "the Conquistador." In the following years, skepticism grew as nothing seemed to happen. In 2016, the site was cleaned—it was in better shape than expected. On May 16th, 2017, the largest renovation project in North America broke ground with a sixteen million dollar investment for the renovation of the 121,000-square-foot administration building and the bridge over East Grand Boulevard within a period of eighteen months. Seventy percent of the space is already leased for offices, the Detroit Training Center, a gallery and event space, a coffee shop, and a restaurant. In contrary to the rough reuse of RIC, the project here is a rather conventional, complete refurbishment of the building. More radical adaptive ideas were proposed in the 2014 Reanimate the Ruins competition promoted by AIA and Detroit Future City. French architects Nadau Lavergne won with a proposal of an autonomous community of urban farms. But there are three more phases scheduled over fifteen years to raise the bar: a recreational complex with a go-kart track, live-work units, and a nightlife destination developed in partnership with Berlin Kraftwerk techno club owner Dimitri Hegemann. Hegemann was originally lured to Detroit by idea of reusing the Fisher Body plant, a vacant 500,000-square-foot building one mile from here. The proposed cooperation will include a ground-floor music venue, a large hostel, another restaurant, and a spa on the top floor. This increasingly complex mix of activities and spaces will require more daring solutions. Stay tuned, for Packard might truly become the next big thing.

18

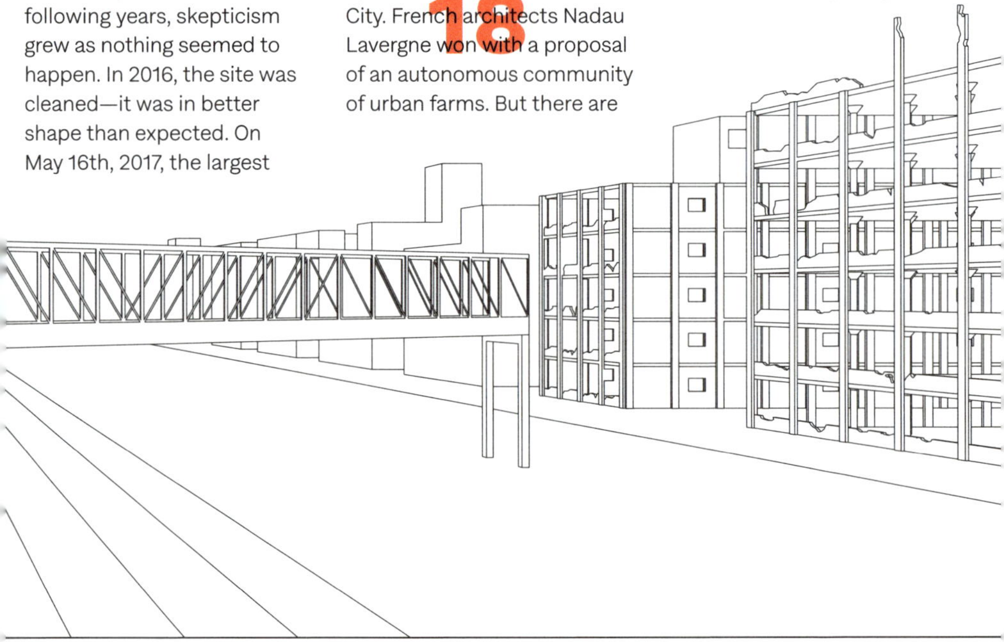

PACKARD

18

detroit

New York
19
19
20

High-end along the High Line

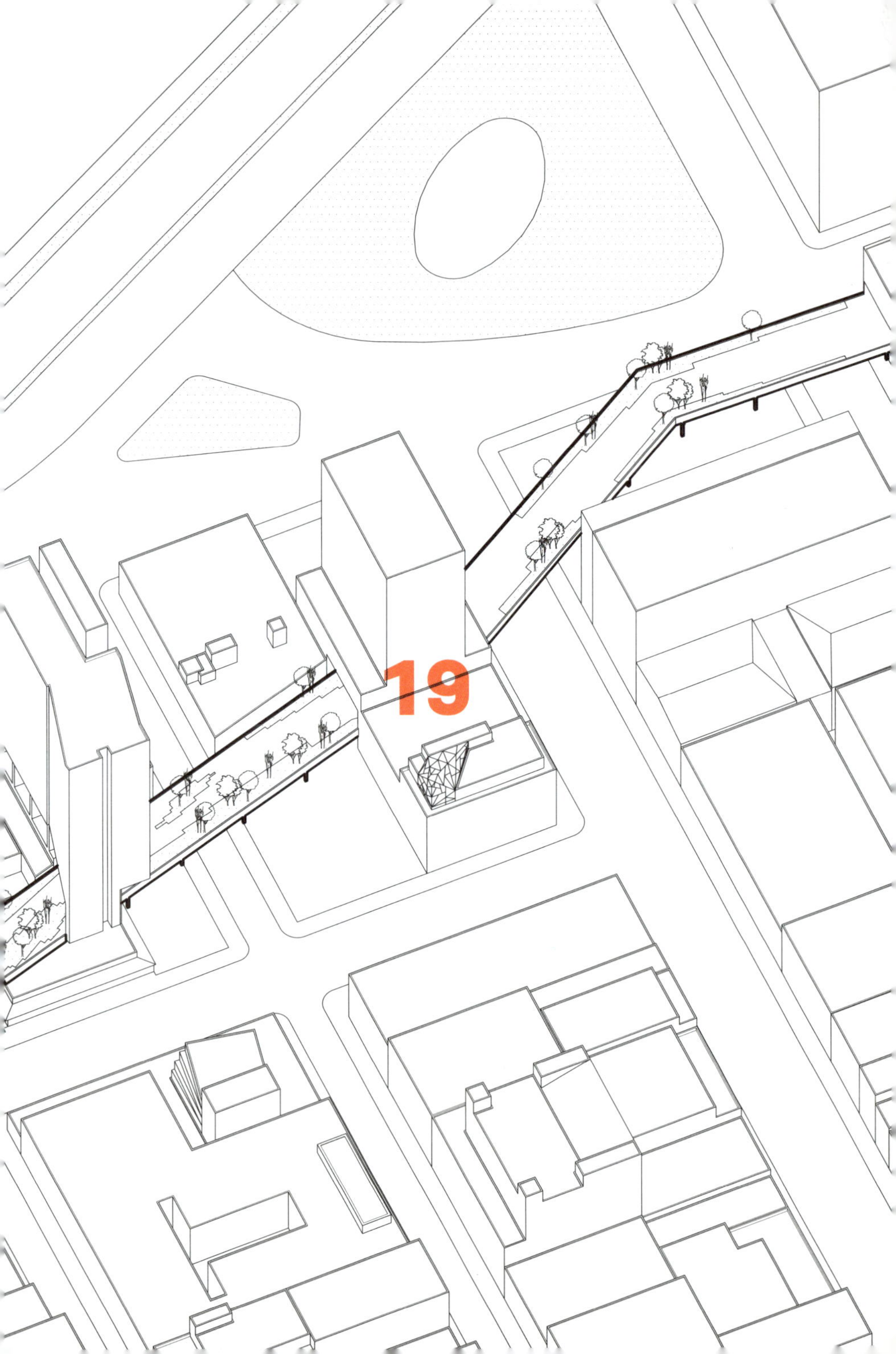
19

There's no adaptive reuse success as celebrated as the 1.45-mile-long High Line in the Lower West Side of Manhattan. Rarely is a project acclaimed by critics as an "icon" in contemporary landscape architecture. The High Line has been flooded by enthusiastic visitors—over 7.7 million in 2016, far from the initial forecast of 300,000—making it the most visited attraction in New York City. It is the vanguard of a new urban genre—a recent survey listed eighteen rail-to-trail projects in the making all over the world. The project has attracted both cultural institutions—the Whitney Museum opened its new building at the southern end in 2015—and real estate investors—twenty projects are listed along and near the line, lured by a twofold increase in values deemed high even for Manhattan standards: an average apartment in a building directly adjacent to the park can sell for six million dollars. And a further boom is expected with the twenty-eight acre mixed-use development currently under construction over the Hudson rail yards, promised as a new kind of data-driven and energy-wise urban environment targeted to tech firms and smart users. Robert Moses would appreciate the fortune of his West Side Improvement Project, a large urban renewal initiative that included the High Line viaduct for the New York Central Railroad's West Side Line, opened to trains in 1934. One of the improvements was the elimination of 105 street level crossings on a line which had operated in a dense urban setting since 1847. Factories and warehouses lifted their loading areas to the new rail level, producing interesting typological hybrids when infrastructure had to be incorporated into buildings. This integrated feeder delivered fresh produce, meat, milk, and raw materials daily to booming Manhattan.

The last train ran in 1980, trucks had taken the lead. Repeatedly scheduled for demolition, the High Line was protected initially by its mere solidity, then by growing attention. In the 1990s, urban explorers and local activists started to climb the abandoned viaduct for botanic walks among the wild vegetation growing in the gravel and in search of startling views of Chelsea and the Hudson piers. In 1999, they formed the non-profit "Friends of the High Line" to fight demolition projects and reclaim it as public space. They succeeded in building an unusual coalition of grassroots activists and global elite, raising more than one hundred and fifty million dollars in funding. In 2004, the New York City government committed fifty million dollars to the project and rezoned West Chelsea for luxury development—the High Line is expected to generate one billion dollars in tax revenues to the city over the next twenty years. Designed by New York-based landscape architecture firm James Corner Field Office, architects

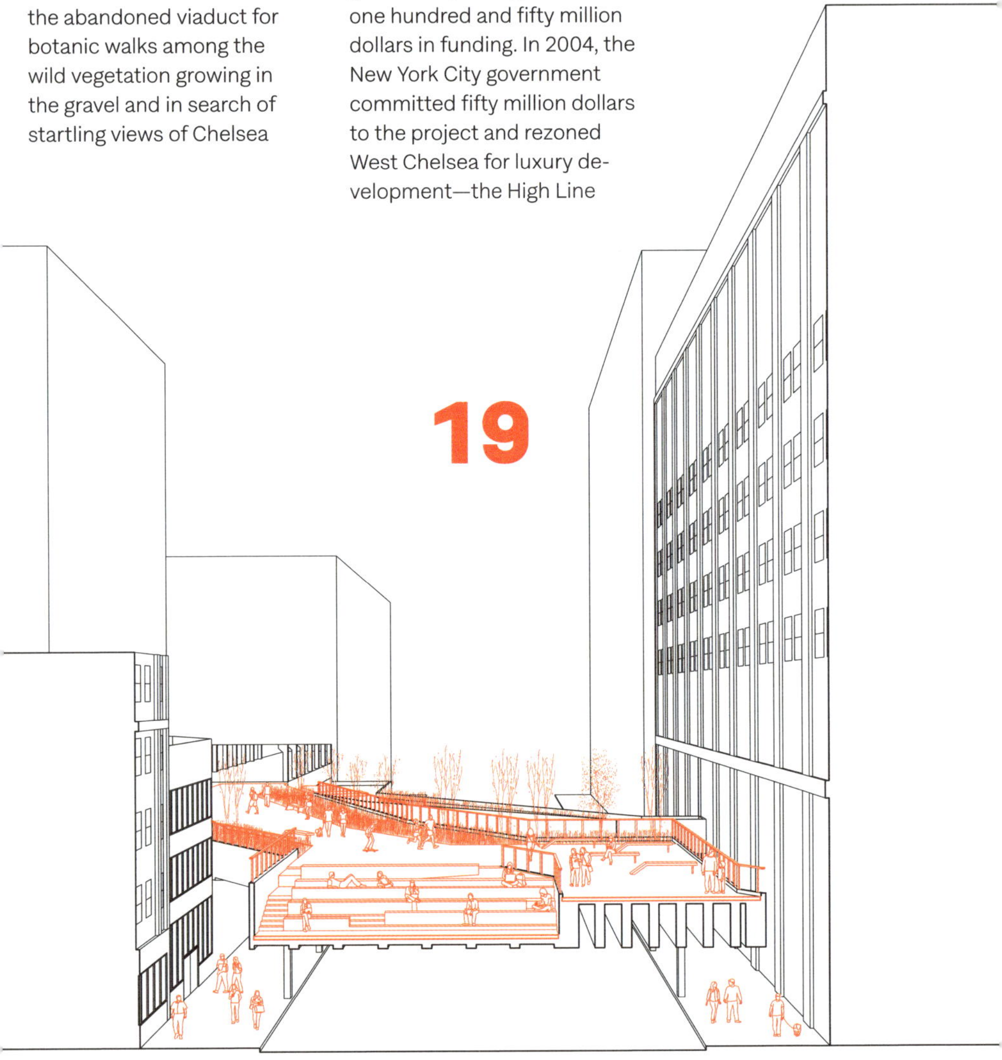

Diller, Scofidio and Renfro, and Dutch botanist Piet Oudolf, the High Line Park was progressively opened to the public as sections were completed in 2009, 2010, and 2014. It's equally rare that such a success story gets disowned by its initiator. "Friends of the High Line" founder Robert Hammond spoke openly of the High Line as a "failure" in a February 2017 interview, referring to his initial goal of reclaiming public green space for the local community. Chelsea was a mix of working-class residents and light-industrial businesses. What started for the benefit of the neighborhood is now changing its social and economic structure: new housing is inaccessible to locals, rising rents expel the traditional activities both under and around the line. A recent City University of New York study found that public visiting the High Line was "overwhelmingly white" —the neighborhood is mixed, but most visitors are tourists, not locals. In 2012, *The New York Times* wrote already that "the High Line has become a tourist-clogged catwalk and a catalyst for some of the most rapid gentrification in the city's history [...] another chapter in the story of New York City's transformation into Disney World." Part of this is inherent to what Rem Koolhaas defined as "manhattanism" or "the exploitation of congestion," part is specific to the design and management of the site. Elevation and concentrated access points separate the park from street life. High design is in itself a means of cultural distinction. Curated planting commands respect and contemplation. Rules exclude active uses—no skating, music, bikes, dogs, no "throwing objects"—i.e. ball games—no gatherings of more than twenty people.

In spite of recent integration efforts by the "Friends," this is a selective space. If public parks have since the 19th century been a balanced mix of freedom and control, nature and artifice, safety and surprise, proximity and estrangement, spontaneity and show, the High Line has rapidly lost its balance. As extreme cases are, it is a precious laboratory to observe and measure changes that could profoundly reshape our notion of public space, a vital ingredient of urban democracy. Here the contradictions implicit in all adaptive reuse processes become explicit, with the maximum of clarity that Manhattan always offers.

19

So you can't parallel park.
It'll be our little secret.
parkfast.com
888-parkfast
PARK
FAST

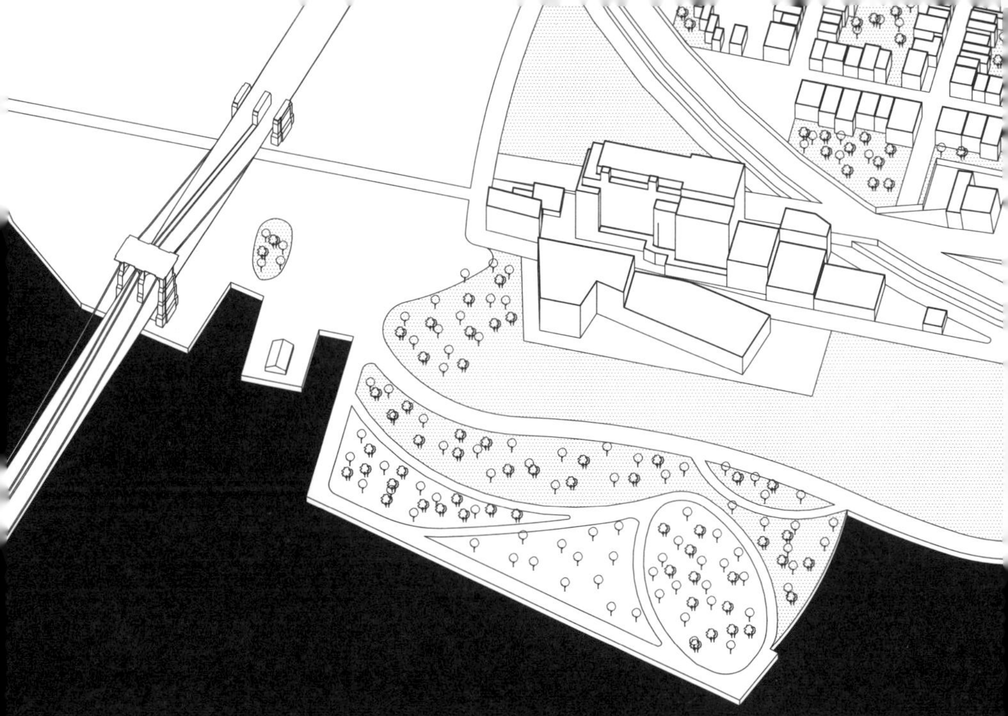

The people of Brooklyn Bridge Park

20

While enjoying your meal with other BBQers on one of the fifty-seven tables and twenty-five hibachi-style grills of Pier 5's "picnic peninsula," you profit from the most iconic view of Manhattan with the Brooklyn Bridge, participate in an informal feast, celebrate a social and civic all-American ritual, and contribute the liveliness of one of the most inclusive and active contem-porary public spaces in New York City.
The variety and animation of Brooklyn Bridge Park's eighty-five acres and 1.3 mile waterfront are the result of an incremental and adaptive planning, design, and construction process that started more than thirty years ago and is still ongoing.
The Port Authority decided to sell the vacant piers below Dumbo and Brooklyn Heights for commercial development in 1984—cargo traffic started declining in the 1970s and ended in 1983. In 2005, local citizens established the non-profit "Friends of Fulton Ferry Landing" to advocate for a park and preservation—this had been "het Veer," the ferry, since 1642: the place where George Washington escaped to Manhattan in 1776, the place where the first steam-boat ferry service was created by Robert Fulton and memo-rialized by Walt Whitman.
The debate was not only development vs. park, but also one of an "active" vs. a "passive" park. The balance between economy and leisure was decided in 2002, when the Port Authority, the city, and the state agreed to develop the area as a "self-sustaining" public parkland, meaning that development incomes were to balance park maintenance costs.
The choice sent a very clear message to future designers: low construction costs, low maintenance costs, no frills, reuse. The "Brooklyn Bridge Park Coalition," the advocacy group that stemmed from the "Friends of Fulton Ferry" envisioned a passive land-scape park enhancing the rich history and unique views of the site. The borough had another idea: it envisioned a harbor market retaining the industrial character of the site, promoting local economy, and attracting people with stalls selling ethnic food, fresh produce, arts, and crafts. The dense neighborhoods behind the Brooklyn Queens Express-way lacked public space, green areas, and sport facilities.
The 2005 park masterplan by Michael Van Valkenburgh Associates—the designers of the 606—set the balance by defining a flexible framework to be developed in phases, each one delivering one fully functioning reclaimed site by reusing existing port infrastructures and piers to project activities on the water. Demolition is minimized. His-torical buildings such as the Empire Stores are reused for offices, retail, and public uses.

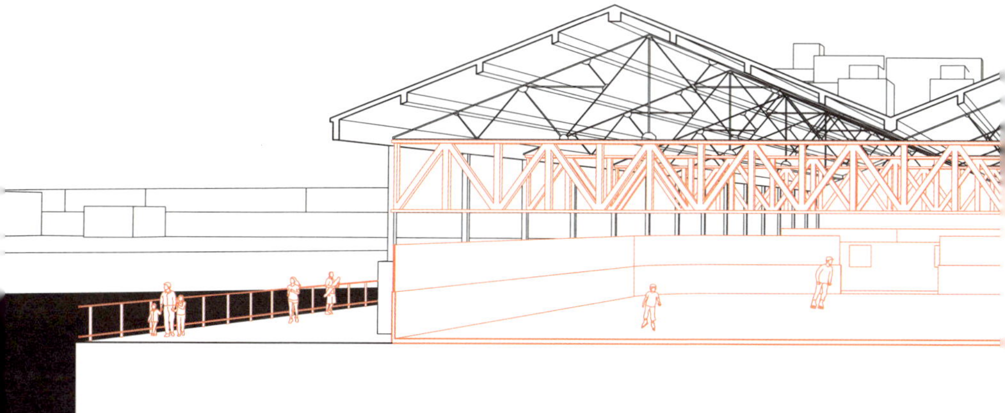

20

Non-reusable structures, like the pier wooden pilings left in the water all along the waterfront, have been designated as landmarks. Reused materials from on and off site are included in the design: thirty miles of pine boards from the demolition of the Cold Storages have been recycled for benches, vendors' stalls, and light poles; three hundred pieces of the Granite Prospect at Pier 1 come from the demolished Roosevelt Island Bridge, and the Pier 3 granite terrace is made with blocks from the Willis Avenue Bridge in the Bronx. The hill at Pier 1 was constructed with rock debris from the excavation of the Long Island Railroad tunnel under Manhattan. Construction began in 2008 with the first six acres of Pier 1, which opened in 2010, and is ongoing with several parts of the park still being designed. The evolving park alternates "hard" activity forms on the water, which reuse the piers and warehouse roofs for sport playgrounds, picnics, and gatherings, with "soft" areas dedicated to contemplation and relaxation—like the thirty-foot hill at Pier 1. These active spaces are complemented by areas dedicated to ecology and biodiversity like freshwater gardens a man-made natural sandy beach, the offshore Bird Island built from the remnants of a transfer bridge, or the upland planted hills that reduce the noise generated by the Brooklyn Queens Expressway. Boat launching and kayaking is possible at Pier 4, and a "community marina" between Piers 4 and 5 accommodates one hundred and two slips on four floating docks. Attractions like the old fire boat station reused as an ice cream factory, Jane's vintage carousel, the future Pier 6 viewing platform by BIG architects, and temporary art installations like Anish Kapoor's 2017 work "Descension"—a giant pool of continuously spiralling water—mix high design and vernacular. Similarly, daily programs satisfy the tastes of a wide variety of different publics: the ordinary summer day offers kayak polo matches, body combat, basketball clinics, sunrise yoga, zumba, broadway dance, hip-hop aerobics, ballet barre, gardening, orienteering, open air readings, birdwatching, piyo workouts, open air cinema, and night stargazing. This incredible mix of infrastructure and programs, reuse and ecology, excitement and peace, monuments and daily life is what attracts all kinds of people here, making the waterfront of Brooklyn Bridge Park a living demonstration of the integrative power of public space in the city—a precious ingredient of democracy.

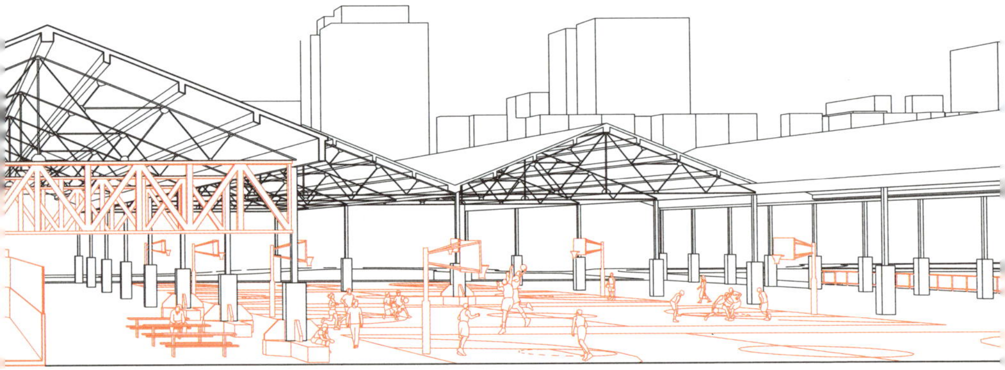

STAFF

POP-UP POOL